DAY BY DAY
WITH
C.H.SPURGEON

D1285432

DAY BY DAY
WITH
C.H. SPURGEON

COMPILED BY
AL BRYANT

WORD PUBLISHING

WORD (UK) LTD
Northbridge Road, Berkhamsted, Herts, England

WORD BOOKS AUSTRALIA
Heathmont, Victoria, Australia

SUNDAY SCHOOL CENTRE WHOLESALE
Salt River, South Africa

First published in the USA 1980 by Word Incorporated, Waco, Texas as "Near the Sun": a source book of daily meditations from Charles Haddon Spurgeon

First British edition 1985.

ISBN 0 85009 063 6

Unless otherwise indicated, scripture quotations are from the King James version of the Bible.

Scripture quotations marked RSV are from the revised standard version of the Bible, copyright 1946, 1952, © 1971, 1973 by the Division of Christian Education of the National Council of the Churches of Christ in the USA.

Scripture quotations marked TLB are from *The Living Bible Paraphrased* published by Tyndale House Publishers, © 1971, Wheaton, IL.

Scripture quotations marked *Modern Language* are from *The Modern Language Bible: The New Berkeley Version in Modern English* © 1945, 1959, 1969 by Zondervan Publishing House.

Foreword

The meditations in this book have been gleaned from various sources. I am particularly indebted to the little volume, *Daily Help,* still being published, for many of the meditations. However, I have tried to get "inside Spurgeon's skin" in arranging and in some cases combining the meditations. In most instances, I have selected a suitable scripture text based on the passage or passages which flashed through my mind as I read Spurgeon's words.

In addition, I have drawn heavily upon Spurgeon's published sermons for many of the meditations herein. They are indeed a treasure-trove of devotional as well as doctrinal writings. To my knowledge, this material has never before appeared in a devotional collection. Here again I have selected the scripture verse that begins the meditation based on the passage that came to mind as I "digested" Spurgeon's original words and tried to think as he would have thought had he selected the daily verses for this book.

One further acknowledgment: it was frequently necessary, I felt, to "modernize" the language in these meditations. You will note that the "thees" and "thous" along with other archaic expressions are missing in this collection. However, I have generally chosen to use the King James Version for the scripture passages, since that was the translation Spurgeon used in his remarkable pulpit ministry.

His is indeed a rich legacy of literature. Even today, if one checks the *Books in Print* listing so important to modern publishers and booksellers, he will discover more books listed under Spurgeon's name than virtually any other single author included in these ponderous volumes.

Charles Haddon Spurgeon was called "the prince of preachers" and this collection of devotional thoughts on a wide range of subjects include meditations on such subjects as: divine providence, the Cross, worship and service, prayer, victory, love, faith, adversity, the Bible, friendship, joy, the Christian life, and many others.

Spurgeon has been described by J. G. G. Norman in *The New International Dictionary of the Christian Church* as:

> Preeminently a preacher. His clear voice, his mastery of Anglo-Saxon, and his keen sense of humor, allied to a sure grasp of Scripture and deep love for Christ, produced some of the noblest preaching of any age . . . an evangelical Calvinist, he read widely and especially loved the seventeenth century Puritans. A diverse author, he wrote biblical expositions, lectures to students, hymns, and the homely philosophy of "John Ploughman," among other works.

Spurgeon speaks just as eloquently to our modern day, and this careful collection of his choicest thoughts is designed to help the modern Christian deal with the pressures of twentieth-century life realistically and in biblical perspective.

I hope you will enjoy the meditations in this book. They spoke to me along the way, and I trust they will speak to you as well.

AL BRYANT

January

And the evening and the morning were the first day.
Genesis 1: 5

1

The evening was "darkness" and the morning was "light," and yet *the two together are called by the name that is given to the light alone!* In every believer there is darkness and light, and yet he is not a sinner because there is sin in him, but he is a saint because he possesses some degree of holiness. This will be a most comforting thought to those who ask, "Can I be a child of God while there is so much darkness in me?" Yes; for you, like the day, take not your name from the evening, but from the morning; and you are spoken of in the Word of God as if you were even now perfectly holy.

If His dark nights are as bright as the world's days, what shall His days be? If even His starlight is more splendid than the sun, what must His sunlight be? If I can praise the Lord in the fires, how will I extol Him before the eternal throne! If evil be good to me *now*, what will the overflowing goodness of God be to me *then?* Oh, blessed "afterward!" Who would not be a Christian? Who would not bear the present cross for the crown which comes afterwards? But herein is work for patience, for the rest is not for today, nor the triumph for the present, but "afterward." Wait, O soul, and let patience have her perfect work.

January

| 2 | *And the Lord said, My spirit shall not always strive with man.* |

Genesis 6: 3

The imagination will sometimes fly up to God with such a power that eagles' wings cannot match it. It sometimes has such might that it can almost see the King in His beauty, and the land which is very far off. But if it is potent one way, it is another, for imagination has taken us down to the lowest plains of earth. But I rejoice and think of one thing, that I can cry out when this imagination comes upon me. So it is with the Christian. If he cries out, there is hope. Can you chain your imagination? No; but the power of the Holy Ghost can. Ah, it shall do it! and it does do it at last, it does it even on earth.

It may be, that during a sermon two men are listening to the same truth; one of them hears as attentively as the other, and remembers as much of it; the other is melted to tears or moved with solemn thoughts; but the one though equally attentive, sees nothing in the sermon, except, maybe, certain important truths well set forth; as for the other, his heart is broken within him and his soul is melted. Ask me how it is that the same truth has an effect upon this one, and not upon the other: because the mysterious Spirit of the living God goes with the truth to one heart and not to the other.

| 3 | *And the dove came in to him in the evening, and, lo, in her mouth was an olive leaf. . . .* |

Genesis 8: 11

What a picture of peace and virtue is the dove, the little bird so often used as a sacrifice by God's people. She reminds me of another of God's creations.

Laden boughs hang low. The nettle mounts above its fellow weeds, but the violet lies shrouded under its leaves, and is only discovered by its own scent. Walking one day by a stream we were conscious of a delicious perfume, and only then did we perceive the little blue flowers which were looking up to us so meekly from the ground on which we stood. Virtue is always modest, and modesty is itself a virtue. He who is discovered by his real excellence, and not by his egotistical advertisements of his own perfections, is a man worth knowing.

Blessed Lord Jesus, be with me, reveal Yourself, and abide with me all night, so that when I awake, I may be still with You. I note that the dove brought in her mouth an olive branch plucked off, the memorial of the past day, and a prophecy of the future. Have I no pleasing record to bring home? No pledge and earnest of loving-kindness yet to come? Yes, my Lord, I present to You my grateful acknowledgments for tender mercies which have been new every morning and fresh every evening; and now, I pray You, put forth Your hand and take me, Your dove, into Your bosom.

While the earth remaineth, seedtime and harvest, and cold and heat, and summer and winter, and day and night shall not cease.

Genesis 8: 22

I have seen in our mortal life summer and winter, prosperity and adversity. Do not expect, dear brother, while you are in this world, always to dwell among the lilies and roses of prosperity. Summer will come, and you will be wise to make hay while the sun shines by using all opportunities for usefulness; but look for winter. I do not know into what trade you can enter to be secure against losses, nor what profession you could follow in which you would escape disappointments. I know no corner of the earth without its night, no land without its stones, no sea without its storms. As to spiritual and mental experience, it seems to me within myself that while the earth remains I will have my ebbs and flows, my risings and my sinkings. Do not therefore begin to kick and quarrel with the dispensations of God's providence. When it is summertime say, "The Lord gave, and blessed be His name." When it is winter say, "The Lord hath taken away, and blessed be His name." Keep to the same music, even though you sometimes have to pitch an octave lower. Still praise and magnify the Lord whether you be

January

sowing or reaping. Let Him do what seems good to Him, but to you let it always seem good to praise.

The bow shall be seen in the cloud.

Genesis 9: 14

When may we expect to see the token of the covenant? The rainbow is only to be seen painted upon a *cloud.* Beloved, our God, who is as the sun to us, always shines, but we do not always see Him—clouds hide His face; but no matter what drops may be falling, or what clouds may be threatening, if *He* does but shine, there will be a rainbow at once. It is said that when we see the rainbow the shower is over. Certain it is, that when Christ comes our troubles are removed, when we behold Jesus our sins vanish, and our debts and fears subside. When Jesus walks the waters of the sea, how profound the calm!

And the bow shall be in the cloud; and I will look upon it, that I may remember the everlasting covenant between God and every living creature of all flesh that is upon the earth.
Genesis 9: 16

Oh, it is not my remembering God, it is God's remembering *me,* which is the ground of my safety; it is not *my* laying hold of His covenant, but His covenant's laying hold on me. Glory be to God! the whole of the bulwarks of salvation are secured by divine power, and even the minor towers, which we may imagine might have been left to man, are guarded by almighty strength. Even the *remembrance* of the covenant is not left to our memories, for *we* might forget; but our Lord cannot forget the saints whom He has graven on the palms of His hands.

Now the Lord had said unto Abram, Get thee out of thy country, and from thy kindred, and from thy father's house, unto a land that I will show thee.

Genesis 12: 1

A long period passed without a voice from God. Man seemed left to himself, and in danger of being given up to idols. The nations wandered each a different way, but all the downward road. Yet grace had not ended its reign; and therefore, before the lamp of God had wholly gone out, the Lord determined to reveal Himself, and establish His worship in the world. He would select a family to be His peculiar servants; He would manifest Himself to the father of that family, and would make with him a covenant. He would reveal to him the great things which He intended to do in the fullness of time, and He would bid him hand down the revelation to his children from generation to generation. This family should grow into a nation, and to that nation should be committed the oracles of God. Out of that nation should come prophets, and priests, and heroes, who should believe in God and maintain the true faith against all comers, even until the Son of God Himself should come to manifest the glory of God in a preeminent degree. In the midst of that nation the Lord resolved to set up ordinances, and a settled organization, by which truth should be taught through type and symbol, and by the hallowed speech of godly men. This, in His wisdom, He judged to be best for the future of the race.

At this moment God is working in much the same manner in the midst of the world by His church. A church is an assembly called out. The true church consists of men who are called, and faithful, and chosen. They are redeemed from among men, and called out from among their fellows by effectual grace. God the Holy Spirit continues to call out, and bring to the Lord Jesus, those who are chosen of God according to the good pleasure of His will. Practically, conversion is the result of the call—"Get thee out from thy country." It is a repetition of that searching word, "Come ye out from among them, and be ye separate, saith the Lord, and touch not the unclean thing." The church is a repetition of the camp of Abram in the midst of Canaan. It is the Lord's portion among men, and it keeps His oracles. The church of the living God is the pillar and ground of the truth; and it is the design of God to find a home for His gospel in His church, till the dispensation of grace shall close, and the Judge shall ascend the throne.

January

8

And God said, Sarah thy wife shall bear thee a son indeed; and thou shalt call his name Isaac: and I will establish my covenant with him for an everlasting covenant, and with his seed after him.

Genesis 17: 19

The pedigree of God's chosen nation Israel may be traced back to one man and one woman—to Abraham and Sarah. Both of them were well along in years when the Lord who had called them verified His promise, yet, in the fulfillment of His covenant engagement, He built up of their seed a great nation, which, for number, was comparable to the stars of heaven.

Take heart, brethren; these things are written for our example and for our encouragement. His church can never sink to so low an ebb that He cannot soon build her up again, nor in our own hearts can the work of grace ever decline so grievously that the same mighty power which once quickened cannot revive and restore us.

Think of Abraham and Sarah, childless till they were old, then rejoicing in one son, who became their heir. Hence sprang the great multitude that peopled Palestine. With such a panorama unfolding before you there is no excuse for despair; but you may find ten thousand reasons for confidence in God.

9

And Abraham called the name of that place Jehovah-jireh: as it is said to this day, In the mount of the Lord it shall be seen.

Genesis 22: 14

Jehovah-jireh means "the Lord will provide" or "will give a means of deliverance." That is why Abraham called the place "Jehovah-jireh." When he offered a sacrifice on the mount it was called a "burnt offering"; but when the Lord Jesus Christ died on Calvary it was not only a burnt offering, but a sin offering, a meat offering, and a peace offering, and every other kind of sacrifice in one. Under the oldest of all dispensations, before the Mosaic economy, God had not taught to men the distinctions of sacrifice, but an offering unto the Lord meant all that was afterwards set forth by many types. When the venerable patriarch offered a sacrifice, it was an offering for sin, and a sweet-smelling savor besides.

So was it with our Lord Jesus Christ. When He died He made His soul an offering for sin, and "put away sin by the sacrifice of himself." When He died, He *also* offered unto God a burnt offering, for we read, "And walk in love, as Christ also hath loved us, and hath given himself for us an offering and a sacrifice to God for a sweetsmelling savor" (Eph. 5: 2). When Jesus died He gave to us a peace offering; for we come to feast upon Him with God, and to us "[his] flesh is meat indeed, [his] blood is drink indeed" (John 6: 55). One would need many a day in which to expatiate upon the infinite virtues and excellencies of Christ, in whom all perfections are sweetly hived. Blessed be His name; God has most gloriously provided for us in the day of our need. Jehovah-jireh!

And the servant said unto him, Peradventure the woman will not be willing to follow me unto this land: must I needs bring thy son again unto the land from whence thou camest?
Genesis 24: 5
Read also Genesis 6–8

10

Genesis is both the book of beginnings and the book of dispensations. You know what use Paul makes of Sarah and Hagar, of Esau and Jacob, and the like. Genesis is, all through, a book instructing the reader in the dispensations of God towards man. Paul said, in a certain place, "which things are an allegory," by which he did not mean that they were not literal facts, but that, being literal facts, they might also be used instructively as an allegory. So may I say of this chapter. It records what actually was said and done; but at the same time, it bears within it allegorical instruction with regard to heavenly things. The true minister of Christ is like this Eleazar of Damascus; he is sent to find a wife for his Master's Son. His great desire is, that many shall be presented unto Christ in the day of His appearing, as the bride, the Lamb's wife.

The faithful servant of Abraham, before he started, communed with his master; and this is a lesson to us, who go on our Lord's errands. Let us, before we engage in actual service, see the Master's face, talk with Him, and tell to Him any difficulties which occur

January

to our minds. Before we get to work, let us know what we are at, and on what footing we stand. Let us hear from our Lord's own mouth what He expects us to do, and how far He will help us in the doing of it. Never go forth to plead with men for God until you have first pleaded with God for men. Do not attempt to deliver a message which you have not first of all yourself received by His Holy Spirit. Come out of the chamber of fellowship with God into the pulpit of ministry among men, and there will be a freshness and a power about you which none shall be able to resist.

I am not worthy of the least of all the mercies, and of all the truth, which thou hast showed unto thy servant; for with my staff I passed over this Jordan; and now I am become two bands.

Genesis 32: 10

I call your attention to the present tense as it is used in the text— Jacob does not say, as we might half have thought he would have said, "I *was* not worthy of the least of all the mercies and of all the truth which thou hast made to pass before thy servant," but he says, "I *am not* worthy." He does not merely allude to his unworthiness when he crossed this Jordan with a staff in his hand, a poor solitary banished man: he believes that he was unworthy then; but even now, looking upon his flocks and his herds and his great family, and all that he had done and suffered, he cries, "*I am not* worthy."

What, has not all God's mercy made you worthy? Brethren, free grace is neither the child nor the father of human worthiness. If we get all the grace we ever can get we shall never be worthy of that grace; for grace as it enters where there is no worthiness, so it imparts to us no worthiness afterwards as we are judged before God. When we have done all, we are unprofitable servants; we have only done what it was our duty to have done.

To touch the praise which comes to us through the operations of divine grace, even with our little finger, were treason against the Most High. To assume for a moment that we deserve anything of the Lord God, is so vainglorious, so false, so unjust that we

14

ought to loathe the very thought of it, and cry like Jacob, "I am not worthy." Job, who had defended himself with vigor and possibly with bitterness, no sooner heard God speaking to him in the whirlwind than he cried, "I have heard of thee by the hearing of the ear; but now mine eye seeth thee: Wherefore I abhor myself, and repent in dust and ashes" (Job 42: 5, 6). Prostrate before the throne is the proper attitude of prayer: in humility is our strength for supplication.

Fear not to go down into Egypt; for I will there make of thee a great nation. I will go down with thee into Egypt; and I will also surely bring thee up again.

Genesis 46: 3, 4

12

Jacob must have shuddered at the thought of leaving the land of his fathers and dwelling among heathen strangers. It was a new scene, and likely to be a trying one. Who shall venture among strangers without anxiety? Yet the way was evidently appointed for him, and therefore he resolved to go.

This is frequently the position of believers today. They are called upon to change jobs, to face situations new and untried: at such times let them imitate Jacob's example by offering sacrifices of prayer to God, and seeking His direction; let them not take a step until they have waited upon the Lord for His blessing. Then they will have Jacob's Companion to be their friend and helper.

How blessed to feel assured that the Lord is with us in all our ways, to know that He condescends to go down into our humiliations and difficulties with us! Even beyond the ocean, our Father's love beams like the sun in its strength. We cannot hesitate to go where Jehovah promises His presence; even the valley of death grows bright with the radiance of this assurance.

Marching onwards with faith in their God, believers shall have Jacob's promise. They shall be brought up again, whether it be from troubles of life or chambers of death. Jacob's seed came out of Egypt in due time, and so shall all the faithful pass unscathed through the tribulation of life, and terror of death.

January

<table>
<tr><td>

13

</td><td>

Now the eyes of Israel were dim for age, so that he could not see. And he brought them near to him; and he kissed them, and embraced them.

Genesis 48: 10

</td></tr>
</table>

Jacob died as one who had been delivered from all evil, aye, even the evil of old age. His eyes were dim; but that did not matter, for his faith was clear. I love to think that we are going where our vision of God will not be through the eye, but through the spiritual perceptions. These were brighter in Jacob in his old age than ever before; his faith and love, which are the earthly forms of those perceptions, were apprehending God in a more forcible manner than ever, and therefore it signified little that the eyes which he would need no longer were failing him. We cannot say that he was in decay, after all; for he was losing what he only needed in this world of shadows, and was gaining fitness for the higher state. His gracious faculties grew as his bodily faculties declined; and, therefore, he felt that his life was ending in a fullness of blessing such as he wished for the children of his dearest son.

<table>
<tr><td>

14

</td><td>

He blessed Joseph, saying, "The God in whose presence my fathers Abraham and Isaac walked, the God who shepherded me through life to this moment."

Genesis 48: 15
Modern Language

</td></tr>
</table>

The old man's voice faltered as he said, "The God which fed me all my life long," or "The God which shepherded me all my life long."

He spoke of the Lord as his Shepherd. Jacob had been a shepherd, and therefore he knew what shepherding included; the figure is full of meaning. There had been a good deal of Jacob about Jacob, and he had tried to shepherd himself. Poor sheep that he was, while under his own guidance he had been caught in many thorns, and had wandered in many wildernesses. Because he would be so much a shepherd to himself, he had been hard put to it. But over all, despite his willfulness, the shepherding of the covenant

God had been exercised towards him, and he acknowledged it.

O dear saints of God, you to whom years are being multiplied, give praise to your God for having been your Shepherd. You delight in the twenty-third Psalm, sing it sometimes with variations by using the past tense: "The Lord has been my shepherd; and I have known no want. He hath made me to lie down in green pastures; he hath led me beside the still waters. Yea, though I have walked through the valley of the shadow of death in times of great darkness, yet I have feared no evil: for he has been with me, his rod and his staff have comforted me." Bear your witness to the shepherding of God, for this may lead others to become the sheep of His pasture.

And he blessed Joseph, and said, God, before whom my fathers Abraham and Isaac did walk, the God which fed me all my life long unto this day.

Genesis 48: 15

This shepherding had been perfect. Our version rightly says that the Lord had *fed* Jacob all his life long. Take that sense of it, and you who have a daily struggle for subsistence will see much beauty in it. Jacob had a large family, and yet they were fed. Some of you say, "It is all very well of you to talk of providence who have few to provide for." I answer, it is better still to talk of providence where a large household requires large provision. Remember Jacob had thirteen children yet his God provided them bread to eat and raiment to put on. None of that large company were left to starve.

You think perhaps that Jacob was a man of large estate. He was not so when he began life. He was only a working man, a shepherd. When he left his father's house he had no attendants with camels and tents. I suppose he carried his little bit of provision in a handkerchief, and when he laid down that night to sleep, with a stone for his pillow, the hedges for curtains, the heavens for his canopy, and the earth for his bed, he had no fear of being robbed. God was with him; apart from this, he had nothing to

January

begin life with but his own hands. Whatever he received from his father Isaac afterwards, he had at first to fight his own way; but he knew no lack either at the beginning or at the end, for he could speak of the great Elohim as "the God which fed me all my life long." Hundreds of us can say the same.

16

And he blessed Joseph, and said, God, before whom my fathers Abraham and Isaac did walk, the God which fed me all my life long unto this day, the Angel which redeemed me from all evil, bless the lads.

Genesis 48: 15, 16

Joseph was unique. In Jacob's family he was like a swan in a duck's nest; he seemed to be of a different race from the rest, even from his childhood. He was the son of old age, the son of the elders, that is, a child who was old when he was young, in thoughtfulness and devotion. He reached an early ripeness, which did not end in early decay. In consequence of this, Joseph was one by himself in the peculiarity of his trials. Through his brothers' hatred of him he was made to suffer greatly, and at last was sold into slavery, and underwent trials in Egypt of the severest kind. "The archers have sorely grieved him, and shot at him, and hated him" (Gen. 49: 23). But, brethren, see the recompense; for he had blessings which were altogether his own. "His bow abode in strength, and the arms of his hands were made strong by the hands of the mighty God of Jacob" (Gen. 49: 24). He was as distinguished by the favor of God as by the disfavor of his brethren. When Jacob was old and about to die, he gave Joseph a blessing all to himself, in addition to that which he received with his brothers.

Had not his tribulations abounded, his consolations would not so have abounded. Do you seem yourself, my friend, to be marked out for peculiar sorrows? Do the arrows of affliction make your life their target, and are you chastened above all other men? Do not be regretful, for the arrows are winged by a covenant love, which designs by their wounds to prepare you for a special work which will lead up to a special benediction from your Father who is in heaven. The day will come when you will be grateful for every smart you now endure; yes, grateful for that bitter pang of unkindness from your brethren, though now it tortures your heart. The abundance of the revelation of God is usually joined with a thorn in the flesh either before or after it. Notwithstanding your grief, there shall yet be born to you as to Joseph a Manasseh, for God shall make you to forget all your toil, and an Ephraim, for God shall make you fruitful in the land of your affliction.

The Angel which redeemed me from all evil, bless the lads; and let my name be named on them, and the name of my fathers Abraham and Isaac; and let them grow into a multitude in the midst of the earth.

Genesis 48: 16

17

Jacob had spoken of ancestral mercies, personal mercies and redeeming mercies, and now he deals with *future mercies*, as he cries, *"Bless the lads."* He began with blessing Joseph, and he finishes with blessing his lads. O dear friends, if God has blessed you, I know you will want Him to bless others. There is the stream of mercy, deep, broad, and clear: you have drunk of it, and are refreshed, but it is as full as ever. It will flow on, will it not? You do not suppose that you and I have dammed up the stream so as to keep it to ourselves. No, it is too strong, too full a stream for that. It will flow on from age to age. God will bless others as He has blessed us. Unbelief whispers that the true church will die out. Do not believe it. Christ will live, and His church will live with Him till the heavens be no more. Has He not said, "Because I live, ye shall live also"? "Oh," you say, "but we shall not see such holy men in the next generation as in past ages." Why not? I hope the next age will see far better men than any of those who are with us at this time. Pray that it may be so. Instead of the fathers, may there be the children, and may these be princes before the Lord!

The stream of divine grace will flow on. Oh, that it may take our sons and daughters in its course! "Bless the lads."

January

18

> *And Moses said unto the people, Fear ye not, stand still, and see the salvation of the Lord, which he will show to you to-day: for the Egyptians whom ye have seen to-day, ye shall see them again no more for ever.*
>
> Exodus 14: 13

These words contain God's command to the believer when he is reduced to great straits and brought into extraordinary difficulties. He cannot retreat; he cannot go forward; he is shut up on the right hand and on the left; what is he now to do? The Master's word to him is, "Stand still." It will be well for him if at such times he listens only to his Master's word, for other and evil advisers come with their suggestions. *Despair* whispers, "Lie down and die; give it all up." But God would have us put on a cheerful courage, and even in our worst times, rejoice in His love and faithfulness. *Cowardice* says, "Retreat; go back to the worldling's way of action; you cannot play the Christian's part, it is too difficult. Relinquish your principles." But, however much Satan may urge this course upon you, you cannot follow it if you are a child of God. *Precipitancy* cries, "Do something. Stir yourself; to stand still and wait is sheer idleness." We *must* be doing something at once— we must do it, so we think—instead of looking to the Lord, who will not only do something but will do everything. *Presumption* boasts, "If the sea be before you, march into it and expect a miracle." But Faith listens neither to Presumption, nor to Despair, nor to Cowardice, nor to Precipitancy, but it hears God say, "Stand still," and immovable as a rock it stands. *"Stand* still"—keep the posture of an upright man, ready for action, expecting further orders, cheerfully and patiently awaiting the directing voice; and it will not be long ere God shall say to you, as distinctly as Moses said it to the people of Israel, "Go forward."

19

> *The pillar of the cloud . . . stood behind them: and it came between the camp of the Egyptians and the camp of Israel; . . . so that the one came not near the other all the night.*
>
> Exodus 14: 19, 20

Note in the text that it is said the pillar went, and *"stood behind them."* I like that, for it is a settled, permanent matter. The Lord had removed, but He was not removing still. He would stay as long as was needful where He then was. That glorious angel, shrouded in the clouds, stood with his drawn sword in the rear of Israel, saying to Pharaoh, "You dare not come further; you cannot break in upon my chosen." He lifted up His vast shield of darkness, and held it up before the tyrant king, so that he could not strike, nay, could not see. All that night his horses champed their bits, but could not pursue the flying host. "They were as still as a stone till thy people passed over, O Lord, till thy people passed over whom thou hadst purchased" (Exod. 15: 16).

It is glorious to think that the Lord stood there, and the furious enemy was compelled to halt. Even thus the Lord remains with the dear child of God. You cannot see anything before you to make you glad, but the living God stands behind you to ward off the adversary. He cannot forsake you. He says to you out of the pillar of cloud, "Can a woman forget her sucking child, that she should not have compassion on the son of her womb? yea, they may forget, yet will I not forget thee" (Isa. 49: 15). He stands fast as your rock, steadfast as your safeguard, sleepless as your watcher, valiant as your champion.

> God is near thee, therefore cheer thee,
> Sad mind!
> He'll defend thee, all around thee,
> And behind.

And Moses stretched out his hand over the sea; and the Lord caused the sea to go back by a strong east wind all that night, and made the sea dry land, and the waters were divided.

Exodus 14: 21

| 20 |

Was it not because the Lord rebuked the sea? The strong east wind did not of itself divide the sea; for a wind naturally strong enough for that would have blown all the people into the air. The wind was used of God to move the waters, but its chief object was to dry up the damp from the floor of the sea, and to make marching easier for the vast host of Israel. Truly the Lord was there, triumphing gloriously. No cloudy pillar was seen across the

January

waters as Israel looked forward to the shore; but yet the Lord was there majestically; and you may have but little comfort of the Lord's presence at this time, and yet God may be with you wondrously. Do not so much set your heart upon comfort, but rejoice in the fact which gladdened Hagar in the wilderness: "Thou God seest me" (Gen. 16: 13). It does not matter to the fire whether the logs are cast upon it from the front, or the oil poured upon it secretly from behind the wall, so long as it finds its fuel. To you the daily supply of grace is more important than the supply of comfort, and this shall never fail you so long as you live.

And the children of Israel went into the midst of the sea upon the dry ground: and the waters were a wall unto them on their right hand, and on their left.

Exodus 14: 22

After all, the host of Israel did not require any guide in front when they came to the sea. "How is that?" you ask. Why, beloved, there were no two ways to choose from: they could not miss the way, for they must needs march through the sea. No room for wandering remained: their road was walled up, and they could not miss it. So when men come into deep trouble, and cannot get out of it, they scarcely need a guide; for their own plain path is submission and patience.

Tried child of God, you have to bear your trouble, and when that is quite clear your way is no longer doubtful. Cast all your care on Him who cares for you, and in patience possess your soul. "Oh, but I thought I was going to find a way of escape made for me." Listen! "God is faithful, who will not suffer you to be tempted above that ye are able; but will with the temptation also make a way to escape, *that ye may be able to bear it*" (1 Cor. 10: 13). You have to bear it, you see. Your great want for this present is faith in God, who has said: "I will bring again from Bashan, I will bring my people again from the depths of the sea" (Ps. 68: 22).

What they did want was the pillar of cloud behind them, and that is where they had it. We read that Israel lifted up their eyes and saw the Egyptians, and then they began to tremble, and cry out: and so God drew the blinds down that His poor children could not see their frightful taskmasters. It is a great mercy when God does not let us see everything. What the eye does not see, perhaps the heart will not rue.

Then sang Moses and the children of Israel this song unto the Lord, and spake, saying, I will sing unto the Lord, for he hath triumphed gloriously: the horse and his rider hath he thrown into the sea. The Lord is my strength and song, and he is become my salvation: he is my God, and I will prepare him a habitation; my father's God, and I will exalt him.

Exodus 15: 1, 2

22

The first verse of this song was quoted by David. I think you will find it in almost the same words three times in the Psalms; but especially in the hundred and eighteenth Psalm you have the exact words, "The Lord is my strength and song; and is become my salvation." As if the Holy Spirit, when He furnished Isaiah with his noblest minstrelsy, could not excel the earlier strains of Moses. Isaiah himself, in chapter twelve, has the same words: "Jehovah is my strength and my song; he also is become my salvation." It is evident that this patriotic song was interwoven with the life of Israel, and that when good and gracious men would express themselves in praise at their very best, they fell back upon this song of Moses, and they sang unto the Lord who had triumphed gloriously. So full of significance then as this song is, there is something for us to learn from it today. May God the Holy Ghost, who dictated this song to Moses, now write it afresh upon His people's hearts! Breathe on us, Holy Spirit, that we also may be filled with the praises of Jehovah.

The Lord is my strength and song, and he is become my salvation. . . .

Exodus 15: 2
Read Exodus 15: 1–18

23

Take up the first note: "The Lord is my *strength.*" What a noble utterance! Poor Israel had no strength! She had cried out by reason

January

of her sore bondage, making bricks without straw. Poor Israel was weakness itself! but Jehovah drew near in power. The Lord is my strength when I have no strength of my own. By the strength of the Lord, Israel came forth with a high hand and an outstretched arm; Egypt was glad when they departed, and the Egyptians gave them jewels of silver and jewels of gold that they might wish them well in departing; for God had given them honor in the sight of the people. Thus the Lord is our strength when we are at the extremity of weakness.

The Lord was also Israel's strength against strength. Pharaoh was exceeding mighty. The kings of the earth trembled at the neighing of his war-horse; the rattling of his chariots made the very heavens to resound; but God was more than a match for him. When strength comes out against God's people, God meets it with his omnipotence. What is Pharaoh's strength when matched against Jehovah's might? A paper pellet thrown against a wall of brass. The enemy said, "I will pursue; I will overtake; I will divide the spoil," and so on; but Jehovah had only to blow with His wind, and the sea covered them. Thus will the Lord be our strength when the mighty are against us.

Thou in thy mercy hast led forth the people which thou hast redeemed: thou hast guided them in thy strength unto thy holy habitation.

Exodus 15: 13

God is love in its highest degree. He is love rendered more than love. Love is not God, but God is love; He is full of grace, He is the plenitude of mercy—He delights in mercy.

I believe that every flower in a garden, which is tended by a wise gardener, could tell of some particular care that the gardener takes of it. He does for the dahlia what he does not for the sunflower; somewhat is wanted by the rose that is not required by the lily; and the geranium calls for an attention which is not given to the honeysuckle. Each flower wins from the gardener a special culture.

He loves us better than we love ourselves.

But I have said unto you, Ye shall inherit their land, and I will give it unto you to possess it, a land that floweth with milk and honey: I am the Lord your God, which have separated you from other people.

Leviticus 20: 24

25

The Lord calls His servants unto the separated life, and because of His authority they are bound to obey. He calls by His Word, either preached or read: it comes to the individual by an application of the Spirit of God, so that the man yields cheerful assent thereto. He is drawn, and therefore he runs. Such a person feels it a pleasure to take Christ for his example, and to put his feet down in the very tracks of the Lord Jesus. It is ours to follow the Lord's precept and example with great care and solemn determination, turning neither to the right hand nor to the left. It was so with Abram: is it so with you?

Because this call comes from God, *it has for us a supreme authority*. We follow our Lord even when darkness is round about Him: though we know not the way, we know the Lord, and therefore we follow Him implicitly. To us the Word of God is more than the decrees of emperors, or the statutes of senators. If this thing were of men, if this thing were ordained by a learned council, or a reverend bench, it would be of small account in our eyes; but when He that made us and redeemed us speaks to us, we can only reply, "Help thy servants to do thy will, for thy will is our delight."

And Moses said unto the Lord, Wherefore hast thou afflicted thy servant? and wherefore have I not found favor in thy sight, that thou layest the burden of all this people upon me?

Numbers 11: 11
Read Numbers 11: 1–15

26

God must explain His dealings to us by revealing Himself to us, because *those ways are in themselves frequently mysterious.* The

January

Lord moved Pharaoh to treat Israel with great severity, and to make them serve with rigor. They made bricks without straw, and the tale of bricks was doubled, till they cried by reason of their taskmasters. How was Israel to perceive that Jehovah was at the back of all this? Yet the Lord was thus accomplishing His design of bringing His chosen out of Egypt.

The most difficult thing was not for Pharaoh to be compelled to let Israel go, but to bring the people into such a state that they would be willing to quit the fertile land. They lived in plenty in the land of Goshen, and did eat of the leeks, and the garlic, and the onions of Egypt; and had they been let alone, they would have had no wish to go forth to Canaan. They would have been satisfied to become Egyptians had they always been treated as they were treated at the first.

How were the Israelites to understand, till God explained it, that this rough usage on the part of Pharaoh was to wean them from Egypt, and make them willing to go out even into a desert, that they might escape from the tyrant? When Pharaoh began to kill their firstborn, when He refused to let them go for a few days to offer sacrifice, and oppressed them more and more, how were they to know that this was a part of the plan of Jehovah who had loved them with an everlasting love?

Even after He had smitten Pharaoh with all His plagues, and Egypt was glad when they departed, how could they comprehend why God led them down to the brink of the Red Sea? Between Migdol and the sea, over against Baal-zephon, the host was made to encamp, even in a place from which there was no escape from their cruel foes, whose chariots they heard rattling behind them. How were they to know that the Lord had His way in the sea, and His path in the mighty waters? How could they guess that He meant to bring Egypt down into the depth of the sea, and there to crush the dragon with so heavy a blow, that through the forty years of Israel's sojourn in the wilderness, upon the Egyptian border, the nation should never be troubled by its old taskmaster?

With a high hand, and an outstretched arm, the Lord brought forth His people, but they understood not His wonders in Egypt till He appeared unto them and said, "I am the Lord thy God, which have brought thee out of the land of Egypt, out of the house of bondage." God's dealings with His chosen are often so mysterious that they cannot know them till they know Himself.

He [*the Lord*] *hath not beheld iniquity in Jacob, neither hath he seen perverseness in Israel: the Lord his God is with him, and the shout of a king is among them. God brought them out of Egypt; he hath as it were the strength of a unicorn.*
Numbers 23: 21, 22

27

The blessing that results when "The Lord . . . is with him" is *strength.* "He hath as it were the strength of a unicorn" (v. 22). It is generally agreed that the creature here meant is an extinct species of urus or ox, most nearly represented by the buffalo of the present period. When God is in a church, what rugged strength, what massive force, what irresistible energy is sure to be there! And how untamable is the living force! You cannot yoke this buffalo to everybody's plow: it has its own free way of living, and it acts after its own style. When the Lord is with a church her power is not in numbers, though very speedily she will increase; her power is not wealth, though God will take care that the money comes when it is needed: her power lies in God, and that power becomes irresistible, untamable, unconquerable. Force and energy are with the Lord. I'm afraid that what many bodies of Christian people need is this force. Examine yonder religious body: it is huge, but it lacks muscle; it is a fine-looking organization, but soul, sinew, backbone are wanting. Where God is there is sure to be life-force. When the Spirit of God descended upon the first saints they began to speak with wondrous power; and though they were persecuted, they were not subdued. No bit could be put into their mouths to hold them in, for they went everywhere preaching the word. Of the true Israel it shall be said—his strength is as the strength of the buffalo: it cannot be controlled or conquered.

Turn you, and take your journey . . . to the land of the Canaanites, and unto Lebanon, unto the great river, the river Euphrates. Behold, I have set the land before you: go in and possess the land which the Lord sware unto your fathers, Abraham, Isaac, and Jacob. . . .
Deuteronomy 1: 7, 8

28

Unless the Lord Himself shall soon descend from heaven with a shout, we shall all die. Yes, the hour of our departure hastens on.

January

Then we shall have to cut ourselves loose from our moorings, be they what they may. Soon shall we hear this word from heaven, "Get thee out of thy country, and from thy kindred, and from thy father's house, unto a land that I will show thee." This will be our summons to the better Canaan, the land that flows with milk and honey. We shall depart out of this world to face an unknown eternity; but we shall by no means dread the migration.

He who has crossed the great river, the river Euphrates, will not fear the Jordan. To give up the world will be no new thing for you or for me: we have given it up many times already. We have frequently given everything into the Lord's hands in real earnest, and we can readily do it once more. We live here as strangers and sojourners, and we find little to charm us in this foreign land. Our treasure is above, and it will be a joy for our souls to rise to the place where our hearts already dwell. We cannot be sorry to quit a dead world. Let us journey, as Abram did, toward the south; that is to say, let us get still further away from the old abode. Let us make for the heart of Immanuel's land. Let us press toward the New Jerusalem, the heavenly city, and rest not till we stand in our lot and behold Him whom Abram saw with gladness.

29

Thou wast a servant in the land of Egypt, and . . . the Lord thy God brought thee out . . . through a mighty hand and by a stretched out arm.

Deuteronomy 5: 15

It is important that we cry for grace from God to see His hand in every trial, and then for grace, seeing His hand, to submit at once to it—not only to submit, but to rejoice in it. "It is the Lord, let him do what seemeth him good." I think there is generally an end to troubles when we get to that, for when the Lord sees we are willing that He should do what He wills, then He takes back His hand and says: "I need not chasten My child; he submits himself to Me. What would have been worked out by My chastisement is worked out already, and therefore I will not chasten him."

There are two ways of getting help. One is to go around to all your friends, be disappointed, and then go to God at last. The other is to go to God first. That is the shortest way. God can make your friends help you afterwards. Seek first God and His righteousness. Out of all troubles the surest deliverance is from God's right hand. Don't go to friends, but pour out your story to God:

> Were half the breath that's vainly spent,
> To heaven in supplication sent;
> Our cheerful song would oftener be,
> Hear what the Lord hath done for me.

Human friends fail us. The strongest arm can be broken, and the most faithful heart will sometimes waver. But our God is eternal and omnipotent; who ever trusted Him in vain?

David learned this lesson well and shared it many times in his songs of love for his Savior God. Here are some of them: "God hath given his angels charge over thee"; "he that dwelleth in the secret place of the Most High, shall abide under the shadow of the Almighty." The Lord said of him: "Because he hath set his love upon me, therefore will I deliver him: I will set him on high, because he hath known my name." He has proved it by trusting in Me alone; therefore will I never fail him. Lean wholly upon God, and since He is everywhere you will stand upright leaning upon Him.

And now, Israel, what doth the Lord . . . require of thee, but to fear the Lord, . . . to walk in all his ways, and to love him, and to serve the Lord thy God with all thy heart and with all thy soul.

Deuteronomy 10: 12

| 30 |

God is glorified by our serving Him in our proper vocations. Every lawful trade may be sanctified by the gospel to noblest ends. Turn to the Bible, and you will find the most menial forms of labor connected either with most daring deeds of faith, or with persons whose lives have been illustrious for holiness. Therefore, do not be discontented with your calling. Whatever God has made your position, or your work, abide in that, unless you are *quite sure*

January

that He calls you to something else. Let your first care be to glorify God to the utmost of your power where you are. Fill your present sphere to His praise, and if He needs you in another He will show it you.

31

The Lord thy God turned the curse into a blessing unto thee, because the Lord' thy God loved thee.

Deuteronomy 23: 5

Poor sinner, do take heart, remember God knows, as we know not, where you are. If you are in the deepest pit in the forest, his almighty eye can see to the bottom. Ay, and in one of the favored moments of the day of salvation—that time accepted— He will send home a promise so sweetly that all your fetters will be scattered and your dawn begin; and He will give you the oil of joy for mourning and the garment of praise for the spirit of heaviness. Believe now, and you will be comforted now; for the time of faith is the time of comfort.

February

The Lord shall establish thee a holy people unto himself, as he hath sworn unto thee, if thou shalt keep the commandments of the Lord thy God, and walk in his ways.

Deuteronomy 28: 9

1

Christ will be master of the heart, and sin must be mortified. If your *life* is unholy your *heart* is unchanged; you are an unsaved person. If the Savior has not sanctified you, renewed you, given you a hatred of sin and a love of holiness, the grace which does not make a man better than others is a worthless counterfeit. Christ saves His people, not *in* their sins, but *from* them. "Without holiness no man shall see the Lord." "Let every one that nameth the name of Christ depart from iniquity" (2 Tim. 2: 19). If not saved from sin, how shall we hope to be counted among His people? Lord, save me even now from all evil, and enable me to honor my Savior.

Only be thou strong and very courageous.

Joshua 1: 7

2

Our God's tender love for His servants makes Him concerned for the state of their inward feelings. He desires them to be of good courage. Some think it a small thing for a believer to be bothered by doubts and fears, but not God. From this text it is plain that our Master would not have us entangled with fears. He would have us without anxiety, without doubt, without cowardice.

Our Master does not take lightly our unbelief, as we do. When we are desponding we are subject to a grievous disease, not to be trifled with, but to be taken at once to the beloved Physician. Our Lord does not like to see us sad. It was the law of Ahasuerus

February

that no one should come into the king's presence dressed in mourning: this is not the law of the King of Kings, for we may come mourning as we are; but still He would have us put on the garment of praise, for there is much reason to rejoice.

The Christian man ought to be of courageous spirit that he may glorify the Lord by enduring trials in a heroic manner. If he is fearful and fainthearted, it will dishonor his God. Besides, it is a bad example.

This disease of doubting and discouragement is an epidemic which soon spreads among the Lord's flock. One downcast believer makes twenty souls sad. Moreover, unless your courage is kept up Satan will be too much for you. Let your spirit be joyful in God your Savior; so the joy of the Lord will be your strength and no servant of Satan will make headway against you: but cowardice throws down the banner.

Moreover, labor is light to a man of cheerful spirit; and success waits upon cheerfulness. The man who toils, rejoicing in his God, believing with all his heart, has success guaranteed. He who sows in hope will reap in joy; therefore, dear reader, "be thou strong, and very courageous."

And the children of Joseph spake unto Joshua, saying, Why hast thou given me but one lot and one portion to inherit, seeing I am a great people, forasmuch as the Lord hath blessed me hitherto?

Joshua 17: 14

Can you not say, "The Lord hath blessed me *hitherto*"? Has He ever denied you one of the blessings common to the covenanted family? Has He ever told you that you may not pray, or that you may not trust? Has He forbidden you to cast your burden on the Lord? Has He denied you fellowship with Himself and communion with His dear Son? Has He laid an embargo on any one of the promises? Has He shut you out from any one of the provisions of His love? I know that it is not so if you are His child, but you can heartily exclaim, "The Lord hath blessed me hitherto." "Such honor have all the saints." By His gracious past of love the Lord guarantees to His redeemed a future of equal blessedness, for His loving-kindness never departs from those on whom it lights.

[Joshua said:] If it seem evil unto you to serve the Lord, choose you this day whom ye will serve . . . but as for me and my house, we will serve the Lord.

Joshua 24: 15

You cannot hold two opinions in the matter of soul-religion. If God be God, serve Him, and do it thoroughly; but if this world be God, serve it, and make no profession of religion. If you think the things of the world the best, serve them. But remember, if the Lord be your God, you cannot have Baal too; you must have one thing or else the other. "No man can serve two *masters.*" If God be served, He will be a master; and if the devil be served, it will not be long before he will be a master; and "ye cannot serve two *masters.*" Oh! be wise, and think not that the two can be mingled together.

And the Spirit of the Lord came mightily upon him [Samson] and he rent him [the lion] as he would have rent a kid, and he had nothing in his hand. . . .

Judges 14: 6

I invite you to remember that *it was by the Spirit of God that the victory was won.* We read, "And the Spirit of the Lord came mightily upon him, and he rent him as he would have rent a kid." Let the Holy Spirit help us in our trouble and we need neither company nor weapon; but without him what can we do? Good Bishop Hall says, "If that roaring lion, that goes about continually seeking whom he may devour, find us alone among the vineyards of the Philistines, where is our hope? Not in our heels, he is swifter than we: not in our weapons, we are naturally unarmed: not in our hands, which are weak and languishing; but in the Spirit of

February

God, by whom we can do all things. If God fight in us, who can resist us? There is a stronger lion in us than that against us."

Here is our one necessity—to be endowed with power from on high: the power of the Holy Ghost. Helped by the Spirit of God, the believer's victory will be complete: the lion shall not just be driven away but it shall be rent in pieces. Girt with the Spirit's power, our victory shall be as easy as it will be perfect: Samson rent the lion as though it were a little lamb, or a kid of the goats. Well said Paul, "I can do all things through Christ that strengtheneth me."

If we were surrounded by all the devils in hell we need not fear them for an instant if the Lord be on our side. We are mightier than all hell's legions when the Spirit is mightily upon us. Sometimes a raging corruption, or a strong habit, wars upon us, and then we conquer by the might of the sanctifying Spirit of God, who is with us and shall be in us evermore. Or else it is the world which tempts, and our feet have almost gone; but we overcome the world through the victory of faith: and if Satan raises against us the lust of the flesh, the lust of the eye, and the pride of life, all at once, we are still delivered, for the Lord is a wall of fire round about us.

And after a time he [Samson] returned to take her, and he turned aside to see the carcass of the lion: and behold, there was a swarm of bees and honey in the carcass. . . . And he took thereof in his hands, and went on eating, and came to his father and mother and he gave them, and they did eat. . . .

Judges 14: 8, 9

But, beloved, it is written, "As he is, so are we also in this world." All that are true Christians are, in a measure, like the Christ whose name they bear, and it is to His image that we are finally to be conformed. When He shall appear we shall be like Him, for we shall see Him as He is; and meanwhile, in proportion as we see Him now, "we are changed into the same image, from glory to glory, even as by the Spirit of the Lord." The Samson type may well serve as the symbol of every Christian in the world. The believer has been helped by divine grace in his spiritual conflicts, and he has known "the victory which overcometh the world, even our faith." He has thus been made more than a conqueror through Him that loved us, and now he stands in the midst of his fellowmen inviting them to Jesus. With the honey in his hands, which he continues still to feast upon, he displays the heavenly sweetness to all that are round about him, saying, "O taste and see that the Lord is good: blessed is the man that trusteth in him."

Howbeit the hair of his head began to grow again after he was shaven.

Judges 16: 22
Read Judges 16

7

Many a man have I seen come back to the dear Savior on account of the oppression which he has endured from his old master, the prince of darkness! If he had been treated well, he might never have returned to Christ any more; but it is not possible for the citizens of the far country to treat prodigals well; sooner or later they starve them and oppress them, so that they run away home.

When Samson's hair began to grow, what did it prophesy? Well, first, it prophesied *hope for Samson.* I will be bound to say that he put his hand to his head, and felt that it was getting bristly, and then he put his hand to his beard, and found it rough. Yes, it was coming, and he thought within himself, "It will be all right soon, I shall not get my eyes back. *They* will not grow again. I am an awful loser by my sin, but I shall get my strength back again, for my hair is growing. I shall be able to strike a blow for my people and for my God yet." So round the mill he went, grinding away, grinding away, but every now and then putting his hand to his head, and thinking, "My hair is growing; oh, it is growing again! My strength is returning to me." The mill went round merrily to the tune of hope, for he felt that he would get his old strength back again. Then they loaded it, and tightened it to make

February

the work heavier, yet his hair was growing; and so he found the burden lighter than it had been before, and his heart began to dance within him, in prospect of being his former self again.

Now, if any of you have signs of restoring grace in your hearts, and you are coming back to your God and Savior, be glad, be thankful. Do not hesitate to let your renewed devotion to God be seen by those round about you. If the grace of God is moving you at all, be hopeful and quicken your steps, and come to Jesus. Come to Him just now even as you came at first.

And he shall be as the light of the morning, when the sun riseth, even a morning without clouds; as the tender grass springing out of the earth by clear shining after rain.
2 Samuel 23: 4

The way of Christ as King, according to David's description, is like "clear shining after rain," whereby the tender grass is made to spring out of the earth. So have we often seen it. After a heavy shower of rain, or after a continued rainy season, when the sun shines, there is a delightful clearness and freshness in the air that we seldom perceive at other times. Perhaps the brightest weather is just when the rain has ceased, when the wind has driven away the clouds, and the sun peers forth from his chambers to gladden the earth with smiles.

And thus is it with the Christian's exercised heart. Sorrow does not last forever. After the pelting rain of adversity comes ever and anon the clear shining. Tried believer, consider this. After all your afflictions there remains a rest for the people of God. There is a clear shining coming to your soul when all this rain is past. When your time of rebuke is over and gone, it shall be to you as the earth when the tempest has sobbed itself to sleep, when the clouds have rent themselves to rags, and when the sun peers forth once more as a bridegroom in his glorious array. To this end, sorrow cooperates with the bliss that follows it, like rain and sunshine, to bring forth the tender blade. The tribulation and the consolation work together for our good.

[Solomon prayed] The Lord our God be with us, as he was with our fathers: let him not leave us, nor forsake us.

1 Kings 8: 57

$\boxed{9}$

O Christian, do you doubt as to whether God will fulfill His promise? Shall the munitions of rock be carried by storm? Shall the storehouses of heaven fail? Do you think that your heavenly Father knows not that you have need of food and raiment? Do you think He will forget you? When not a sparrow falls to the ground without your Father's knowledge, and the very hairs of your head are all numbered, will you mistrust and doubt Him? Full many there be who have been tried till at last they have been driven to exercise faith in God, and the moment of their faith has been the instant of their deliverance.

The believer commits his soul to the hand of his God; it came from Him, it is His own. Up until now He has sustained it, He is able to keep it, and it is most fitting that He should receive it. All things are safe in His hands; what we entrust to the Lord will be secure, both now and in that day of days toward which we are hastening. It is peaceful living and glorious dying to repose in the care of Heaven. At all times we should commit our all to Jesus' faithful hand; then, though life may hang on a thread, and adversities may multiply as the sands of the sea, our soul shall dwell at ease, and delight itself in quiet resting places.

The barrel of meal wasted not, neither did the cruse of oil fail, according to the word of the Lord, which he spake by Elijah.

1 Kings 17: 16

$\boxed{10}$

See here the faithfulness of divine love. You observe that this woman had daily necessities. She had herself and her son to feed in a time of famine; and now, in addition, the prophet Elijah was to be fed too. But though the need was threefold, yet the supply of meal wasted not, for she had a constant supply. Each day she made calls upon the barrel, but yet each day it remained the same.

You, dear reader, have daily necessities, and because they come so frequently, you are apt to fear that the barrel will fail you.

February

Rest assured that, according to the Word of God, this shall not be the case.

Each day, though it bring its trouble, shall bring its help; and though you should live to outnumber the years of Methuselah, and though your needs should be as many as the sands of the seashore, yet shall God's grace and mercy last through all your necessities, and you shall never know a real lack.

For three long years, in this widow's days, the heavens never saw a cloud, and the stars never wept a holy tear of dew upon the wicked earth: famine, and desolation, and death made the land a howling wilderness, but this woman never was hungry, but always joyful in abundance.

So shall it be with you. "Your bread shall be given you, and your water shall be sure." Better have God for your guardian, than the Bank of England for your possession. You might spend the wealth of the Indies, but the infinite riches of God you can never exhaust.

11

For the arrows of the Almighty are within me, the poison whereof drinketh up my spirit: the terrors of God do set themselves in array against me.

Job 6: 4

The path of the Christian is not always bright with sunshine; he has his seasons of darkness and storm. True, it is written in God's Word, "Her ways are ways of pleasantness, and all her paths are peace." It is a great truth that the Christian faith is calculated to give a man happiness below as well as bliss above; but experience tells us that if the course of the just be "as the shining light that shineth more and more unto the perfect day," yet sometimes *that* light is eclipsed. At certain periods clouds cover the believer's sun, and he walks in darkness and sees no light.

There are many who have enjoyed the presence of God for a season; they have basked in the sunshine of the earliest stages of their Christian experience; they have walked among the "green pastures" by the side of the "still waters," but suddenly they find their glorious sky is clouded; instead of the land of Goshen they have to tread the sandy desert; in the place of sweet waters, they find troubled streams, bitter to their taste, and they say, "Surely, if I were a child of God, this would not happen."

Don't say that, you who are walking in present darkness. The best of God's children must drink from the bitter well; the dearest of His people must bear the cross. No Christian has enjoyed perpetual prosperity; no believer can always keep his harp from the willows. Perhaps the Lord allotted you at first a smooth and unclouded path because you were weak and timid. He tempered the wind for the shorn lamb, but now that you are stronger in the spiritual life, you must enter upon the riper and rougher experience of God's full-grown children.

We need winds and tempests to exercise our faith, to tear off the rotten bough of self-dependence, and to root us more firmly in Christ. The day of evil reveals to us the value of our glorious hope.

Now my days are swifter than a post [runner]: they flee away, they see no good. They are passed away as the swift ships. . . .
Job 9: 25, 26

12

You have sometimes seen how the ship cuts through the billows, leaving a white furrow behind her, and causing the sea to boil around her. Such is life, says Job, "like the swift ships." I cannot stop its motion; I may direct it with the rudder of God's Holy Spirit; but nevertheless, like a swift ship, my life must speed on its way until it reaches its haven. Where is that haven to be? Shall it be found in the land of bitterness and barrenness, that dreary region of the lost? Or shall it be that sweet haven of eternal peace?

For his eyes are upon the ways of man, and he seeth all his goings. . . . The steps of a good man are ordered by the Lord: and he delighteth in his way.
Job 34: 21; Psalm 37: 23

13

"The steps of a good man are ordered by the Lord." An all-wise God disposes His people according to His sovereign will. Let us

February

not seek to alter our destiny, but let us try to make the best of our circumstances. This is what Joshua exhorted Ephraim and Manasseh to do. "You have a hill country crowned with forests: hew them down. You have fat valleys occupied by Canaanites: drive out the present inhabitants." O, if we would but thoroughly enjoy what God has freely given us, we should be happy to the full, and even anticipate the joys of heaven. We have a deep river of delights in the covenant of grace, yet we are content to paddle about its shores. We are only up to our ankles, the most of us, whereas the waters are "waters to swim in." A great sun of everlasting love shines upon the globe of our life with tropical force, but we get away to the North Pole of doubt and fear, and then complain that the sun has such little heat, or that he is so long below the horizon. He who will not go to the fire ought not to complain that the room is cold. If we would heartily feed upon what the Lord has set on our table, accept the ring which He has prepared for our finger, and wear the garments which He has provided for our comfort, we might here on earth make music and dancing before the Lord.

14
Behold, God is mighty, and despiseth not any: he is mighty in strength and wisdom.

Job 36: 5

Each of God's saints is sent into the world to prove some part of the divine character. In heaven we shall read the great book of the experience of all the saints, and gather from that book the whole of the divine character as having been proved and illustrated. Each Christian man is a manifestation and display of some position or other of God; a different part may belong to each of us, but when the whole shall be combined, when all the rays of evidence shall be brought, as it were, into one great sun, and shine forth with meridian splendor, we shall see in Christian experience a beautiful revelation of our God.

Wherever the church is, there is God. God is pleased, in His mercy and condescension, to stoop from the highest heavens to dwell in this lower heaven—the heaven of His church. It is here, among the household of faith, He deigns—let me say it with sacred reverence—to unbend Himself, and be familiar with those round about Him whom He hath adopted into His family. He may be a consuming fire abroad, but when He comes into His own house He is all mercy, mildness, and love. Abroad He does great works of power; but at home in His own house He does great works of grace.

Canst thou bind the sweet influences of Pleiades, or loose the bands of Orion?

Job 38: 31

15

In mythology, Orion was a giant-sized hunter who pursued Pleiades, the seven daughters of Atlas. He was eventually slain by Artemis and then placed in the sky as a constellation of stars. Job says of the Lord that He looses the bands of Orion, and none but He. What a blessing it is that He can do it! O that He would perform the wonder tonight! Lord, end my winter, and let my spring begin. I cannot, with all my longings, raise my soul out of her death and dullness, but all things are possible with You. I need celestial influences, the clear shinings of Your love, the beams of Your grace, the light of Your countenance; these are the Pleiades to me. I suffer much from sin and temptation; these are my wintry signs, my terrible Orion. Lord, work wonders in me, and for me.

We are so little, that if God should manifest His greatness without condescension, we should be trampled under His feet; but God, who must stoop to view the skies, and bow to see what angels do, turns His eye yet lower, and looks to the lowly and contrite, and makes them great.

"Thy gentleness hath made me great" (Ps. 18: 35). How marvelous has been our experience of God's gentleness! How gentle have been His corrections! How gentle His teachings! How gentle His drawings! Meditate upon this theme, O believer. Let gratitude be awakened; let humility be deepened; let love be quickened, ere this day close.

February

16

Salvation belongeth unto the Lord. . . . But the salvation of the righteous is of the Lord: he is their strength in the time of trouble.

Psalms 3: 8; 37: 39

It is well to be the sheep of God's pasture, even if we have been wandering sheep. The straying sheep has an owner, and however far it may stray from the fold, it ceases not to belong to that owner. I believe that God will yet bring back into the fold every one of His own sheep, and they shall all be saved. It is something to feel our wanderings, for if we feel ourselves to be lost, we shall certainly be saved; if we feel ourselves to have wandered, we shall certainly be brought back.

The city of refuge set apart by the Lord had round it suburbs of a very great extent. Two thousand cubits were allowed for grazing land for the cattle of the priests, and a thousand cubits within these for fields and vineyards. Now, no sooner did a man reach the outside of the city, the suburbs, than he was safe; it was not necessary for him to get within the walls, but the suburbs themselves were sufficient protection. Learn, hence, that if you but touch the hem of Christ's garment, you will be made whole; if you but lay hold of him with "faith as a grain of mustard seed," with faith which is scarcely a believing, but is truly a believing, you are safe.

17

Stand in awe, and sin not: commune with your own heart upon your bed, and be still. Selah. Offer the sacrifices of righteousness, and put your trust in the Lord.

Psalm 4: 4, 5

David was surrounded with many wicked and cruel enemies. They touched him in a tender place when they mocked his religion, and so turned his glory into shame. They invented all kinds of lies against him; but the worst of all was that they said, "There is no help for him in God."

David first made his appeal to God in prayer. Herein he showed his wisdom. You can drive a better business at the mercy-seat than in the world's jangling markets. You will get more relief from the righteous Lord than from ungodly men. To enter into debate is never so profitable as to enter into devotion. Carry not your complaint into the lower courts, but go at once to the Court of King's

February

Bench, where the Judge of all presides. Copy David and David's Lord, who in the days of His flesh with strong crying and tears poured out His soul before the Father.

For thou hast made him a little lower than the angels, and hast crowned him with glory and honor.

Psalm 8: 5
Read Psalm 8

18

I understand by "glory" our perfected manhood. When God made Adam he was a far superior being to any of us. Man's place in creation was very remarkable. The Psalmist says, "For thou hast made him a little lower than the angels, and hast crowned him with glory and honor. Thou madest him to have dominion over the works of thy hands; thou hast put all things under his feet: all sheep and oxen, yea, and the beasts of the field; the fowl of the air, and the fish of the sea, and whatsoever passeth through the paths of the seas."

Can we ever rise to this honor? Brethren, listen, "It doth not yet appear what we shall be, but we know that when Christ shall appear we shall be like him, for we shall see him as he is." Is there any limit to the growth of the mind of man? Can we tell what we may reach? Then we shall know even as we are known by God. Now we see, but it is "through a glass darkly," but then we shall see "face to face." We shall not always be as we are today, contracted and hampered because of our little knowledge, and our slender faculties, and our dull perceptions.

What a man will become we can scarcely tell when he is remade in the image of God, and made like unto our divine Lord who is "the firstborn among many brethren." Our bodies are to be developed into something infinitely brighter and better than the bodies of men here below: and as for the soul, we cannot guess to what an elevation it shall be raised in Christ Jesus. There is room for the largest expectation here, as we conjecture what will be the full accomplishment of the vast intent of eternal love, an intent which has involved the sacrifice of the only-begotten Son of God. That can be no mean design which has been carried on at the expense of the best that heaven itself possessed.

February

19 *The Lord also will be a refuge for the oppressed, a refuge in times of trouble.*

Psalm 9: 9

It will always give a Christian the greatest calm, quiet, ease and peace, to think of the perfect righteousness of Christ. How often are the saints of God downcast and sad! I do not think they ought to be. I do not think they would if they could always see their perfection in Christ. When the believer says, "I live on Christ alone; I rest on Him solely for salvation; and I believe that, however unworthy, I am still saved in Jesus"; then there rises up as a motive of gratitude this thought—"Shall I not live to Christ? Shall I not love Him and serve Him, seeing that I am saved by His merits?" "The love of Christ constraineth us," "that they which live should not henceforth live unto themselves, but unto Him which died for them." If saved by imputed righteousness, we shall greatly value imparted righteousness.

It certainly is not possible for us to be in a position where Omnipotence cannot assist us. God hath servants everywhere. There are "treasures hid in the sand," and the Lord's chosen shall eat thereof. When the clouds hide the mountains they are as real as in the sunshine; so the promise and the Providence of God are unchanged by the obscurity of our faith, or the difficulties of our position.

When we are at our worst let us trust with unshaking faith. Recollect that then is the time when we can most glorify God by faith.

20 *Lord, thou hast heard the desire of the humble: thou wilt prepare their heart, thou wilt cause thine ear to hear.*

Psalm 10: 17

Apply this logic to prayer. God has answered prayer, and therefore He will answer it. Of this first statement many of us are witnesses. The evidences of that truth are with us in daily experience; we have proofs of the power of prayer as innumerable as the stars of heaven. Because the Lord has heard us out of His holy place we infer that He will still hear us, and therefore as long as we live will we call upon Him. This is no casual thing, but it is Jehovah's perpetual name and standing memorial—the God that hears prayer. Never while the earth endures will He forsake the throne of grace and turn a deaf ear to the cries of His suppliant Israel.

It is necessary that you pray, for the needy must cry to their Helper; and it is profitable that you pray, for the bosoms of suppliants are filled with benedictions. It is not a vain thing to wait upon God; it is your comfort, your strength, your life. If you seek honor it should be your delight to pray; for nothing is more ennobling than to win the ear of the Lord of all. A man admitted to audience with the Most High is honored in an unspeakable degree.

The Lord trieth the righteous.

Psalm 11: 5

21

All events are under the control of Providence; consequently all the trials of our outward life are traceable at once to the great First Cause. All providences are doors to trials. Even our mercies, like roses, have their thorns. Our mountains are not too high, and our valleys are not too low, for temptations: trials lurk on all roads. Everywhere, above and beneath, we are beset and surrounded with dangers. Yet no shower falls unpermitted from the threatening cloud; every drop has its order before it hastens to the earth. The trials that come from God are sent to prove and strengthen us.

If the most precious are tried in the fire, are we to escape the crucible? If the diamond must be ground upon the wheel, are we to be made perfect without suffering? Who has commanded the wind to cease from blowing because our bark is on the deep? Why and for what reason should we be treated better than our Lord? The Firstborn felt the rod, and why not the younger brethren? It is pride which would choose a downy pillow and a silken couch for a soldier of the cross. Wiser far is he who, being first resigned to the divine will, grows by the energy of grace to be pleased with it, and so learns to gather lilies at the foot of the cross, and, like Samson, to find honey in the lion.

February

22

I will sing unto the Lord, because he hath dealt bountifully with me.

Psalm 13: 6

"Return unto thy rest, O my soul; for the Lord hath dealt bountifully with thee" (Ps. 116: 7). It was at the still hour, when the gates of the day were closing, that with weary wing the dove came back to her master: O Lord, enable me this evening thus to return to Jesus. She could not endure to spend a night hovering over the restless waste, nor can I bear to be even for another hour away from Jesus, the rest of my heart, the home of my spirit. She did not merely alight upon the roof of the ark, she "came into him"; even so would my longing spirit look into the secret of the Lord, pierce to the interior of truth, enter into that which is within the veil, and reach to my Beloved in very deed.

"The Lord is slow to anger, and great in power" (Nahum 1: 3), but the greatness of His power brings us mercy. Dear reader, what is your state this day? Can you by humble faith look to Jesus and say, "My substitute, You are my rock, my trust"? Then, beloved, be not afraid of God's power; for now that you are forgiven and accepted, now that by faith you have fled to Christ for refuge, the power of God need no more terrify you, than the shield and sword of the warrior need terrify those whom he loves. Rather rejoice that He who is "great in power" is your Father and Friend.

23

The fool hath said in his heart, There is no God. . . .

Psalm 14: 1

I say, "Does the fool think he can argue me out of my peace of heart, my joy in the Lord, my hope of heaven?" It cannot be: the experienced believer is invulnerable from head to foot against anything and everything that can be hurled against him by skepticism.

We are as sure of the truth of the gospel as we are of our own existence. The old philosopher heard a man assert that we do not exist, and his only reply was to get up and walk: so when we hear arguments against our holy faith, all we have to do is just to live on in the power of the Spirit, and silence gainsayers. May the Holy Spirit thus lead you into all truth—into the secret of the Lord may He conduct you, and there feast you upon fat things, full of marrow, and upon wines on the lees well refined.

We will rejoice in thy salvation, and in the name of our God we will set up our banners. . . .

Psalm 20: 5

24

Let not your exertions end in tears, mere weeping will do nothing without action. Get on your feet; you who have voices and might, go forth and preach the gospel, preach it in every street and lane of this huge city; you who have wealth, go forth and spend it for the poor, the sick, the needy, the dying, the uneducated, the unenlightened; you who have time, go forth and spend it in deeds of goodness; you who have power in prayer go forth and pray—every one to his post, every one of you to your gun in this day of battle; now for God and for His truth; for God and for the right; let every one of us who knows the Lord seek to fight under His banner!

Now I know that the Lord saveth his anointed; he will hear him from his holy heaven with the saving strength of his right hand.

Psalm 20: 6

25

You see yonder ship. After a long voyage, it has neared the harbor, but is much injured; the sails are rent to ribbons. That is like the righteous being "scarcely saved." But do you see that other ship? It has made a prosperous voyage; and now, laden to the water's edge, with the sails all up and with the white canvas filled with the wind, it rides into the harbor joyously and nobly. That is an "abundant entrance"; and if you and I are helped by God's Spirit

February

to add to our faith, virtue, and so on, we shall have at the last an "abundant entrance into the kingdom of our Lord Jesus Christ."

If you might go to Heaven and hold communion with some person whom you dearly loved, you would often be found there. But here is Jesus, the King of Heaven, and He gives you that which can open the gates of Heaven and let you in to be with Him, and yet you live without meditating upon His work, meditating upon His person, meditating upon His offices, and meditating upon His glory. Ah! there is nothing that can so console your spirits, and relieve all your distresses and troubles, as the feeling that now you can meditate on the person of Jesus Christ.

The Lord is my Shepherd. . . . And we have seen and do testify that the Father sent the Son to be the Saviour of the world.

Psalm 23: 1; 1 John 4: 14

If I once wandered on yon mountain top, and Jesus climbed up and caught me, and put me on His shoulders, and carried me home, I cannot and dare not doubt that He is my Shepherd. If I had belonged to some other sheep owner, He would not have sought me. And from the fact that He did seek, I learn that He must be my Shepherd. Could I trace my deliverance to the hand of a creature, I should think that some creature might be my shepherd; but since he who has been reclaimed of God must confess that God alone has done it, such a one will feel persuaded that the Lord must be his Shepherd, because He brought him, He delivered him.

My Shepherd is also my Savior. There is none other name under heaven given among men whereby we must be saved, but Jesus Christ and Him crucified. There were not two arks, but one ark: so there are not two Saviors, but one Savior. There was no other means of salvation except the ark: so there is no plan of deliverance except by Jesus Christ, the Savior of sinners. In vain you climb the lofty top of Sinai. In vain you climb to the highest pinnacles of your self-conceit and your worldly merit: you shall be drowned—

for "other foundation can no man lay than that which is laid—Jesus Christ and him crucified."

I will fear no evil: for thou art with me.

Psalm 23: 4

27

Behold, how independent of outward circumstances the Holy Ghost can make the Christian! What a bright light may shine within us when it is all dark without! How firm, how happy, how calm, how peaceful we may be, when the world shakes to and fro, and the pillars of the earth are removed! Even death itself, with all its terrible influences, has no power to suspend the music of a Christian's heart, but rather makes that music become more sweet, more clear, more heavenly, till the last kind act which death can do is to let the earthly strain melt into the heavenly chorus, the temporal joy into the eternal bliss! Let us have confidence, then, in the blessed Spirit's power to comfort us.

Dear reader, are you looking forward to poverty? Fear not; the divine Spirit can give you, in your want, a greater plenty than the rich have in their abundance. You know not what joys may be stored up for you in the cottage around which grace will plant the roses of content. Are you conscious of a growing failure of your bodily powers? Do you expect to suffer long nights of languishing and days of pain? O be not sad! That bed may become a throne to you. You little know how every pang that shoots through your body may be a refining fire to consume your dross—a beam of glory to light up the secret parts of your soul. Are the eyes growing dim? Jesus will be your light. Do the ears fail you? Jesus' name will be your soul's best music, and His person your dear delight. Socrates used to say, "Philosophers can be happy without music"; and Christians can be happier than philosophers when all outward causes of rejoicing are withdrawn. In Thee, my God, my heart shall triumph, come what may of ills without! By Thy power, O blessed Spirit, my heart shall be exceeding glad, though all things should fail me here below.

February

<table>
<tr><td>

28

</td><td>

Lead me in thy truth, and teach me: for thou art the God of my salvation; on thee do I wait all the day.

Psalm 25: 5

</td></tr>
</table>

Oh! it is a happy way of smoothing sorrow when we can say, "We will wait only upon God." Oh, you agitated Christians, do not dishonor your religion by always wearing a brow of care; come cast your burden upon the Lord. I see you staggering beneath a weight which He would not feel. What seems to you a crushing burden would be to Him but as the small dust of the balance. See! the Almighty bends His shoulders, and He says, "Here, put thy troubles here."

"Come unto Me, and I will give you rest."

It will not save me to know that Christ is a Savior; but it will save me *to trust* Him to be *my* Savior. I shall not be delivered from the wrath to come by believing that His atonement is sufficient; but I shall be saved by making that atonement my trust, my refuge, and my all. The pith, the essence of faith lies in this—a casting of oneself on the promise. It is not the life jacket on board ship that saves the man when he is drowning, nor is it his belief that it is an excellent and successful invention. No! he must have it around him, or his hand upon it, or else he will sink.

<table>
<tr><td>

29

</td><td>

Judge me, O Lord; for I have walked in mine integrity: I have trusted also in the Lord; therefore I shall not slide.

Psalm 26: 1

</td></tr>
</table>

This confidence in God makes men *strong*. I should advise the enemy not to oppose the man who trusts in God. In the long run he will be beaten, as Haman found it with Mordecai. He had been warned of this by Zeresh, his wife, and his wise men, who said, "If Mordecai be of the seed of the Jews, before whom thou hast begun to fall, thou shalt not prevail against him, but shalt surely fall before him." Contend not with a man who has God at his back.

Years ago, the Mentonese desired to break away from the dominion of the Prince of Monaco. They therefore drove out his agent. The prince came with his army, not a very great one, it is true, but still formidable to the Mentonese. I know not what the high and mighty princeling was not going to do; but news came that the King of Sardinia was coming up in the rear to help the Mentonese, and therefore his lordship of Monaco prudently retired to his own rock. When a believer stands out against evil he may be sure that the Lord of hosts will not be far away. The enemy will hear the dash of his horse-hoof and the blast of his trumpet, and shall flee before him. Wherefore be of good courage, and compel the world to say of you, "He trusted in the Lord that he would deliver him."

March

Examine me, O Lord, and prove me; try my reins and my heart.

Psalm 26: 2

David knew what it meant to be tried and proven. And we modern Davids cannot expect to escape the school of trial.

Most of the grand truths of God have to be learned by trouble; they must be burned into us with the hot iron of affliction, otherwise we shall not truly receive them. No man is competent to judge in matters of the kingdom until first he has been tried; since there are many things to be learned in the depths which we can never know in the heights. He shall best meet the wants of God's people who has had those wants himself; he shall best comfort God's Israel who has needed comfort; and he shall best preach salvation who has felt his own need of it.

He that loves much must weep much; much love and much sorrow must go together in this vale of tears. Ofttimes tears are the index of strength. There are periods when they are the noblest thing in the world. The tears of penitents are precious; a cup of them was worth a king's ransom. It is no sign of weakness when a man weeps for sin; it shows that he has strength of mind; nay, more, that he has strength imparted by God, which enables him to forswear his lusts and overcome his passions, and to turn unto God with full purpose of heart.

The Lord is my light and my salvation.

Psalm 27: 1

"The Lord is my light and my salvation." Here is personal interest, *"my light," "my salvation"*; the soul is assured of it, and therefore

declares it boldly. Into the soul at the new birth divine light is poured as the precursor of salvation. Where there is not enough light to reveal our own darkness, and to make us long for the Lord Jesus, there is no evidence of salvation. After conversion our God is our joy, comfort, guide, teacher, and in every sense our light: He is light within, light around, light reflected from us, and light to be revealed to us. He, then, who by faith has laid hold upon God, has all covenant blessings in his possession.

For in the time of trouble he shall hide me in his pavilion: in the secret of his tabernacle shall he hide me; he shall set me up upon a rock.

Psalm 27: 5

3

Choice discoveries of the wondrous love and grace of Jesus are most tenderly vouchsafed unto believers in the times of grief. Then it is that He lifts them up from His feet, where, like Mary, it is their delight to sit, and exalts them to the position of the favored John, pressing them to His breast and bidding them lean on His bosom.

The love of Christ in its sweetness, its fullness, its greatness, its faithfulness, passes all human comprehension.

Heaven on earth is abounding love to Jesus. This is the first and last of true delight—to love Him who is the first and the last. To love Jesus is another name for paradise.

Weeping may endure for a night, but joy cometh in the morning.

Psalm 30: 5

4

Christian! If you are in a night of trial, think of the morrow; cheer up your heart with the thought of the coming of your Lord. Be patient, for "Lo! He comes with clouds descending."

Be patient! The Husbandman waits until He reaps His harvest.

March

Be patient; for you know who has said, "Behold, I come quickly; and my reward is with me, to give to every man according as his work shall be." If you are feeling wretched now, remember

> A few more rolling suns, at most,
> Will land thee on fair Canaan's coast.

Your head may be crowned with thorny troubles now, but it shall wear a starry crown ere long; your hand may be filled with cares—it shall sweep the strings of the harp of heaven soon. Your garments may be soiled with dust now; they shall be white by-and-by. Wait a little longer. Ah! How despicable our troubles and trials will seem when we look back upon them! Looking at them here in the prospect, they seem immense; but when we get to heaven we shall then

> With transporting joys recount,
> The labors of our feet.

Our trials will then seem light and momentary afflictions. Let us go on boldly; even though the night be dark, the morning comes, which is more than they can say who are shut up in the darkness of hell. Do you know what it is thus to live on the future—to live on expectation—to anticipate heaven? Happy believer, to have so sure, so comforting a hope.

5

O love the Lord, all ye his saints: for the Lord preserveth the faithful, and plentifully rewardeth the proud doer. Be of good courage, and he shall strengthen your heart, all ye that hope in the Lord.

Psalm 31: 23, 24

> Jesus, the name that charms our fears,
>   That bids our sorrows cease;
> 'Tis music in the sinner's ears,
>   'Tis life, and health, and peace.

The faith which we hold is our daily and hourly joy and hope. The doctrines which I believe in connection with the divine Person in whom I trust are the pillow of my weariness, the anodyne of my care, the rest of my spirit. Jesus gives me a look-out for years to come which is celestial, and at the same time I can look back with thankfulness on the years which are past. For all time the Lord Jesus is our heart's content. Nothing can separate us from His love, and therefore nothing can deprive us of our confident hope. Through this blessed name and this blessed faith believers are themselves made glad and strong. On the name of Jesus we feed, and in that name we wrap ourselves. It is strength for our weakness, yea, life for our death.

Blessed is he whose transgression is forgiven, whose sin is covered.

Psalm 32: 1

6

Men have their own ideals of blessedness. Those ideals are often altogether contrary to the sayings which our Savior uttered in His Sermon on the Mount. They count those to be blessed who are strong in health, who are abundant in riches, who are honored with fame, who are entrusted with command, who exercise power—those, in fact, who are distinguished in the eyes of their fellow-creatures. Yet I find not such persons called "blessed" in God's Word, though I do notice that oftentimes humble souls, who might excite pity rather than envy, are congratulated upon the blessings which they are heirs to, and which they shall soon enjoy. To the penitent there is no voice so pleasant as that of pardon.

God, who cannot lie—God, who cannot err—tells us what it is to be blessed. Here He declares that "Blessed is he whose transgression is forgiven, whose sin is covered." This is an oracle not to be disputed. Forgiven sin is better than accumulated wealth. The remission of sin is infinitely to be preferred before all the glitter and the glare of this world's prosperity. The gratification of creature passions and earthly desires is illusive—a shadow and a fiction; but the blessedness of the justified, the blessedness of the man to whom God imputeth righteousness is substantial and true.

March

7

Be glad in the Lord, and rejoice, ye righteous: and shout for joy, all ye that are upright in heart.

Psalm 32: 11

God helping us, we can always rejoice *in God.* What a God we have! "God my exceeding joy," said the Psalmist. "Delight thyself also in the Lord." Every attribute of God, every characteristic of God, is an inexhaustible gold mine of precious joy to every man who is reconciled to God. Delight yourself in God the Father, and His electing love, and His unchanging grace, and His illimitable power, and His transcending glory; and in the fact that you are His child, and in that providence with which He orders all things for you. Delight in your Father God. Delight also in the Son, who is "God with us." God with us before the earth was, in the covenant council when He became our surety and our representative. God with us when His delights were with the sons of men. Delight in Him as man suffering, sympathizing with you. Delight in Him as God putting forth infinite wisdom and power for you.

8

Let all the earth fear the Lord: let all the inhabitants of the world stand in awe of him.

Psalm 33: 8

But how is this to be: How is the world to be brought back to its original perfection? How is it to be restored? We answer, the reason why there was this original harmony between earth and heaven was because there was love between them, and our great reason for hoping that there shall be at last reestablished or undiscordant harmony between heaven and earth is simply this, that God has already manifested His love toward us, and that in return, hearts touched by His grace do even now love him; and when they shall be multiplied, and love reestablished, then shall harmony be complete.

You know in a wheel there is one portion that never turns round, that stands steadfast, and that is the axle. So, in God's Providence there is an axle which never moves. Christian, here is a sweet thought! Your state is ever changing: sometimes you are exalted, and sometimes depressed; yet there is an unmoving point in your state. What is that axle? What is the pivot upon which all the machinery revolves? It is the axle of God's everlasting love toward His covenant people. The exterior of the wheel is changing; but the center stands forever fixed. Other things may move; but God's love never moves; it is the axle of the wheel, and will endure. And ultimately triumph!

O magnify the Lord with me, and let us exalt his name together.

Psalm 34: 3

9

Many men believe in the existence of a God, but they do not love that belief. But to the Christian the thought that there is a God is the sunshine of his existence. His intellect bows before the Most High; like the angel who prostrates himself because he loves to adore his Maker. His intellect is as fond of God as his imagination. "Oh!" he says, "my God, I bless You that You are; for You are my highest treasure, my richest and my rarest delight. I love You with all my intellect; I have neither thought nor judgment, nor conviction, nor reason, which I do not lay at Your feet, and consecrate to Your honor."

Before the throne of God angels and redeemed saints extol His name. Thus heaven sings evermore. And this world is singing too; sometimes with the loud noise of the rolling thunder, of the boiling sea, of the dashing cataract, and of the lowing cattle; and often with that still, solemn harmony which flows from the vast creation, when in its silence it praises God.

In heaven they sing, "The Lord be exalted; let his name be magnified forever." And the earth sings the same: "'Great art Thou in Thy works, O Lord! and unto Thee be glory.'"

This poor man cried, and the Lord heard him, and saved him out of all his troubles.

Psalm 34: 6

10

Your desires have voices of their own: they knock hard at heaven's door, and it shall be opened unto them. This desire may be unac-

March

companied by any confident expectation. When you pray you ought to believe the promise and expect its fulfillment. It is the duty and the privilege of every suppliant to believe that when he prays in the name of Jesus he must and shall be heard. But sometimes humility, which is a good thing, is attended by a want of faith, which is an evil thing; and this much hinders prayer.

Humility is deceived by unbelief, and so it gives way to the dark thought that its poor feeble prayer will not speed with God. I fear that in some cases this want of expectancy is an effectual barrier to prayer, and prevents its being answered; but it is forgiven to naturally despondent, heavily laden spirits, whose fears are not so much doubts of God as a deeply humiliating judgment of themselves. It is not so much the case that this faith is sinfully defective as that they have a painfully acute sense of their own unworthiness; and so when they cry they hope that the Lord will hear them, and they mean to wait upon Him till He does; but they are sore afraid. They will go nowhere else, for other hope they have none but that which lies in the free grace and sovereign mercy of God; but yet they do not exercise that happy expectancy which the sure promise warrants their enjoying. My brethren, I would chide your unbelief, but I would still encourage your desires; for that desire which God hears is not to be despised. The text says, "Lord, thou hast heard the desire of the humble," and the Lord will yet hear your humble sighs and groans; and you shall be surprised to find the Lord doing for you exceeding abundantly above what you asked or even thought. May your faith grow exceedingly, being fed upon the heavenly food which the Lord deals out to those who hunger and thirst after righteousness.

11 *O taste and see that the Lord is good: blessed is the man that trusteth in him.*

Psalm 34: 8

The Lord Jesus Christ is not only the ideal bread, but *He is in Himself a sufficient bread.* That manna which the Israelites ate in the wilderness was all that they really wanted. They began lusting, and they cried after flesh, and they sighed for the leeks, and the garlic, and the onions, which had charmed their degenerate palates when they lived among the Egyptians.

How wretched was their taste. They must have been of a coarse mold to grow weary of the food of angels, and sigh for something more rank, more tasty, more heavy. Something injurious they wanted; yet had they been wise and right, they would have known that within the manna there was everything that was sufficient and suitable for them; for the God that made man, made manna, and He knew exactly what man wanted. Out of the ovens of heaven He sent man down bread, fresh and hot, each morning, that he might eat to the full, and yet never be surfeited, nor filled with evil humors.

They called the manna "light bread," but what should the food be for those who were always on the march but light, and easy of digestion? Our Lord Jesus is simple in doctrine; but what else do we wish for, even we who are wayfaring men, and all too apt to err?

My brethren, if we do but get a hold of Jesus Christ, and feed on Him, He is sufficient for us—sufficient for gigantic labors, sufficient for anguish, and grief, and sorrow; sufficient for the weakest of the babes, for He is the unadulterated milk; sufficient for the full-grown men among us, for He is the strong meat of the kingdom. His flesh is meat indeed.

The Lord is nigh unto them that are of a broken heart; and saveth such as be of a contrite spirit.

Psalm 34: 18

12

To this man will I look, even to him that is poor and of a contrite spirit, and trembleth at my word" (Isa. 66: 2). Stoop if you would climb to heaven. Do we not say of Jesus, "He descended that he might ascend"? So must you. You must grow downwards, that you may grow upwards; for the sweetest fellowship with heaven is to be had by humble souls, and by them alone. God will deny no blessing to a thoroughly humbled spirit. Humility makes us ready to be blessed by the God of all grace, and fits us to deal efficiently

March

with our fellow-men. Whether it be prayer or praise, whether it be work or suffering, the genuine salt of humility cannot be used in excess.

Jesus is the great teacher of lowliness of heart. We need daily to learn of Him. See the Master taking a towel and washing His disciples' feet! Follower of Christ, will you not humble yourself? See Him as the Servant of servants, and surely you cannot be proud! "He humbled himself!" Was He not on earth always stripping off first one robe of honor, and then another, till, naked, He was fastened to the cross? And there did He not empty out His inmost self, pouring out His life-blood, giving up all for us? How low was our dear Redeemer brought! How, then, can we be proud?

13

The Lord is nigh unto them that are of a broken heart; and saveth such as be of a contrite spirit.

Psalm 34: 18

"*All my springs* are in thee" (Ps. 87: 7), and if you have all your springs in God, your heart will be full enough. If you do go to the foot of Calvary, there will your heart be bathed in love and gratitude. If you do linger in the vale of meditation, and there talk with your God, it is there that your heart will be full of calm resolve. If you go out with your Master to the hill of Olivet, and there with Him look down upon a wicked Jerusalem, and weep over it with Him, then will your heart be full of love for never-dying souls.

The river of God is full of water; but there is not one drop of it that takes its rise in earthly springs. God will have no strength used in His own battles but the strength which He Himself imparts; and I would not have you that are now distressed discouraged by it. Your emptiness is but the preparation for your being filled; and your casting down is but the making ready for your lifting up.

Unexpected help will come to us when affairs are at their worst. Let us learn from our Master to reckon upon forces invisible.

March

*Many are the afflictions of the righteous: but the Lord deliver-
eth him out of them all.*

Psalm 34: 19

Losses, too, are frequently the means God uses to fetch home His
wandering sheep; like fierce dogs, they bring wanderers back to
the shepherd. How often have we seen the Christian rendered
obedient to his Lord's will by straightness of bread and hard labor.
When rich and increased with goods, many professors carry their
heads much too loftily, and speak much too boastfully. Like David,
they boast: "My mountain standeth fast; it shall never be moved."
When the Christian grows wealthy, is in good repute, has good
health, and a happy family, he too often wanders away. If he be
a true child of God, there is a rod preparing for him.

We never live so well as when we live on the Lord Jesus simply
as He is, and not upon our enjoyments and raptures. Faith is never
more likely to increase in strength than in times which seem ad-
verse to her. When she is lightened of trust in joys, experiences,
frames, feelings, and the like, she rises the nearer heaven. Trust
in your Redeemer's strength, benighted soul; exercise what faith
you have, and by and by He shall rise upon you with healing beneath His wings. Go from faith to faith and you shall receive blessing upon blessing.

*My soul shall be joyful in the Lord: it shall rejoice in his
salvation.*

Psalm 35: 9

Nothing gives the believer so much joy as fellowship with Christ.
He has enjoyment as others have in the common mercies of life,
he can be glad both in God's gifts and God's works; but in all
these separately, yea, and in all of them added together, he does
not find such substantial delight as in the matchless person of his
Lord Jesus.

Where can such sweetness be found as we have tasted in communion with our Beloved?

If you know anything of the inner life, you will confess that
our highest, purest, and most enduring joys must be the fruit of
the tree of life which is in the midst of the Paradise of God.

March

There are moments when the eyes glisten with joy: and we can say: "We are persuaded, confident, certain." I do not wish to distress anyone who is under doubt. Often gloomy doubts will prevail; there are seasons when you fear you have not been called, when you doubt your interest in Christ. Ah! what a mercy it is that it is not your hold of Christ that saves you, but His hold of you! What a sweet fact that it is not how you grasp His hand, but His grasp of yours, that saves you.

The Lord's promise once given is never recalled.

16

Delight thyself also in the Lord; and he shall give thee the desires of thine heart.

Psalm 37: 4

Blessed is that man who no longer follows the devices and desires of his own heart, and no longer trusts to his own understanding. Blessed is he who bows his mind to the mind of God. My own desire is not to believe what I may imagine, or invent, or think out; but I would believe what the Lord God has taught us in the inspired Scriptures. I submit myself to the guidance of the Spirit of God in connection with the written word. This is safe walking.

Combine the two descriptive clauses of this text: "There is therefore now no condemnation to them which are in Christ Jesus, who walk not after the flesh, but after the Spirit" (Rom. 8: 1). On the one hand look to Christ alone, and abide in Him; and then, on the other hand, look for the guidance of the Holy Spirit who is to be in you. By faith we are in Christ, and the Holy Spirit is in us. All who can go with me in this are delivered from condemnation: for how shall he be condemned who is in Christ? And how shall he be condemned who has the Holy Ghost within him?

17

Those that wait upon the Lord . . , shall inherit the earth.

Psalm 37: 9

God has clearly revealed that He *will* hear the prayer of those who call upon Him, and that declaration cannot be contravened.

He has so firmly, so truthfully, so righteously spoken, that there can be no room for doubt. He does not reveal His mind in unintelligible words, but He speaks plainly and positively, "Ask, and ye shall receive." Believe, O trembler, this sure truth—your prayer must and will be heard, and that never, even in the secrets of eternity, has the Lord said unto any living soul, "Seek ye me in vain" (Isa. 45: 19).

It is a happy thing when we can address the Lord with the confidence which David manifests; it gives us great power in prayer, and comfort in trial. "My soul, wait thou only upon God; for my expectation is from him" (Ps. 62: 5). Patience is the fair handmaid and daughter of faith; we cheerfully wait when we are certain that we shall not wait in vain. It is our duty and our privilege to wait upon the Lord in service, in worship, in expectancy, in trust, all the days of our life. Our faith will be tried faith, and if it be of the true kind, it will bear continued trial without yielding. We shall not grow weary of waiting upon God if we remember how long and how graciously He once waited for us.

I waited patiently for the Lord; and he . . . heard my cry.
Psalm 40: 1

18

You have no place in which to pour your troubles except the ear of God. If you tell them to your friends, you but put your troubles out a moment, and they will return again. Roll your burden unto God, and you have rolled it into a great deep, out of which it will never by any possibility rise. Cast your troubles where you cast your sins; you have cast your sins into the depths of the sea, there cast your troubles also. Never keep a trouble half an hour on your own mind before you tell it to God. As soon as the trouble comes, quick, the first thing, tell it to your Father.

Stars may be seen from the bottom of a deep well when they cannot be discerned from the top of a mountain: so are many things learned in adversity which the prosperous man dreams not of. We need affliction as the trees need winter, that we may collect

March

sap and nourishment for future blossoms and fruit. Sorrow is as necessary for the soul as medicine is to the body:

> The path of sorrow, and that path alone,
> Leads to the land where sorrow is unknown.

The adversities of today are a preparatory school for the higher learning.

But I am poor and needy; yet the Lord thinketh upon me [and] art my help and my deliverer. . . .

Psalm 40: 17

Divine omniscience affords no comfort to the ungodly mind, but to the child of God it overflows with consolation. Always thinking upon us, God never turns aside His mind from us, for it would be dreadful to exist for a moment beyond the observation of our heavenly Father. His thoughts are always tender, loving, far-reaching, and they bring to us countless benefits. The Lord always did think upon His people: hence their election and the covenant of grace by which their salvation is secured; He always will think upon them: hence their final perseverance by which they shall be brought safely to their final rest.

In all our wanderings the watchful glance of the Eternal Watcher is evermore fixed upon us—we never roam beyond the Shepherd's eye. In our sorrows He observes us incessantly, and not a pang escapes Him; in our toils He marks all our weariness, and writes in His book all the struggles of His faithful ones. These thoughts of the Lord encompass us in all our paths, and penetrate the innermost region of our being.

Dear reader, is this precious to you? Then hold to it. The Lord lives and thinks upon us, this is a truth far too precious for us to be lightly robbed of it. If the Lord thinks upon us, all is well, and we may rejoice evermore.

Why go I mourning?

Psalm 42: 9

Can you answer this, believer? Can you find any reason why you are so often mourning instead of rejoicing? Why yield to gloomy anticipations? Who told you that the night would never end in day? Who told you that the winter of your discontent would proceed from frost to frost, from snow and ice, and hail, to deeper snow, and yet more heavy tempest of despair? Don't you know that day follows night, that flood comes after ebb, that spring and summer succeed to winter? Have hope then! Hope now and ever! for God fails not.

[*David prayed:*] *Cast me not away from thy presence; and take not thy Holy Spirit from me. Restore unto me the joy of thy salvation; and uphold me with thy free spirit.*

Psalm 51: 11, 12

Because you thus have Christ by His Spirit, you cannot be orphans, for the Spirit of God is always with you. It is a delightful truth that the Spirit of God always dwells in believers—not sometimes, but always. He is not always active in believers, and He may be grieved until His sensible presence is altogether withdrawn, but His secret presence is always there. At no single moment is the Spirit of God wholly gone from a believer. The believer would die spiritually if this could happen, but that cannot be, for Jesus has said, "Because I live, ye shall live also." Even when the believer sins, the Holy Spirit does not utterly depart from him, but is still in him to make him smart for the sin into which he has fallen. The believer's prayers prove that the Holy Spirit is still within him. "Take not thy Holy Spirit from me," was the prayer of a saint who had fallen very foully, but in whom the Spirit of God still kept His residence, notwithstanding all the foulness of his guilt and sin.

March

22

As for me, I will call upon God; and the Lord shall save me.

Psalm 55: 16

If we had the blessings without asking for them, we should think them common things; but prayer makes the common pebbles of God's temporal bounties more precious than diamonds; and spiritual prayer cuts the diamond, and makes it glisten more.

When you are wrestling, like Jacob with the angel, and are nearly thrown down, ask the Holy Spirit to strengthen your arm. Consider how the Holy Spirit is the chariot-wheel of prayer. Prayer may be the chariot, the desire may draw it forth, but the Spirit is the very wheel by which it moves.

If I desired to put myself in the most likely place for the Lord to meet with me, I should prefer the house of prayer, for it is in preaching that the Word is most blessed; but still I think I should equally desire the reading of the Scriptures; for I might pause over every verse, and say, "Such a verse was blessed to so many souls; then, why not to me? I am at least in the pool of Bethesda; I am walking among its porches, and who can tell but that the angel will stir the pool of the Word, while I lie helplessly by the side of it, waiting for the blessing?"

23

Thou crownest the year with thy goodness.

Psalm 65: 11

All the year round, every hour of every day, God is richly blessing us; both when we sleep and when we wake His mercy waits upon us. The sun may leave us a legacy of darkness, but our God never ceases to shine upon His children with beams of love. Like a river, His loving-kindness is always flowing with a fullness inexhaustible as His own nature. Like the atmosphere which constantly surrounds the earth, and is always ready to support the life of man, the benevolence of God surrounds all His creatures; in it, as in their element, they live, and move, and have their being.

March

It is well with the righteous *always*. From the beginning of the year to the end of the year, from the first gathering of evening shadows until the day-star shines, in all conditions, and under all circumstances, it shall be well with the righteous. It is so well with him that we could not imagine it to be better, for he is *well fed*, he feeds upon the flesh and blood of Jesus; he is *well clothed*, he wears the imputed righteousness of Christ; he is *well housed*, he dwells in God; he is *well married*, his soul is knit in bonds of marriage union to Christ; he is *well provided for*, for the Lord is his Shepherd; he is *well endowed*, for heaven is his inheritance.

The chariots of God are twenty thousands, even thousands of angels: the Lord is among them, as in Sinai, in the holy place.

Psalm 68: 17

24

If we fear the Lord, we may look for timely interpositions when our case is at its worst. Angels are not kept from us by storms, or hindered by darkness. Seraphs think it no humiliation to visit the poorest of the heavenly family. If angels' visits are few and far between at ordinary times, they shall be frequent in our nights of tempest and tossing.

Dear reader, is this an hour of distress with you? Then ask for peculiar help. Jesus is the angel of the covenant, and if His presence be now earnestly sought, it will not be denied. What that presence brings is heart cheer.

This Savior was "a man of sorrows," but every thoughtful mind has discovered the fact that down deep in His innermost soul He carried an inexhaustible treasury of refined and heavenly joy. Of all the human race, there was never a man who had a deeper, purer, or more abiding peace than our Lord Jesus Christ. "[He] was anointed with the oil of gladness above [His] fellows" (Heb. 1: 9). His vast benevolence must have afforded Him the deepest possible delight, for benevolence is joy. There were a few remarkable seasons when this joy manifested itself. "At that hour Jesus rejoiced in spirit, and said, I thank Thee, O Father, Lord of heaven and earth" (Luke 10: 21).

March

25

Remember thy congregation, which thou hast purchased of old. . . .

Psalm 74: 2

At this hour the church expects to walk in sympathy with her Lord along a thorny road; through much tribulation she is forcing her way to the crown. To bear the cross is her office, and yet the church has a deep well of joy, of which none can drink but her own children. There are stores of wine, and oil, and corn, hidden in the midst of our Jerusalem, upon which the saints of God are evermore sustained and nurtured; and sometimes, as in our Savior's case, we have our seasons of intense delight, for "There is a river, the streams whereof shall make glad the city of our God." Exiles though we be, we rejoice in our King; yea, in Him we exceedingly rejoice.

Jesus gave His blood for us; what shall we give to Him? We are His, and all that we have, for He has purchased us into Himself—can we act as if we were our own? Oh for more consecration! and to this end, oh for more love! Blessed Jesus, receive with favor the smallest sincere token of affection! Receive our poor forget-me-nots and love-tokens, as though they were intrinsically precious, though indeed they are but as the bunch of wild flowers which the child brings to his mother. We will give You the first fruits of our increase, and pay You tithes of all, and then we will confess "of thine own have we given thee."

26

The Lord will give grace and glory.

Psalm 84: 11

Bounteous is Jehovah in His nature; to give is His delight. His gifts are beyond measure precious, and are as freely given as the light of the sun. He gives grace to His elect because He wills it, to His redeemed because of His covenant, to the called because of His promise, to believers because they seek it, to sinners because they need it. He gives grace abundantly, seasonably, constantly, readily, sovereignly; doubly enhancing the value of the boon by the manner of its bestowal. Grace in all its forms He freely renders to His people: comforting, preserving, sanctifying, directing, instructing, assisting grace, He generously pours into their souls without ceasing, and He always will do so, whatever may occur. Sickness may befall but the Lord will give grace; poverty may happen to us, but grace will surely be afforded; death must come, but grace will light a candle at the darkest hour. Reader, how blessed it is as years roll round, and the leaves begin again to fall, to enjoy such an unfading promise as this, "The Lord will give grace."

The little conjunction *and* in this verse is a diamond rivet binding the present with the future; grace and glory always go together. God has married them, and none can divorce them. The Lord will never deny a soul glory to whom He has freely given grace. Glory, the glory of heaven, the glory of eternity, the glory of Jesus, the glory of the Father, the Lord will surely give to His chosen. Oh, rare promise of a faithful God!

In his hand are the deep places of the earth: the strength of the hills is his also. The sea is his, and he made it: and his hands formed the dry land.

Psalm 95: 4, 5

27

The book of nature is an expression of the thoughts of God. We have God's terrible thoughts in the thunder and lightning; God's loving thoughts in the sunshine and the balmy breeze; God's bounteous, prudent, careful thoughts in the waving harvest and in the ripening meadow. We have God's brilliant thoughts in the wondrous scenes which are beheld from mountaintop and valley; and we have God's most sweet and pleasant thoughts of beauty in the little flowers that blossom at our feet. "God giveth us richly all things to enjoy."

In the very beginning, when this great universe lay in the mind of God, like unborn forests in the acorn-cup; long ere the echoes walked the solitudes; before the mountains were brought forth; and long ere the light flashed through the sky, God loved His chosen creatures. Before there was creatureship—when the ether was not fanned by the angel's wing; when space itself had not

March

an existence; when there was nothing save God alone; even then, in that loneliness of Deity, and in that deep quiet and profundity, His love moved for His chosen. Their names were written on His heart, and then were they dear to His soul.

28

O come, let us worship and bow down: let us kneel before the Lord our maker.

Psalm 95: 6

Oh newborn soul, trembling with anxiety, if you have not yet beheld the fair face of your Beloved, if you cannot as yet delight in the majesty of His offices, and the wonders of His person, let your soul be fully alive to the richness of His grace, and the preciousness of His blood. These you have in your possession, the pledges of your interest in Him; love Him then for these, and in due time He will reveal to you fresh wonders and glories, so that you will be able to exclaim, "O staff of my life and strength of my heart, I will sit and sing under thy shadow, yea, I will sing a song of loves touching my Well-beloved!"

When the soul is led by the Holy Spirit to take a clear view of Jesus in His various offices, how speedily the heart is on fire with love! To see Him stooping from His throne to become man, next yielding to suffering to become man's sympathizing friend, and then bowing to death itself to become his ransom, is enough to stir every passion of the soul. To discern Him by faith as the propitiation for sin, sprinkling His own blood within the veil, and nailing our sins to His cross, is a sight which never fails to excite the reverent, yet rapturous admiration of the beholder.

29

Serve the Lord with gladness.

Psalm 100: 2

Delight in divine service is a sure sign of genuine gladness. Those who serve Christ with a long face and a sad countenance, as if what they are doing is unpleasant to them, are not serving Him at all; they bring the form of homage, but the life is absent. They have a form of godliness, but deny the power thereof.

Our God requires no slaves to grace His throne; He is the Lord of the empire of love and would have His servants dressed in uniforms of joy. The angels of God serve Him with joy and songs, not with groans and grumblings; a murmur or a sigh would be a mutiny in their ranks. That obedience which is grudging and not voluntary is disobedience, for the Lord looks on the heart, and if He sees we serve Him from force, and not because we love Him, He will reject our offering.

Service coupled with cheerfulness is heart-service, and therefore true. Take away joyful willingness from the Christian, and you have removed the test of his sincerity. If a man must be driven into battle, he is no patriot; but he who marches into the fight singing, with flashing eye and beaming face, proves himself to be sincere in his patriotism.

Cheerfulness is the support of our strength; in the joy of the Lord are we strong. It acts as the remover of difficulties. It is to our service what oil is to the wheels of industry. Without oil the axle soon grows hot, and accidents occur; and if there be not holy cheerfulness to oil our wheels, our spirits will be clogged with weariness. The man who is cheerful in his service of God, proves that obedience is his element; that true joy is his portion.

Reader, let me ask you this question—do *you* serve the Lord with *gladness?* Let us show the people of the world, who think our religion to be slavery, that it is to us a delight and a joy! Let our gladness proclaim that we serve a good Master.

Forget not all his benefits.

Psalm 103: 2

30

It is a delightful and profitable occupation to mark the hand of God in the lives of ancient saints, and to observe His goodness in delivering them, His mercy in pardoning them, and His faithfulness in keeping His covenant with them. But would it not be even

March

more interesting and profitable for us to notice the hand of God in our own lives? Ought we not to look upon our own history as being at least as full of God, as full of His goodness and of His truth, as much a proof of His faithfulness and veracity, as the lives of any of the saints who have gone before? We do our Lord an injustice when we suppose that He performed all His mighty acts, and showed Himself strong for those in the early time, but does not perform wonders or lay bare His arm for the saints who are now upon the earth.

31 *But the mercy of the Lord is from everlasting to everlasting upon them that fear him, and his righteousness unto children's children; To such as keep his covenant, and to those that remember his commandments to do them.*

Psalm 103: 17, 18

How encouraging is the thought of the Redeemer's never-ceasing intercession for us. When we pray, He pleads for us; and when we are *not* praying, He is advocating our cause, and by His supplications shielding us from unseen dangers. We little know what we owe to our Savior's prayers. When we reach the hilltops of heaven, and look back upon all the way whereby the Lord our God has led us, how we shall praise Him who, before the eternal throne, has pleaded our cause against our unseen enemies. *"But I have prayed for thee,* that thy faith fail not."

If any one should ask me for an epitome of the Christian religion, I should say, it is in that one word—*prayer.* If I should be asked, "What will take in the whole of Christian experience?" I should answer, "prayer." A man must have been convinced of sin before he could pray; he must have had some hope that there was mercy for him before he could pray. All the Christian virtues are locked up in the word *prayer.*

In troubled times our best communion with God will be carried on by supplication. Tell Him your case; search out His promise, and then plead it with holy boldness. This is the best, the surest, the speediest way of relief.

April

For he satisfieth the longing soul, and filleth the hungry soul with goodness.

Psalm 107: 9

From the cross of Calvary, where the bleeding hands of Jesus drop mercy; from the garden of Gethsemane, the cry comes, "Look unto me, and be saved, all the ends of the earth." From Calvary's summit, where Jesus cries, "It is finished," I hear a shout, "Look, and be saved." But there comes a cry from our soul, "Nay, look to yourself!" Ah, look to yourself, and you will be lost. As long as you look to yourself there is no hope for you. It is not a consideration of what you are, but a consideration of what God is, and what Christ is, that can save you.

If you know these two things—yourself a sinner and Christ a Savior—it is looking from yourself to Jesus. Oh! there be men that quite misunderstand the gospel; they think that righteousness qualifies them to come to Christ; whereas sin is the only qualification for a man to come to Jesus. Good old Crisp says, "Righteousness keeps me from Christ: the whole have no need of a physician, but they that are sick. Sin makes me come to Jesus, when sin is felt; and in coming to Christ, the more sin I have the more cause I have to hope for mercy."

He shall not be afraid of evil tidings: his heart is fixed, trusting in the Lord.

Psalm 112: 7

Elsewhere the Psalmist says, "for thou art my strength" (Ps. 31: 4). What strong reason for trust is here! What an inexpressible

April

sweetness is to be found in these few words! How joyfully may we encounter toils, and how cheerfully may we endure sufferings, when we can lay hold upon celestial strength. He is a happy man who has such matchless might engaged upon his side. Our own strength would be of little service when caught in the nets of base cunning, but the Lord's strength is ever available; we have but to invoke it, and we shall find it near at hand. If by faith we are depending alone upon the strength of the mighty God of Israel, we may use our holy reliance as a plea in supplication.

Let me command to you a life of trust in God in temporal things. Walk in your path of integrity with steadfast steps, and show that you are invincibly strong in the strength which confidence in God alone can confer. Thus you will be delivered from anxious care, you will not be troubled with evil tidings, your heart will be fixed, trusting in the Lord. How pleasant to float along the stream of providence! There is no more blessed way of living than a life of dependence upon a covenant-keeping God. We have no care, for He cares for us; we have no troubles, because we cast our burdens upon the Lord.

3

The Lord shall increase you more and more, you and your children. Ye are blessed of the Lord which made heaven and earth. The heaven, even the heavens, are the Lord's: but the earth hath he given to the children of men.

Psalm 115: 14–16

The Psalmist declares what the Lord will yet do. It is not about what evil men are doing, or what we are afraid will happen through their malice; but of what the Lord alone will do. He pictures the whole affair finished, and Israel settled in the Promised Land, and this is His song. Come, brethren, let us sing the music of the future, the music of what God will do. Do you believe that the Lord will be defeated in the long run? Do you fear that at the end Jehovah's everlasting purpose will fail—that Christ will have died in vain? Think you the eternal truth promulgated in this book will be driven out of the earth by modern thought? Or that our old Christianity, for which our fathers bled, will become extinct? By no means. We shall conquer yet in the great name of Jehovah. Therefore let us take heart of hope to ourselves, and sing of what the Lord has done so often; for again and again, "The horse and his rider hath he thrown into the sea" (Exod. 15: 1).

The heaven, even the heavens, are the Lord's.

Psalm 115: 16

4

The best enjoyments of Christ on earth are but as the dipping of our finger in water for the cooling of our thirst; but heaven is bathing in seas of bliss: even so our love here is but one drop of the same substance as the waters of the ocean, but not comparable for magnitude or depth. Oh, how sweet it will be to be married to the Lord Jesus, and to enjoy forever, and without any interruption, the heavenly delights of His society! Surely, if a glimpse of Him melts our souls the full fruition of Him will be enough to burn up our hearts with affection.

An honored saint was once so ravished with a revelation of his Lord's love, that feeling his mortal frame to be unable to sustain more of such bliss, he cried, "Hold, Lord, it is enough, it is enough!" In heaven we shall be able to bring the bottomless well of love to our lips, and drink on forever. Ah, that will be love indeed which shall overflow our souls forever in our Father's house above! Who can tell the transports, the raptures, the amazements of delight which that love shall beget in us? And who can guess the sweetness of the song, or the swiftness of the obedience which will be the heavenly expressions of love made perfect?

Because he hath inclined his ear unto me, therefore will I call upon him as long as I live.

Psalm 116: 2

5

What! is Christ your Brother, and does He live in your house, and yet you have not spoken to Him for a month? I fear there is

April

little love between you and your Brother, for you have had no conversation with Him for so long. What! is Christ the Husband of His Church, and has she had no fellowship with Him for all this time?

Prayer is the outcome of that sense of need which arises from the new life; a man would not pray to God if he did not feel that he had urgent need of blessings which only the Lord can bestow.

Prayer is the autograph of the Holy Ghost upon the renewed heart.

Some persons say they cannot bear to be an hour in solitude; they have got nothing to do, nothing to think about. No Christian will ever talk so, surely; for if I can but give him one word to think of—*Christ*—let him spell that over forever; let me give him the word *Jesus,* and only let him try to think it over, and he shall find that an hour is nothing, and that eternity is not half enough to utter our glorious Savior's praise.

From a sweet fountain of thought we shall have sweet waters of talk. It is sweet to live in the thoughts of those we love. This should be the spirit in which we go to prayer.

6 *Because he hath inclined his ear unto me, therefore will I call upon him as long as I live.*

Psalm 116: 2

"Jesus lifted up his eyes, and said, Father, I thank Thee. . . ." It was the habit and life of Jesus to talk to God. May *we* likewise have silent fellowship with the Father, so that often we may answer Him, and though the world knows not to whom we speak, may we be responding to that secret voice unheard of any other ear, which our own ear, opened by the Spirit of God, recognizes with joy. What a privilege is intimate communion with the Father of our spirits! It is a secret hidden from the world, a joy with which even the nearest friend cannot interfere.

This very day may our hearts be in such a state, that when God speaks to us, we, like Jesus, may be prepared at once to *answer* Him.

Boldly come unto the King of kings, from whom no sincere petitioner ever was dismissed unheard.

Whenever there is a heart big with sorrow, wherever there is an eye suffused with tears, wherever there is a lip quivering with agony, wherever there is a deep groan, or a penitential sigh, the ear of Jehovah is wide open. He puts our prayers, like rose leaves, between the pages of His book of remembrance, and when the volume is opened at last, there shall be a precious fragrance springing up therefrom.

I shall not die, but live, and declare the works of the Lord.
Psalm 118: 17

7

There are some people who are like what is fabled of the swan. The ancients said that the swan never sang in his lifetime, but always sang just when he died. Now, there are many of God's desponding children who seem to go all their life under a cloud; but they get a swan's song before they die. The river of their life comes running down, perhaps black and miry with troubles, and when it begins to touch the white foam of the sea there comes a little glistening in its waters. So, beloved, though we may have been very much dispirited by reason of the burden of the way, when we get to the end we shall have sweet songs.

You who have lost your friends, come to the grave of your best friend—your brother, yea, one who "sticketh closer than a brother." Come to the grave of your dearest relative, O Christian, for Jesus is your husband. "Thy maker is thy husband, the Lord of Hosts is his name." Does affection not draw you? Do not the sweet lips of love woo you? Is not the place sanctified where one so well beloved slept, although but for a moment? Surely you need no eloquence. I have but the power, in simple, but earnest accents, to repeat the words, "Come, see the place where the Lord lay."

April

8

Thy word have I hid in mine heart, that I might not sin against thee.

Psalm 119: 11

Never, never neglect the Word of God; that will make your heart rich with precept, rich with understanding; and then your conversation, when it flows from your mouth, will be like your heart, rich, unctious and savory. Make your heart full of rich, generous love, and then the stream that flows from your hand will be just as rich and generous as your heart. Oh! go, Christian, to the great mine of riches, and cry unto the Holy Spirit to make your heart rich unto salvation. So shall your life and conversation be a blessing to your fellows; and when they see you, your face shall be as the angel of God to them.

The gospel is the sum of wisdom; an epitome of knowledge; a treasure-house of truth; and a revelation of mysterious secrets. Our meditation upon it enlarges the mind; and as it opens to our soul in successive flashes of glory, we stand astonished at the profound wisdom manifest in it. Ah, dear friends! if you seek wisdom, you shall see it displayed in all its greatness. But turn aside and see this great sight—an incarnate God upon the cross; a substitute atoning for mortal guilt; a sacrifice satisfying the vengeance of heaven, and delivering the rebellious sinner. Here is essential wisdom; enthroned, crowned, glorified.

9

Remember the word unto thy servant, upon which thou hast caused me to hope.

Psalm 119: 49

Whatever your particular need may be, you will readily find some promise in the Bible suited to it. Are you faint and feeble because your way is rough and you are weary? Here is the promise, "He giveth power to the faint." When you read such a promise, take it back to the great Promiser and ask Him to fulfill His own word. Are you seeking after Christ and thirsting for closer communion with Him? This promise shines like a star upon you, "Blessed are they that hunger and thirst after righteousness for they shall be filled." Take that promise to the throne continually; do not plead anything else, but go to God over and over again with this—"Lord, Thou hast said it; do as Thou hast said."

Are you distressed because of sin, and burdened with the heavy load of your iniquities? Listen to these words, "I, even I, am He that blotteth out thy transgressions, and will no more remember thy sins." You have no merit of your own to plead why He should pardon you, but plead His written engagements and He will perform them. Are you afraid lest you should not be able to hold on to the end, lest, after having thought yourself a child of God, you should prove a castaway? If that is your state, take this word of grace to the throne and plead it: "The mountains may depart, and the hills may be removed, but the covenant of My love shall not depart from thee."

If you have lost the sweet sense of the Savior's presence and are seeking Him with a sorrowful heart, remember the promises: "Return unto Me, and I will return unto you"; "For a small moment have I forsaken thee, but with great mercies will I gather thee." Banquet your faith upon God's own Word, and whatever your fears or wants, repair to the Bank of Faith with your Father's note of hand, saying, "Remember the word unto Thy servant, upon which Thou hast caused me to hope."

The Lord hath chosen Zion.

Psalm 132: 13

10

He would have those upon whom His choice is fixed be glad and happy. The elect of a great king have cause for thankfulness, but the chosen of the King of kings should rejoice continually in the God who chose them. He would have His church rejoice because He has not only chosen her, but He has cleansed her. Jesus has put away the sin of His people by His blood, and by His Spirit He is daily renewing the nature of His children. Sin is the cause of sorrow, and when sin is put away, sorrow shall be put away too. The sanctified should be happy. The Lord will, therefore, com-

April

fort them, because He has cleansed them. The church of God is placed where God dwells—

> Where God doth dwell sure heaven is there:
> And singing there should be.

What can you conceive of weeping and lamenting in the house where the Holy Spirit dwells? In all our afflictions we may draw near to the Lord, but His presence should dispel our sorrow and sighing; for the children of Zion should be joyful in their King. If the Lord dwells in the midst of His people, there ought to be shoutings of joy. The presence of the King of heaven is the heaven of their delight. Moreover, Zion enjoys her Monarch's love, and therefore He would have her comforted.

11 *Behold, how good and how pleasant it is for brethren to dwell together in unity!*

Psalm 133: 1

The best way to make a Christian man happy is to make him useful in plowing the fields which God has watered, and gathering the fruits which he has ripened. A Christian church never enjoys so much concord, love, and happiness as when every member is kept hard at work for God, every soul upon the stretch of anxiety to do good and communicate, every disciple a good soldier of the Cross, fighting the common enemy. Thus the Lord will comfort Zion, and He comforts her by turning her desert into a garden, and her wilderness into an Eden. And oh! my brethren, how happy is the church when all the members are active, all the trees bearing fruit; when sinners are converted, and daily added to the fellowship of the saved; when instead of the thorn, there comes up the myrtle, and instead of the briar there comes up the fir tree; when God is turning hard hearts, that were like rocks, into good soil, where the corn of the kingdom may grow. Oh, the joy of having the Holy Spirit. There is no joy like it!

April

If I ascend up into heaven, thou art there: if I make my bed in hell, behold, thou art there.

Psalm 139: 8

12

The most important part of human life is not its end, but its beginning. Our death day is the child of the past, but our opening years are the sires of the future. At the last hour men summon to their bedsides a solemnity of thought which arrives too late for any practical result. The hush and awe and faraway look, so frequent in departing moments, should have come much sooner. Commend us to the example of David and the Hebrew king, who fasted and wore sackcloth while the child was yet alive. Wisely did he foresee the uselessness of lamenting when the scene should close.

If the Lord be with us through life, we need not fear for our dying confidence; for *when we come to die,* we shall find that "the Lord is there"; where the billows are most tempestuous, and the water is most chill, we shall feel the bottom, and know that it is good: our feet shall stand upon the Rock of Ages when time is passing away. Beloved, from the first of a Christian's life to the last, the only reason why he does not perish is because *"the Lord is there."* When the God of everlasting love shall change and leave his elect to perish, then may the Church of God be destroyed; but not till then, because it is written, *Jehovah Shammah,* "the Lord is there."

Surely the righteous shall give thanks unto thy name: the upright shall dwell in thy presence.

Psalm 140: 13

13

The distinguishing mark of a Christian is his confidence in the love of Christ, and the yielding of his affections to Christ in return. First, faith sets her seal upon the man by enabling the soul to say with the apostle, "Christ loved me and gave himself for me." Then love gives the countersign, and stamps upon the heart gratitude and love to Jesus in return. "We love him because he first loved us." In those grand old ages, which are the heroic period of the Christian religion, this double mark was clearly to be seen

81

April

in all believers in Jesus; they were men who knew the love of Christ, and rested upon it as a man leans upon a staff whose trustiness he has tried.

His presence will be most realized by those who are most like Him. If you desire to see Christ, you must grow in conformity to Him. Bring yourself, by the power of the Spirit, into union with Christ's desires, and motives, and plans of action, and you will be in fellowship with Him. Remember *His presence may be had.* His promise is as true as ever. He delights to be with us. If he does not come, it is because we hinder Him by our indifference. He will reveal Himself to our earnest prayers, and graciously suffer Himself to be detained by our entreaties, and by our tears, for theses are the golden chains which bind Jesus to His people.

14

> *Great is the Lord, and greatly to be praised; and his greatness is unsearchable.*
>
> Psalm 145: 3

I gaze on beauty, and may be myself deformed. I admire the light, and may yet dwell in darkness; but if the light of the countenance of God rests upon me, I shall become like Him; the lineaments of His visage will be on me, and the great outlines of His attributes will be mine. Oh, wondrous glass, which thus renders the beholder lovely. Oh, admirable mirror, which reflects not self with its imperfections, but gives a perfect image to those that are uncomely.

If you continually draw your impulse, your life, the whole of your being from the Holy Spirit, then shall you see God and Jesus face to face.

Behold the unpillared arch of heaven; see how it stretches its gigantic span; and yet it falls not, though it is unpropped and unbuttressed. "He hangeth the world upon nothing." What chain is it that binds up the stars, and keeps them from falling? A Christian should be a second exhibition of God's universe; his faith should be an unpillared confidence, resting on the past, and on the eternity to come, as the sure groundwork of its arch. His faith should be like the world, it should hang on nothing but the promise of God, needing nothing to uphold him but the right hand of his Father.

April

He who lives without prayer—he who lives with little prayer—he who seldom reads the Word— he who seldom looks up to heaven for a fresh influence from on high—he will be the man whose heart will become dry and barren; but he who calls in secret on his God—who spends much time in holy retirement—who delights to meditate on the words of the Most High—whose soul is given up to Christ—such a man must have an overflowing heart; and as his heart is, such will his life be.

Prayer is the rustling of the wings of the angels that are on their way bringing us the boons of heaven. Have you heard prayer in your heart? You shall see the angel in your house. When the chariots that bring us blessings do rumble, their wheels do sound with prayer. We hear the prayer in our own spirits, and that prayer becomes the token of the coming blessings. Even as the cloud foreshadows the rain, so prayer foreshadows the blessing; even as the green blade is the beginning of the harvest, so is prayer the prophecy of the blessing that is about to come.

Praise ye the Lord. Sing unto the Lord a new song, and his praise in the congregation of saints.

Psalm 149: 1

16

We will be glad and rejoice in God. We will not open the gates of the year to the dolorous notes of the sackbut, but to the sweet strains of the harp of joy. "O come, let us sing unto the Lord: let us make a joyful noise unto the rock of our salvation." What heavens are laid up in Jesus! What rivers of infinite bliss have their source, ay, and every drop of their fullness in Him! Since, O sweet Lord Jesus, You are the present portion of Your people, favor us this year with such a sense of Your preciousness, that from its first to its last day, we may be glad and rejoice in You.

Suppose you see a lake, and there are twenty or thirty streamlets running into it: why, there will not be one strong river in the

April

whole country; there will be a number of little brooks which will be dried up in the summer, and will be temporary torrents in winter. They will every one of them be useless for any great purpose, because there is not water enough in the lake to feed more than one great stream. Now, a man's heart has only enough life in it to pursue one object fully. You must not give half your love to Christ, and the other half to the world. No man can serve God and mammon.

My son, despite not the chastening of the Lord; neither be weary of his correction: For whom the Lord loveth he correcteth; even as a father the son in whom he delighteth.

Proverbs 3: 11, 12

There are occasions when God's servants shrink from duty. But what is the consequence? *They lost the presence and comfortable enjoyment of God's love.* When *we* obey our Lord Jesus as believers should, our God is with us; and though we have the whole world against us, if we have God with us, what does it matter? But the moment we start back, and seek our own inventions, we are at sea without a pilot. Then may we bitterly lament and groan out, "O my God, where have You gone? How could I have been so foolish as to lose all the bright shinings of Your face? This is a price too high. Let me return to my allegiance, that I may rejoice in Your presence."

When God seems most to leave His church, His heart is warm toward her. History shows us that whenever God uses a rod to chasten His servants, He always breaks it afterwards, as if He loathed the rod which gave His children pain. "Like as a father pitieth his children, so the Lord pitieth them that fear him." His blows are no evidences of a lack of love. You may fear that the Lord has passed you by, but it is not so: He who counts the stars, and calls them by their names, is in no danger of forgetting His own children. He knows your case as thoroughly as if you were the only creature He ever made, or the only saint He ever loved. Approach Him and be at peace.

Happy is the man that findeth wisdom, and the man that getteth understanding.

Proverbs 3: 13

18

If trained by the Great Teacher, we follow where He leads, we shall find good, even while in the dark abode. But where shall this wisdom be found? Many have dreamed of it, but have not possessed it. Where shall we learn it? Let us listen to the voice of the Lord, for He has declared the secret; He has revealed to the sons of men where true wisdom lies, and we have in it the text, "Whoso trusteth in the Lord, happy is he" (Prov. 16: 20). *The true way to handle a matter wisely is to trust in the Lord.* This is the sure clue to the most intricate labyrinths of life. Lord, in this sweet evening, walk with me in the garden and teach me the wisdom of faith.

The Lord by wisdom hath founded the earth; by understanding hath he established the heavens.

Proverbs 3: 19

19

Better have two lights than only one. The light of creation is a bright light. God may be seen in the stars; His name is written in golden letters on the brow of night; you may discover His glory in the ocean waves, yea, in the trees of the field; but it is better to read it in two books than in one. You will find it here more clearly revealed; for He has written this Book Himself, and He has given you the key to understand it, if you have the Holy Spirit. Ah, beloved, let us thank God for this Bible; let us love it; let us count it more precious than much fine gold.

The canon revelation is closed; there is no more to be added; God does not give a fresh revelation, but He rivets the old one. When it has been forgotten, and laid in the dusty chamber of our memory, He brings it forth and cleans the picture, but does not paint a new one. It is not by any new revelation that the Spirit comforts. He does so by telling us old things over again; He brings a fresh lamp to manifest the treasures hidden in Scripture; He unlocks the strong chests in which the truth has long

April

lain, and He points to secret chambers filled with untold riches;
but He coins no more, for enough is done.

20

*I love them that love me; and those that seek me early shall
find me.*

Proverbs 8: 17

Omnipotence may build a thousand worlds, and fill them with bounties; Omnipotence may powder mountains into dust, and burn the
sea, and consume the sky, but Omnipotence cannot do an unloving
thing toward a believer. Oh! rest quite sure, Christian, a hard thing,
an unloving thing from God toward one of His own people is quite
impossible. He is as kind to you when He casts you into prison
as when He takes you into a palace; He is as good when He sends
famine into your house as when He fills your barns with plenty.
The only question is, Are you his child? If so, He has rebuked
you in affection, and there is love in His chastisement.

Do you not know that God is an eternal self-existent Being; that
to say He loves *now*, is, in fact, to say He always did love, since
with God there is no past, and can be no future. What we call
past, present, and future, He wraps in one eternal now. And if
you say He loves you now, you say He loved yesterday; He loved
in the past eternity; and He will love forever; for *now* with God
is past, present, and future.

Christ's love is the sun and our love is the moonlight, which
we are able to give forth because the sun has looked upon us.

21

The righteous hath hope in his death.

Proverbs 14: 32

The saints in Jesus, when their bodies sleep in peace, have perpetual fellowship with him—ay, better fellowship than we can enjoy.

We have but the transitory glimpse of His face; they gaze upon it every moment. We see Him "in a glass, darkly"; they behold Him "face to face." We sip of the brook by the way; they plunge into the very ocean of unbounded love. We look up sometimes, and see our Father smile; look whenever they may, His face is always full of smiles for them. We get some drops of comfort, but they get the honeycomb itself. They are full of peace, full of joy forever. They "sleep in Jesus."

The death of the saints is precious in the sight of the Lord. On their account we have cause rather to rejoice than to weep. Yes, we have the fond and firm persuasion that already their redeemed spirits have flown up to the eternal throne. We do believe that they are at this moment joining in the hallelujahs of paradise, feasting on the fruits of the tree of life, and walking by the side of the "river, the streams whereof make glad the heavenly city of our God." We know they are supremely blest; we think of them as glorified spirits above who are present with the Lord Jesus.

When a man's ways please the Lord, he maketh even his enemies to be at peace with him.

Proverbs 16: 7

22

I must see that my ways please the Lord. Even then I shall have enemies; and, perhaps, all the more certainly because I endeavored to do that which is right. But what a promise this is! The Lord will make the wrath of men to praise Him, and abate it so that it shall not distress me. When I meet death, who is called the last enemy, I pray that I may be at peace. Only let my great care be to please the Lord in all things.

Ever to be remembered is that best and brightest of hours when first we saw the Lord, lost our burden, received the roll of promise, rejoiced in full salvation, and went on our way in peace. It was springtime in the soul; the winter was past. Then the flowers appeared in our heart: hope, love, peace and patience sprung from the sod; and our resolve was, "Lord, I am yours, wholly yours; all I am, and all I have, I would devote to You. You have bought me with Your blood; let me spend myself and be spent in Your

April

service. In life and in death let me be consecrated to You." *How have we kept this resolve?*

23 *A man that hath friends must show himself friendly: and there is a friend that sticketh closer than a brother.*

Proverbs 18: 24

Friendship, though very pleasing and exceedingly blessed, has been the cause of the greatest misery to men when it has been unworthy and unfaithful; for just in proportion as a good friend is sweet, a false friend is full of bitterness. "A faithless friend is sharper than an adder's tooth." It is sweet to repose in some one; but O! how bitter to have that support snapped, and to receive a grievous fall as the effect of your confidence. Solomon declares that "there is a friend that sticketh closer than a brother." That friend, I suppose, he never found in the pomps and vanities of the world. He had tried them all, but he found them empty; he passed through all their joys. For you, that Friend is Jesus!

24 *Faithful are the wounds of a friend; but the kisses of an enemy are deceitful. Ointment and perfume rejoice the heart: so doth the sweetness of a man's friend by hearty counsel. Thine own friend, and thy father's friend, forsake not; neither go into thy brother's house in the day of thy calamity: for better is a neighbor that is near than a brother far off. As in water face answereth to face, so the heart of man to man.*

Proverbs 27: 6, 9, 10, 19

Faithfulness to us in our faults is a certain sign of fidelity in a friend. You may depend upon that man who will tell you of your faults in a kind and considerate manner. Give me for a friend a man who will speak honestly of me before my face; who will not tell first one neighbor, and then another, but who will come straight

April

to my house and say: "I feel there is a wrong in you, my brother, I must tell you of." That man is a true friend. He has proved himself to be so, for we never get any praise for telling people of their faults; we rather hazard their dislike. A man will sometimes thank you for it, but he does not often like you any the better.

Friendship is the only thing in the world concerning the usefulness of which all mankind are agreed. Friendship seems as necessary an element of a comfortable existence in this world as fire and water, or even air itself. A man may drag along a miserable existence in proud solitary dignity, but his life is scarce life; it is nothing but an existence, the tree of life being stripped of the leaves of hope and the fruits of joy. He who would be happy here must have friends; and he who would be happy hereafter, must, above all things, find a friend in the world to come, in the person of God, the Father of His people.

He that trusteth in his own heart is a fool: but whoso walketh wisely, he shall be delivered.

Proverbs 28: 26

25

How bitter is the enmity of the world against the people of Christ. Men will forgive a thousand faults in others, but they will magnify the most trivial offense in the follower of Jesus. Instead of vainly regretting this, let us turn it to account, and since so many are watching for our halting, let this be a special motive for walking very carefully before God. If we live carelessly, the lynx-eyed world will soon see it, and they will shout triumphantly, "See how these Christians act!" The cross of Christ is in itself an offense to the world; let us take heed that we add no offense of our own, for thus can much damage be done to the cause of Christ, and much insult offered to His name.

A true believer, called by grace and washed in the precious blood of Jesus, has tasted of better drink than the river of this world's pleasure can give him; we have had fellowship with Christ; we have felt the joy of seeing Jesus, and leaning our heads upon His bosom. Can the trifles, the songs, the honors, the merriment of this earth content us after that? If you are wandering after the

89

April

waters of Egypt, oh, return quickly to the one living fountain: the waters of Sihor may be sweet to the Egyptians, but they will prove only bitterness to you. *What have you to do with them?* Jesus asks—what will your answer be?

26

An unjust man is an abomination to the just: and he that is upright in the way is abomination to the wicked.

Proverbs 29: 27

You cannot, though you may think you can, preserve a moderation in sin. If you commit one sin, it is like the melting of the lower glacier upon the Alps; the others must follow in time. As certainly as you heap one stone upon the cairn today, the next day you will cast another, until the heap, reared stone by stone, shall become a very pyramid. Set the coral insect at work, you cannot decree where it shall stay its work. It will not build its rock just as high as you please; it will not stay until there shall be soil upon it, and an island shall be created by tiny creatures. Sin cannot be held in with bit and bridle.

"Oh!" cries one, "I wish I could escape the wrath of the law! Oh that I knew that Christ did keep the law for me!" Stop, then, and I will tell you. Do you feel today that you are guilty, lost, and ruined? Do you, with tears in your eyes, confess that none but Jesus can do you good? Are you willing to give up all trusts, and cast yourself alone on Him who died upon the cross? Can you look to Calvary, and see the bleeding Sufferer, all crimson with streams of gore? Then He kept the law for you, and the law cannot condemn whom Christ has absolved.

27

Who hath gathered the wind in his fists? who hath bound the waters in a garment? who hath established all the ends of the earth?

Proverbs 30: 4

It has been asserted that God cannot be known. Those who say this declare that they themselves know nothing but phenomena.

April

He who made the world was certainly an intelligent being, in fact the highest intelligence; for in myriads of ways His works display the presence of profound thought and knowledge. Lord Bacon said, "I had rather believe all the fables of the Talmud and the Koran than that this universal frame is without a mind." This being so, we do in that very fact know God in a measure; ay, and in such a measure that we are prepared to trust Him. He who made all things is more truly an object of confidence than all things that He has made.

But we do not observe God's hand as much as we should. Our good puritanic forefathers, when it rained, used to say, that God had unstopped the bottles of heaven. When it rains nowadays, we think the clouds have become condensed. If they had a field of hay cut, they used to plead of the Lord that He would cause the sun to shine. We, perhaps, are wiser, as we think; and we consider it hardly worth while to pray about such things, thinking they will come in the course of nature. They believed that God was in every storm; nay, in every cloud of dust. They used to speak of a present God in everything.

My beloved is mine, and I am his. . . .
Song of Solomon 2: 16

28

Surely if there be a happy verse in the Bible, it is this—"My Beloved is mine, and I am his." So peaceful, so full of assurance, so overrunning with happiness and contentment is it, that it might well have been written by the same hand which penned the twenty-third Psalm. The verse savors of Him who, an hour before He went to Gethsemane, said, "Peace I leave with you, my peace I give unto you: not as the world giveth, give I unto you." "In the world ye shall have tribulation: but be of good cheer; I have overcome the world." Let us ring the silver bell again, for its notes are exquisitely sweet: "My Beloved is mine, and I am his."

April

29

I sleep, but my heart waketh: it is the voice of my beloved. . . .

Song of Solomon 5: 2

We are none of us so much awake as we should be. With a perishing world around us, to sleep is cruel. Oh, that we may leave forever the couch of ease, and go forth with flaming torches to meet the coming Bridegroom! *My heart waketh.* This is a happy sign. Life is not extinct, though sadly smothered. When our renewed heart struggles against our natural heaviness, we should be grateful to sovereign grace for keeping a little vitality within the body of this death. Jesus will hear our hearts, will help our hearts, will visit our hearts; for the voice of the wakeful heart is really the voice of our Beloved, saying, "Open to me." Holy zeal will surely unbar the door.

In the evening of the day opportunities are plentiful: men return from the labor, and the zealous soul-winner finds time to tell abroad the love of Jesus. Have I no evening work for Jesus? If I have not, let me no longer withhold my hand from a service which requires abundant labor. Jesus gave both His hands to the nails; how can I keep back one of mine from His blessed work? Night and day He toiled and prayed for me; how can I give a single hour to selfish indulgence? Up, idle heart; stretch out your hand to work, or uplift it to pray: heaven and hell are in earnest; let me be so, and this evening sow good seed for the Lord my God.

30

Come now, and let us reason together, saith the Lord: though your sins be as scarlet, they shall be as white as snow; though they be red like crimson, they shall be as wool.

Isaiah 1: 18

At this moment, dear reader, whatever your sinfulness, Christ has power to pardon—power to pardon you, and millions such as you are. A word will speak it. He has nothing more to do to win your pardon; all the atoning work is done. He can, in answer to your tears, forgive your sins today, and make you know it. He can breathe into your soul at this very moment a peace with God

92

April

which passes all understanding, which shall spring from perfect remission of your many sins. Do you believe that? I trust that you do. May you experience now the power of Jesus to forgive sin!

What bliss to be a perfectly pardoned soul! My soul dedicates all her powers to Him who, of His own unpurchased love, became my surety, and provided for me redemption through His blood! What riches of grace does free forgiveness exhibit! To forgive at all, to forgive fully, to forgive freely, to forgive ever! Here is a constellation of wonders; and when I think of how great my sins were, how dear were the precious drops which cleansed me from them, I am in a maze of wondering, worshiping affection. I bow before the throne which absolves me; I clasp the cross which delivers me; I serve henceforth the Incarnate God, through whom I am this day a pardoned soul.

May

1

Come ye, and let us go up to the mountain of the Lord.
Isaiah 2: 3

It is exceedingly beneficial to our souls to mount above this present evil world to something nobler and better. The cares of this world and the deceitfulness of riches are apt to choke everything good within us, and we grow fretful, desponding, perhaps proud and carnal. It is well for us to cut down these thorns and briers, for heavenly seed sown among them is not likely to yield a harvest; and where shall we find a better sickle with which to cut them down than communion with God?

May the Spirit of God assist us to leave the mists of fear and the fevers of anxiety, and all the ills which gather in this valley of earth, and to ascend the mountains of anticipated joy and blessedness. May God the Holy Spirit cut the cords that keep us here below, and assist us to mount! We sit too often like chained eagles fastened to the rock, only that, unlike the eagle, we begin to love our chain, and would, perhaps, if it came really to the test, be loath to have it snapped. May God now grant us grace, if we cannot escape from the chain as to our flesh, yet to do so as to our spirits; and leaving the body, like a servant, at the foot of the hill, may our soul, like Abraham, attain the top of the mountain, there to indulge in communion with the Most High.

*Woe unto them that draw iniquity with cords of vanity, and
sin as it were with a cart rope. . . . Woe to those who drag
their sins behind them like a bullock on a rope.*

Isaiah 5: 18, KJV, TLB

2

> E'er since by faith I saw the stream
> His flowing wounds supply,
> Redeeming love has been my theme,
> And shall be till I die.

Oh, my beloved readers, believe in Christ as I did. The gospel
comes to each sorrowing sinner and it says—Trust the Savior and
there is joy for you. There is but a veil of gauze between you
and peace; move the hand of faith, and that veil will be torn to
pieces. There is but a step between your misery and music and
dancing and a life of perpetual delights; take that step out of self
and into Christ, and all is changed forever. Ask Jesus to break
your bonds, and with a touch of His pierced hand, He will make
you free as the swallow on the wing which no cage can hold. You
will see *Him*, and see your sins never again.

God bless you and break the cart ropes, and remove the cords
of vanity, for Jesus' sake.

*And the Spirit of the Lord shall rest upon him, the spirit
of wisdom and understanding, the spirit of counsel and
might, the spirit of knowledge and of the fear of the Lord.*

Isaiah 11: 2

3

As a man does not make himself spiritually alive, so neither can
he keep himself so. He can feed on spiritual food, and so preserve
his spiritual strength; he can walk in the commandments of the
Lord, and so enjoy rest and peace, but still the inner life is dependent upon the Spirit as much for its after existence as for its first
begetting. No man himself, even when converted, has any power,
except as that power is daily, constantly, and perpetually infused
into him by the Spirit.

The motivating power of action to a believing man lies hard
by the realization that God, for Christ's sake, has forgiven his iniquities.

Salvation is God's highest glory. He is glorified in every dewdrop

May

that twinkles to the morning sun. He is magnified in every wood flower that blossoms in the copse, although it live to blush unseen and waste its sweetness in the forest air. But sing, sing, O Universe, till you have exhausted yourself, you cannot afford a song so sweet as the song of Incarnation. There is more in that than in creation, more melody in Jesus in the manger, than there is in worlds on worlds rolling their grandeur round the throne of the Most High.

Behold, God is my salvation; I will trust, and not be afraid: for the Lord Jehovah is my strength and my song; he also is become my salvation.

Isaiah 12: 2

Note, the word is not "The Lord gives me strength," but "The Lord *is* my strength"! How strong is a believer? I say it with reverence, he is as strong as God—"The Lord is my strength." God, the infinite Jehovah, in the infinity of His nature, is our strength.

The next is, "The Lord is my *song*," that is to say, the Lord is the giver of our songs; He breathes the music into the hearts of His people; He is the creator of their joy. The Lord is also the subject of their songs: they sing of Him and of all that He does on their behalf. The Lord is, moreover, the object of their song; they sing unto the Lord. Their praise is meant for Him alone. They do not make melody for human ears, but unto the Lord. "The Lord is my song." Then I ought always to sing: and if I sing my loudest, I can never reach the height of this great argument, nor come to the end of it. This song never changes. If I live by faith my song is always the same, for "The Lord is my song." Our song unto God is God Himself. He alone can express our intensest joy. O God, You are my exceeding joy. Father, Son, and Holy Ghost, You are my hymn of everlasting delight.

For thou hast been a strength to the poor, a strength to the needy in his distress, a refuge from the storm, a shadow from the heat, when the blast of the terrible ones is as a storm against the wall.

Isaiah 25: 4

Do you not know today how secure, how immutable is your defense? Even as the eagle on the rock cannot be reached by the fowler, so are you secure. Look! You have God's promise—"I will never leave thee nor forsake thee!" "No good thing will he withhold from them that walk uprightly." These promises are the munitions of rocks behind which you are sheltered; the sure words of an unchanging God are your bulwarks. You have also the oath of God as your high tower: for He has sworn by Himself because He could swear by no greater. There stands His covenant made up of promises, secured by oath, and ratified by blood: who shall break within that line of defense? What munitions of rock can be compared with these things in which it is "impossible for God to lie"—these pledges which God can never dishonor, these guarantees of everlasting faithfulness that can never be questioned? Oh, the blessed security of a child of God!

And in that day shall the deaf hear the words of the book, and the eyes of the blind shall see out of obscurity, and out of darkness.

Isaiah 29: 18

6

If Christ is more excellent at one time than another it certainly is in "the cloudy and dark day." We can never so well see the true color of Christ's love as in the night of weeping. Christ in the dungeon, Christ on the bed of sickness, Christ in poverty, is Christ indeed to a sanctified man. No vision of Christ Jesus is so truly a revelation as that which is seen in the Patmos of suffering. This He proves to His beloved, not by mere words of promise, but by actual deeds of affection. As our sufferings abound, so He makes our consolations to abound.

Sunlight is never more grateful than after a long watch in the midnight blackness; Christ's presence is never more acceptable than after a time of weeping, on account of His departure. It is a sad thing that we should need to lose our mercies to teach us to be grateful for them; let us mourn over this crookedness of our nature; and let us strive to express our thankfulness for mercies, so that we may not have to lament their removal. If you desire Christ as a perpetual guest, give Him all the keys of your heart: let not one cabinet be locked up from Him; give Him the range of every room, and the key of every chamber; thus you will constrain Him to remain.

May

7

He shall dwell on high; his place of defense shall be the munitions of rocks: bread shall be given him; his waters shall be sure.

Isaiah 33: 16

It is a matter of fact that the man who believes in the Lord Jesus Christ, and lives as a Christian should live, dwells on the heights. His mind is lifted up above the common cares, and worries, and vexations of life. The Holy Spirit has begotten him again unto a lively hope by the resurrection of Jesus Christ from the dead, and therefore his conversation is in heaven—from whence he looks for his Savior the Lord Jesus. I am sure that many of you know what it is to ride on the high places of the earth, and to look down upon the world as a poor paltry thing. You have walked with God in light, even as He is in the light, and then you have been filled with a joy which no man can take from you, and you have trodden the world beneath your feet, and all that earth calls good or great. Thus has it been true of you, "he shall dwell on high."

You have also found that you have had a place of defense in time of trouble. Though often assailed you have never been really injured; unto this day the rage of man has caused you no real loss. You can understand today the meaning of that word, "Who art thou, that thou shouldest be afraid of a man that shall die, and of the son of man which shall be made as grass?" Even Satan himself has not been able to overthrow you: you have trodden upon the lion and the dragon: in the name of the Lord you have resisted the devil, and he has fled from you. Tell it out this day to all the sons of men, that the Lord thy God has been a wall of fire round about you. All things have worked together for good to us up till now, and we know it; we have had a place of defense, and in this we will rejoice and be glad.

8

And the ransomed of the Lord shall return, and come to Zion with songs and everlasting joy upon their heads: they shall obtain joy and gladness, and sorrow and sighing shall flee away.

Isaiah 35: 10

If there be one place where our Lord Jesus most fully becomes the joy and comfort of His people, it is where He plunged deepest into the depths of woe. Come hither, gracious souls, and behold the Man in the garden of Gethsemane; behold His heart so brimming with love that He cannot hold it in—so full of sorrow that it must find a vent. Behold the Man as they drive the nails into His hands and feet. Look up, repenting sinners, and see the sorrowful image of your suffering Lord. If we would live aright, it must be by the contemplation of His death; if we would rise to dignity, it must be by considering His humiliation and His sorrow.

Most of us know what it is to be overwhelmed in heart. Disappointments and heartbreaks will do this when billow after billow rolls over us, and we are like a broken shell hurled to and fro by the surf. Blessed be God, at such seasons we are not without an all-sufficient solace; our Savior is the harbor of weather-beaten sails, the hospice of forlorn pilgrims. Higher than we are is our God, His mercy higher than our sins, His love higher than our thoughts. A rock He is since He changes not, and a high rock, because the tempests which overwhelm us roll far beneath at His feet. O Lord, our God, by Your Holy Spirit, teach us Your way of faith, lead us unto Your rest.

Now on whom dost thou trust?

Isaiah 36: 5

Reader, this is an important question. Listen to the Christian's answer, and see if it is yours. "On whom dost thou trust?" "I trust," says the Christian, "in a triune God. I trust the Father, believing that He has chosen me from before the foundations of the world; I trust Him to provide for me in providence, to teach me, to guide me, to correct me if need be, and to bring me home to His own house where the many mansions are. I trust the Son. Very God of very God is He—the man Christ Jesus. I trust in Him to take away all my sins by His own sacrifice, and to adorn me with His perfect righteousness. I trust Him to be my Intercessor, to present my prayers and desires before His Father's throne, and I trust Him to be my Advocate at the last great day, to plead my cause, and to justify me. I trust Him for what He is, for what He has done, and for what He has promised yet to do. And I trust the Holy Spirit—I trust Him to drive out all my sins; I trust Him to curb my temper, to subdue my will, to enlighten my understanding, to check my passions, to comfort my despondency, to help my

May

weakness, to illuminate my darkness; I trust Him to dwell in me as my life, to reign in me as my King, to sanctify me wholly, spirit, soul and body, and then to take me up to dwell with the saints in light forever."

Oh, blessed trust! To trust Him whose power will never be exhausted, whose love will never wane, whose kindness will never change, whose faithfulness will never fail, whose wisdom will never be nonplussed, and whose perfect goodness can never know a diminution! Happy are you, reader, if this trust is yours! So trusting, you will enjoy sweet peace now, and glory hereafter, and the foundation of your trust shall never be removed.

The grass withereth, the flower fadeth: but the word of our God shall stand for ever.

Isaiah 40: 8

Between the revelation of God in His Word and that in His works, there can be no actual discrepancy. The one may go farther than the other, but the revelation must be harmonious. Between *the interpretation* of the Works and *the interpretation* of the Word, there may be great differences. It must be admitted that the men of the Book have sometimes missed its meaning. Nay, more: it is certain that, in their desire to defend their Bible, devout persons have been unwise enough to twist its words. If they had always labored to understand what God said, in His Book, and had steadfastly adhered to its meaning, they would have been wise.

One of the marvels of the Bible is its singular fullness. It is not a book of gold leaf beaten thin, as most books are as to thought; but its sentences are nuggets of unalloyed truth. The Book of God is clearly the god of books, for it is infinite. Well said a German author, "In this little book is contained all the wisdom of the world."

He shall feed his flock like a shepherd: he shall gather the lambs with his arm, and carry them in his bosom, and shall gently lead those that are with young.

Isaiah 40: 11

It is true I am weak in faith, and prone to fall, but my very feebleness is the reason why I should always be where You feed Your flock, that I may be strengthened and preserved in safety beside the still waters. Why should I turn aside? There is no reason why I should, but there are a thousand reasons why I should not, for Jesus beckons me to come. If He withdraw Himself a little, it is but to make me prize His presence more. Now that I am grieved and distressed at being away from Him, He will lead me yet again to that sheltered nook where the lambs of His fold are sheltered from the burning sun.

He shall gather the lambs with his arm, and carry them in his bosom. . . .

Isaiah 40: 11

12

Who is he of whom such gracious words are spoken? He is the Good Shepherd. Why does He carry the lambs in His bosom? Because He has a tender heart, and any weakness at once melts His heart. The sighs, the ignorance, the feebleness of the little ones of His flock draw forth His compassion. It is His office, as a faithful High Priest, to consider the weak. Besides, He purchased them with blood, they are His property: He must and will care for that which cost Him so dear. Then He is responsible for each lamb, bound by covenant engagements not to lose one. Moreover, they are all a part of His glory and reward.

Let the people renew their strength.

Isaiah 41: 1

13

All things on earth need to be renewed. No created thing continues by itself. "Thou renewest the face of the year," was the Psalmist's utterance. Even the trees, which wear not themselves with care, nor shorten their lives with labor, must drink of the rain of heaven and suck from the hidden treasures of the soil. The cedars of Lebanon, which God has planted, only live because day by day they are full of sap freshly drawn from the earth. Neither can man's

May

life be sustained without renewal from God. As it is necessary to repair the waste of the body by the frequent meal, so we must repair the waste of the soul by feeding upon the Book of God, or by listening to the preached Word.

Without constant restoration we are not ready for the perpetual assaults of hell, or the stern afflictions of heaven, or even for the strifes within. When the whirlwind shall be loosed, woe to the tree that has not sucked up fresh sap, and grasped the rock with many intertwisted roots. When tempests arise, woe to the mariners that have not strengthened their mast, nor cast their anchor, nor sought the haven. If we suffer the good to grow weaker, the evil will surely gather strength and struggle desperately for the mastery over us; and so, perhaps, a painful desolation, and a lamentable disgrace may follow. Let us draw near to the footstool of divine mercy in humble entreaty, and we shall realize the fulfillment of the promise, "They that wait on the Lord shall renew their strength."

Fear thou not; for I am with thee: be not dismayed; for I am thy God: I will strengthen thee; yea, I will help thee; yea, I will uphold thee with the right hand of my righteousness.

Isaiah 41: 10

"I will help thee," says God. That is very little for Me to do, to help you. Consider what I have done already. What! not help you? Why, I bought you with My blood. What! not help you? I have died for you; and if I have done the greater, will I not do the less? *Help* you, My beloved! It is the least thing I will ever do for you. I have done more, and I will do more. Before the day-star first began to shine I chose you. "I will *help* thee." I made the covenant for you, and exercised all the wisdom of My eternal mind in the plan of salvation. "I will *help* thee."

In the light of this promise, it is the highest stage of manhood to have no wish, no thought, no desire, but Christ—to feel that to die were bliss, if it were for Christ—that to live in penury, and woe, and scorn, and contempt, and misery, were sweet for Christ—to feel that it matters nothing what becomes of one's self, so that our Master is but exalted—to feel that though, like a dry leaf, we are blown in the blast, we are quite careless where we are going, so long as we feel that the Master's hand is guiding us according to His will.

Declaring the end from the beginning, and from ancient times the things that are not yet done, saying, My counsel shall stand, and I will do all my pleasure.

Isaiah 46: 10

15

A fool soon makes up his mind, because there is so very little of it; but a wise man waits and considers. The case is far otherwise with the only wise God. The Lord is not a man that He should need to hesitate; His infinite mind is made up, and He knows His thoughts. With the Lord there is neither question nor debate: "He is in one mind, and none can turn him." His purpose is settled, and He adheres to it. He is resolved to regard them who diligently seek Him, and to honor those who trust in Him. He is resolved to remember His covenant forever, and to keep His promises to those who believe Him.

His thought is that the people whom He has formed for Himself shall show forth His praise. The Lord knows them that are His; He knows whom He gave to His Son, and He knows that these shall be His jewels forever and ever.

Beloved, when you do not know your own mind, God knows *His* mind. Though you believe not, He abides faithfully; when you are in the gloom He is light, and in Him is no darkness at all. Your way may be closed, but His way is open. God knows all when you know nothing at all.

They shall not hunger nor thirst; neither shall the heat nor sun smite them: for he that hath mercy on them shall lead them, even by the springs of water shall he guide them.

Isaiah 49: 10

16

I must not fail to notice that the poetic utterance, "Thy bread shall be given thee" (Isa. 33: 16) is also literally true. It has been

May

true to you, my brethren, concerning your daily bread. That word is true, "Trust in the Lord, and do good, so shalt thou dwell in the land, and verily thou shalt be fed." At times there has been little on the table, but all-sufficiency has still filled the storehouse.

When God multiplied the oil and the meal of the poor woman at Zarepta, I do not believe that at any one moment she ever had more than sufficed for a single meal: every day that Elijah lived with her she had to scrape the bottom of the barrel, for she had never more than a handful of meal and a little oil.

We are not told that either the barrel or the cruse was filled up; but we read—"The barrel of meal shall not waste, neither shall the cruse of oil fail." You may frequently reach the end of your provision, but you can never exhaust your Provider. The meal may come by handfuls, and the oil may only drip out drop by drop, but what matters? Was not the manna from heaven a small round thing, and did it not fall morning by morning? If you have earthly provision as you want it, should it not suffice you? If you get as much as you need at this meal, and as much as you want for the next meal, is it not well? Are not the loaves of heavenly bread all the better for being fresh and fresh? The manna would not keep, but bred worms; who wants such unsavory food?

There is nothing like living from hand to mouth when it is from God's hand to faith's mouth. Daily bread promotes daily gratitude, and from God's hand hourly providence brings multiplied love tokens, and is a surer sign of remembrance than if we could have life's mercies all in a lump.

For the Lord shall comfort Zion: he will comfort all her waste places; and he will make her wilderness like Eden, and her desert like the garden of the Lord; joy and gladness shall be found therein, thanksgiving, and the voice of melody.
Isaiah 51: 3

"Joy and gladness shall be found therein, thanksgiving, and the voice of melody." You notice the doubles. The parallelism of He-

brew poetry, perhaps, necessitated them. Still I am prone to remember how John Bunyan says that "all the flowers in God's garden bloom double." We are told of "manifold mercies," that is, mercies which are folded up one in another, so that you may unwrap them and find a fresh mercy enclosed in every fold. Here we have "joy and gladness, thanksgiving, and the voice of melody." Just so; the Psalmist tells us of our soul being satisfied with "marrow and fatness"—two things. Elsewhere, he speaks of "loving-kindness and tender mercy"—two things again. The Lord multiplies His grace: He is always slow to anger, but He is always lavish of His grace. See here, then, God will give His people an overflowing joy, an inexpressible joy, a sort of double joy, as though He would give them more joy than they could hold—joy, and then gladness; thanksgiving, and the voice of melody.

On mine arm shall they trust.

Isaiah 51: 5

18

In seasons of severe trial, the Christian has nothing on earth that he can trust to, and is therefore compelled to cast himself on his God alone. When his vessel is on its beam-ends, and no human deliverance can avail, he must simply and entirely trust himself to the providence and care of God. Happy storm that wrecks a man on such a rock as this! O blessed hurricane that drives the soul to God and God alone!

There is no getting to our God sometimes because of the multitude of our friends; but when a man is so poor, so friendless, so helpless that he has nowhere else to turn, he flies into his Father's arms, and is blessedly clasped therein. When he is burdened with troubles so pressing and so peculiar, that he cannot tell them to any but his God, he may be thankful for them; for he will learn more of his Lord then than at any other time. Oh, tempest-tossed believer, it is a happy trouble that drives you to the Father.

May

19

For ye shall not go out with haste, nor go by flight; for the Lord will go before you; and the God of Israel will be your rearward.

Isaiah 52: 12

Beloved friends, God is always with those who are with Him. If we trust Him, He has said, "I will never leave thee, nor forsake thee." There is a special and familiar presence of God with those who walk uprightly, both in the night of their sorrow, and in the day of their joy. Yet we do not always in the same way perceive that presence so as to enjoy it. God never leaves us, but we sometimes think He has done so. The sun shines on, but we do not always bask in its beams; we sometimes mourn an absent God— it is the bitterest of all our mourning. As He is the sum total of our joy, so His departure is the essence of our misery. If God does not smile upon us, who can cheer us? If He be not with us, then the strong helpers fail, and the mighty men are put to rout. It is concerning the presence of God that I speak. You and I know how joyous it is. May we never be made to know its infinite value experimentally by the loss of it. If we see no cloud or flame, yet may we know that God is with us, and His power is around us.

20

He was wounded for our transgressions, he was bruised for our iniquities: the chastisement of our peace was upon him; and with his stripes we are healed.

Isaiah 53: 5

He saves us from the punishment of sin because "the chastisement of our peace was upon him." He died as a victim in our stead. He saves us from the power of sin by His Spirit, and by faith in His death: we overcome sin by the blood of the Lamb. Salvation is every department, salvation from its hopeful dawning to its glorious noontide in perfection, is all of Christ Jesus. He is Savior, and He alone. "There is none other name under heaven given among men, whereby we must be saved." He is the unique Savior; there is no other possible salvation now or in the world to come. Do you believe in Christ? Then you have salvation. "But he that believeth not shall be damned."

Seek ye the Lord while he may be found, call ye upon him while he is near. . . . Wherefore the rather, brethren, give diligence to make your calling and election sure: for if ye do these things, ye shall never fall.

Isaiah 55: 6; 2 Peter 1: 10

21

Is, then, your calling a high calling? Has it ennobled your heart, and set it upon heavenly things? Has it elevated your hopes, your tastes, your desires? If man alone call you, you are uncalled. Is your calling of God? Is it a call *to* heaven as well as from heaven? Unless you are a stranger here, and heaven your home, you have not been called with a heavenly calling; for those who have been so called, declare that they look for a city which has foundations, whose builder and maker is God. Is your calling thus holy, high, heavenly? Then, beloved, you have been called of God, for such is the calling with which God calls His people.

They shall not labor in vain, nor bring forth for trouble; for they are the seed of the blessed of the Lord, and their offspring with them.

Isaiah 65: 23

22

Self-reliance is inculcated as a moral virtue, and in a certain sense, with proper surroundings, it is so. Observation and experience show that it is a considerable force in the world. He who questions his own powers, and does not know his own mind, hesitates, trembles, falters, fails; his diffidence is the author of his disappointment. The self-reliant individual hopes, considers, plans, resolves, endeavors, perseveres, succeeds; his assurance of victory is one leading cause of his triumph. A man believes in his own capacity, and unless he is altogether a piece of emptiness he gradually convinces others that his estimate is correct.

This is no unusual occurrence; it is the general rule of the moral universe that those men prosper who do their work with all their hearts, while those are almost certain to fail who go to their labor leaving half their hearts behind them. God does not give harvests to idle men, except harvests of thistles, nor is He pleased to send wealth to those who will not dig in the field to find its hid treasure.

May

It is universally confessed that if man would prosper, he must be diligent in business. It is the same in religion as it is in other things. If you would prosper in your work for Jesus, let it be *heart* work, and let it be done with *all* your heart.

23	*And it shall come to pass, that before they call, I will answer; and while they are yet speaking, I will hear.*
	Isaiah 65: 24

I am sometimes startled at the power of a feeble prayer to win a speedy answer. "Startled," you will say; why am I startled? for it is written, "Before they call, I will answer: and while they are yet speaking, I will hear." Yes, it is so written, but we do not always appreciate the fact. When the promise comes speedily to pass, have you never felt your flesh creep with a solemn awe in the presence of God, who has so remarkably drawn near at the voice of prayer? You turn aside from your business but a minute and pray, and you come back calm and composed. This is the finger of God. You do not leave the counter, but simply dart a glance heavenward, and the thing you sought for is bestowed upon you. Is it not often so, my beloved? You know it is. Is it not easily accounted for by the fact that God is at your right hand, ready to be gracious? There is no need in every case to break the continuity of business, and to get away from the concerns of this life, for the Lord is in the shop, and in the office, as well as in the prayer closet. You are in the midst of a throng of wicked men, but God is there too, if His providence has called you into such company.

24	*Thus saith the Lord, The heaven is my throne, and the earth is my footstool.*
	Isaiah 66: 1

Christ is the chariot in which souls are drawn to heaven. The people of the Lord are on their way to heaven; they are carried in everlast-

May

ing arms; and those arms are the arms of Christ. Christ is carrying them up to His own house, to His own throne; by-and-by His prayer, "Father, I will that they whom thou hast given me be with me where I am," shall be wholly fulfilled. The cross is the great covenant transport which will weather out the storms, and reach its desired heaven. This is the chariot, the pillars wherewith are of gold; it is lined with the purple of the atonement of our Lord Jesus Christ.

Heaven is a place of complete victory and triumph. This is the battlefield; there is the triumphal procession. This is the land of the sword and the spear; that is the land of the wreath and the crown. Oh, what a thrill of joy shall shoot through the hearts of all the blessed when their conquests shall be complete in heaven, when death itself, the last of foes, shall be slain—when Satan shall be dragged captive at the chariot wheels of Christ—when He shall have overthrown sin—when the great shout of universal victory shall rise from the hearts of all the redeemed!

Thy words were found, and I did eat them; and thy word was unto me the joy and rejoicing of my heart: for I am called by thy name, O Lord God of hosts.

Jeremiah 15: 16

We should be abler teachers of others, and less liable to be carried about by every wind of doctrine, if we sought to have a more intelligent understanding of the Word of God. As the Holy Ghost, the Author of the Scriptures, is He who alone can enlighten us rightly to understand them, we should constantly ask His teaching, and His guidance into all truth.

Therefore if, for your own and others' profiting, you desire to be "filled with the knowledge of God's will in all wisdom and spiritual understanding," remember that prayer is your best means of study. You may force your way through anything with the leverage of prayer.

May

26

And I will deliver thee out of the hand of the wicked, and I will redeem thee out of the hand of the terrible.

Jeremiah 15: 21

Note the glorious personality of the promise—*I* will, *I* will. The Lord Jehovah Himself interposes to deliver and redeem His people. He pledges Himself personally to rescue them. His own arm shall do it, that He may have the glory. Neither our strength nor our weakness is taken into the account, but the lone *I*, like the sun in the heavens, shines out resplendent in all-sufficiency. Why then do we calculate our forces, and consult with flesh and blood to our grievous wounding? Peace, unbelieving thoughts, be still, and know that the Lord reigns.

Seeing that we have such a God to trust to, let us rest upon Him with all our weight; let us resolutely drive out all unbelief, and endeavor to get rid of doubts and fears, which so much mar our comfort; since there is no excuse for fear where God is the foundation of our trust. A loving parent would be sorely grieved if his child could not trust him; and how ungenerous, how unkind is our conduct when we put so little confidence in our heavenly Father, who has never failed us, and who never will! We have been in many trials, but we have never yet been cast where we could not find in our God all that we needed.

27

O earth, earth, earth, hear the word of the Lord.

Jeremiah 22: 29

You may think of a doctrine forever, and get no good from it, if you are not already saved; but think of the person of Christ, and that will give you faith. Take Him everywhere, wherever you go, and try to meditate on Him in your leisure moments, and then He will reveal Himself to you, and give you peace.

We should all know more, live nearer to God and grow in grace, if we were more alone. Meditation chews the cud and extracts the real nutriment from the mental food gathered elsewhere.

Read the Bible carefully, and then meditate and meditate and meditate.

The Bible is a vein of pure gold, unalloyed by quartz, or any earthly substance. This is a star without a speck; a sun without a blot; a light without darkness; a moon without its paleness; a glory without a dimness. It cannot be said of any other book, that it is perfect and pure; but of this Book we can declare all wisdom is gathered up in it, without a particle of folly. This is the judge that ends the strife, where wit and reason fail. This is the book untainted by any error; but is pure, unalloyed, perfect truth.

Behold, the days come, saith the Lord, that I will raise unto David a righteous Branch, and a King shall reign and prosper, and shall execute judgment and justice in the earth.
Jeremiah 23: 5

28

Whether we speak of the active or passive righteousness of Christ there is an equal fragrance. There was a sweet savor in His active life by which He honored the law of God, and made every precept to glitter like a precious jewel in the pure setting of His own person. Such, too, was His passive obedience, when He endured, with unmurmuring submission, hunger and thirst, cold and nakedness, and at length was fastened to the cruel cross that He might suffer the wrath of God in our behalf. These two things are sweet before the Most High; and for the sake of His doing and His dying, His substitutionary sufferings and His vicarious obedience, the Lord our God accepts us.

Our Lord Jesus, by His death, did not purchase a right to a *part* of us only, but to the *entire* man. He contemplated in His passion the sanctification of us wholly, spirit, soul, and body. It is the business of the newborn nature which God has given to the regenerate to assert the rights of the Lord Jesus Christ. My soul, so far as you are a child of God, you must conquer all the rest of yourself which yet remains unblest; you must subdue all your powers and passions to the silver scepter of Jesus' gracious reign, and

May

you must never be satisfied till He who is king by purchase becomes also king by gracious coronation and reigns within you supreme.

> *For thus saith the Lord, That after seventy years be accomplished at Babylon I will visit you, and perform my good word toward you, in causing you to return to this place.*
> Jeremiah 29: 10
> Read Jeremiah 29: 10–14

29

Our relation to God should be one of *continual expectancy*, especially expectancy of the fulfillment of His promises. I call your attention to this verse: "I will perform my good word toward you." His promises are good words: good indeed, and sweetly refreshing. When your hearts are faint, then is the promise emphatically *good*. Expect the Lord to be as good as His good word.

Brethren, do not heap up to yourselves sorrow, as some do in these days, by expecting that which the Lord has not promised. I earnestly warn you against those who have been led by a fevered imagination to expect, first, perfection in the flesh, and then perfection of the flesh, and then an actual immortality for the flesh. God will fulfill His promise, but He will not fulfill our misreading of it. I should not wonder if there should arise a race of people who will believe that they can live without eating, because it is said, "Man shall not live by bread alone, but by every word that proceedeth out of the mouth of God shall man live." If healed without medicine, why not fed without food? What absolute need of any visible means when God can work without them? Those who think it needful to lay aside all outward means in order to have a true faith in God, are on the way to any absurdity. Truly, if God had bidden me to live without eating, I would fast at His command and expect to live; but as He has not done so, I shall not presume.

Faith that is not warranted by the Word of God is not faith, but folly; and folly is not the faith of God's elect. The Lord will perform His own word, but He will not perform the delirious declarations of madmen. If it needs a million miracles to fulfill God's promise they shall be forthcoming; but we are not anxious for miracles, because our larger faith believes that the Lord can over-

May

rule the ordinary ways of Providence to perform his good word, and bring us the expected end (Jer. 29: 11).

For I know the plans I have for you, says the Lord, plans for welfare and not for evil, to give you a future and a hope.
Jeremiah 29: 11, RSV

30

The Lord's thoughts are all working toward "an expected end" (KJV), or, as the Revised Version has it, "to give you hope in your latter end." Some read it, "a future and a hope." The renderings are instructive. God is working with a motive. All things are working together for one object: the good of those who love God. We see only the beginning; God sees the end from the beginning. He knows every letter of the Book of Providence; He sees not only what He is doing, but what will come of what He is doing.

As to our present pain and grief, God sees not these things exclusively, but He sees the future joy and usefulness which will come of them. He regards not only the tearing up of the soil with the plow, but the clothing of that soil with the golden harvest. He sees the after consequences of affliction, and He accounts those painful incidents to be blessed which lead up to so much of happiness. Let us comfort ourselves with this. God meant in Babylon to prepare a people that should know Him, of whom He could say, "I will be their God, and they shall be my people." At the end of seventy years, He would bring these people back to Jerusalem like a new race, who, whatever their faults might be, would never again fall into idolatry. He knew what He was driving at in their captivity; and in our case the Lord is equally clear as to His purpose. We do not ourselves know, for "it doth not yet appear what we shall be."

You have never seen the Great Artist's masterpiece; you have seen the rough marble, you have marked the chippings that fall on the ground; you have felt the edge of His chisel, you know the weight of His hammer, and you are full of the memory of these things; but oh, could you see that glorious image as it will be when He has put the finishing stroke to it, you would then understand the chisel, and the hammer, and the Worker better than you now do!

May

The Lord hath appeared of old unto me, saying, Yea, I have loved thee with an everlasting love: therefore with loving-kindness have I drawn thee.

Jeremiah 31: 3

The master-magnet of the gospel is not fear, but love. Penitents are *drawn* to Christ rather than *driven.* The most frequent impulse which leads men to Jesus is hope that in Him they may find salvation. Truly, even then they are moved by fear of the evil which they would escape: but their feet are led to fly toward Him by hope in His gentleness, His goodness, His readiness to receive sinners. Hope in that mercy of God which endures forever is the great cord which draws men to repentance. Consequently, after the Lord had sounded the clarion note of warning, He touched the harp strings of grace and brought forth from them notes both soft and sweet, cheering the sad, and encouraging the despondent: these notes He knew would be heard where even the trumpet sounded not.

I am glad, therefore, that I may write to God's people and set forth God's love as the reason they should love Him in return. "We love him because he first loved us" is the great law of the Christian life. In proportion as we recognize the love of God, and know somewhat of its height, and depth, and length, and breadth, our hearts will be graciously affected by it. When the love of God is shed abroad in our hearts by the Holy Ghost who is given to us, then we love our Lord with all our might.

June

And there is hope in thine end, saith the Lord, that thy children shall come again to their own border.

Jeremiah 31: 17

1

When under affliction we are sorely depressed, and when conscience perceives that there are reasons why the Lord should contend with us, then the enemy whispers, "The Lord has evil thoughts toward you, and will cast you off forever." No, beloved, His thoughts are *not of evil.* Though the Lord hates your sin, He does not hate you. Though He is the enemy of your follies, He is your own firm friend; yea, He is all the truer friend, because He fights against your faults.

He would have you pure and holy, therefore He bathes you in the rivers, and baptizes you in the fires. Not in anger does He afflict you, but in His dear covenant love. The hardest blow that He ever laid upon His child was inflicted by the hand of love. You may rise from your bed in the morning to be chastised, and before you fall asleep in the night you may smart under the rod, and yet be none the less, but all the more, the favorite of heaven. God has no evil thoughts toward His chosen; He has no desire to grieve us, but to save us.

If ye can break my covenant of the day, and my covenant of the night, and that there should not be day and night in their season; then may also my covenant be broken with David my servant.

Jeremiah 33: 20, 21

2

"*If ye can break* my covenant of the day and my covenant of the night, then shall David not have a son to reign upon his throne."

115

June

God has promised never to change the royal line: but while the earth remains, and day and night are seen, the Son of David shall reign King of kings and Lord of lords. Until all enemies are under His feet He must reign. So, then, as I wrap my garment about me, feeling the cold of winter, I will say to myself, "God has, by sending cold, confirmed His covenant with Jesus our Lord and King." Every morning the light greets my eyes, and declares that "his name shall be continued as long as the sun"; and when the shades of evening fall, and the stars look forth from their houses, I hear a sound of "abundance of peace so long as the moon endureth." His dominion is an everlasting dominion, and of His kingdom there is no end. The Lord Jesus is King in Zion, and head over all things to His church while the earth remains.

3	*I will feed them in a good pasture, and upon the high mountains of Israel shall their fold be: there shall they lie in a good fold, and in a fat pasture shall they feed. . . .* Ezekiel 34: 14

God as the good Shepherd is pictured for us here. Though the host that feeds at the Lord's table is countless as the stars of heaven, yet each one has his portion of meat. Think how much grace one saint requires; so much that nothing but the Infinite could supply him for one day; and yet the Lord spreads His table, not for one, but many saints; not for one day, but for many years. The guests at mercy's banquet are satisfied, nay, more "abundantly satisfied"; and that not with ordinary fare, but with fatness, the peculiar fatness of God's own house; and such feasting is guaranteed by a faithful promise to all those children of men who put their trust under the shadow of His wings.

Whenever we are privileged to eat of the bread which Jesus gives, we are satisfied with the full and sweet repast. When Jesus is the host, no guest goes empty from the table. Our *head* is satisfied with the precious truth which Christ reveals; our *heart* is content with Jesus; our *hope* is satisfied, for whom have we in heaven but Jesus? And our *desire* is satiated, for what can we wish for more than "to know Christ and to be found in him"? Jesus fills our *conscience*, till it is at perfect peace; our judgment with the certainty of His teachings; our *memory* with recollections of what He has done, and our *imagination* with the prospects of what He is yet to do.

And I will give you a heart of flesh.

Ezekiel 36: 26

The hard heart does not love the Redeemer, but, the renewed heart burns with affection toward Him. Many are the privileges of this renewed heart: "'Tis here the Spirit dwells, 'tis here that Jesus rests." This heart is fitted to receive every spiritual blessing, and every blessing comes to it. It is prepared to yield every heavenly fruit to the honor and praise of God, and therefore the Lord delights in it. A tender heart is the best defense against sin, and the best preparation for heaven. A renewed heart stands on its watertower looking for the coming of the Lord Jesus. Do you have this heart of flesh?

God neither chose us nor called us because we were holy, but He called us that we might be holy, and holiness is the beauty produced by His workmanship in us. The excellencies which we see in a believer are as much the work of God as the atonement itself. Thus is brought out very sweetly the fullness of the grace of God. Salvation must be of grace, because the Lord is the author of it. Salvation must be of grace, because the Lord works in such a manner that our righteousness is forever excluded. Such is the believer's privilege—*a present salvation;* such is the evidence that he is called to it—*a holy life.* To do this, He must give us a heart of flesh!

The love of the Lord.

Hosea 3: 1

5

Believer, look back through all your experience, and think of the way whereby the Lord your God has led you in the wilderness,

June

and how He has fed and clothed you every day—how He has borne with your bad manners—how He has put up with all your murmurings, and all your longings after the flesh-pots of Egypt—how He has opened the rock to supply you and fed you with manna that came down from Heaven. Think of how His grace has been sufficient for you in all your troubles—how His blood has been a pardon to you in all your sins—how His rod and His staff have comforted you. When you have thus looked back upon the love of the Lord, then let faith survey His love in the future, for remember that Christ's covenant and blood have something more in them than the past. He who has loved you and pardoned you shall never cease to love and pardon. He is Alpha, and He shall be Omega also: He is the first, and He shall be last. Therefore remember, when you shall pass through the valley of the shadow of death, you need fear no evil, for He is with you. When you shall stand in the cold floods of Jordan, you need not fear, for death cannot separate you from His love; and when you shall come into the mysteries of eternity you need not tremble, "For I am persuaded, that neither death; nor life, nor angels, nor principalities, nor powers, nor things present, nor things to come, nor height, nor depth, nor any other creature, shall be able to separate us from the love of God, which is in Christ Jesus our Lord."

Now, soul, is not your love refreshed? Does not this make you love Jesus? Does not a flight through illimitable plains of the ether of love inflame your heart and compel you to delight yourself in the Lord your God? Surely as we meditate on "the love of the Lord," our hearts burn within us, and we long to love Him more.

6

When Israel was a child, then I loved him, and called my son out of Egypt. . . . I drew them with cords of a man, with bands of love. . . .

Hosea 11: 1, 4

Nothing can satisfy the entire man but the Lord's love, and the Lord's own self. To embrace our Lord Jesus, to dwell in His love, and be fully assured of union with Him—this is all in all. Dear reader, you need not try other styles of life to see whether they are better than the Christian's: if you roam the world around, you will see no sights like a sight of the Savior's face; if you could have all the comforts of life, if you lost your Savior, you would be wretched; but if you win Christ, you would find it a paradise; should you live in obscurity, or die with famine, you will yet be satisfied with favor, and full of the goodness of the Lord.

Our heavenly Father often draws us with the cords of love. How slowly do we respond to His gentle impulse! *He draws us to exercise a more simple faith in Him;* but we have not yet attained to Abraham's confidence; we do not leave our worldly cares with God. Our meager faith brings leanness into our souls; we do not open our hearts wide, though God has promised to fill them. Does He not this day draw us to trust Him? Can we not hear Him say, "Come, my child, and trust Me. The veil is rent; enter into My presence, I am worthy of your fullest confidence; cast your cares on Me. Shake off the dust of your cares, and put on your beautiful garments of joy."

I will surely assemble, O Jacob, all of thee; I will surely gather the remnant of Israel; I will put them together as the sheep of Bozrah, as the flock in the midst of their fold: they shall make great noise by reason of the multitude of men. The breaker is come up before them: they have broken up, and have passed through the gate, and are gone out by it; and their king shall pass before them, and the Lord on the head of them.

Micah 2: 12, 13

7

I would have you dwell upon the fact that the sheep are marching under royal leadership: "Their king shall pass before them." Christ is always at the head of His own church. Why? Because He loves it so that He cannot be away from it. He is at the head of His own flock because He has purchased it with His own blood. He will not send an angel to lead His chosen, but He himself will watch over the objects of His everlasting love. He knows the necessities of His church to be such as He, and only He, can meet: therefore as the King He always remains at their head.

Brethren, let us always reverence, honor, and obey Him. Our

June

active, present King must be loyally and earnestly served. As "Breaker" He did us service; as "King" we must render Him service. Remember how the Psalmist put it to the chosen bride: "He is thy Lord, and worship thou him." As a church, we know no other head; as the people of His pasture, we know no other leader. Let us follow Him boldly and gladly.

> But thou, Bethlehem Ephratah, though thou be little among the thousands of Judah, yet out of thee shall he come forth unto me that is to be the ruler in Israel; whose goings forth have been from of old, from everlasting.
>
> Micah 5: 2

"*Whose goings forth* have been from of old, from everlasting." The Lord Jesus had goings forth for His people, *as their representative before the throne, long before they appeared upon the stage of time.* It was "from everlasting" that He signed the compact with His Father, that He would pay blood for blood, suffering for suffering, agony for agony, and death for death, in the behalf of His people; it was "from everlasting" that He gave Himself up, without a murmuring word. His goings forth as our Surety were from everlasting. Pause, my soul, and wonder! There were goings forth in the person of Jesus "from everlasting."

> *My God will hear me.*
>
> Micah 7: 7

What a charming sentence! Can you say it? Only five words, but what meaning! Huge volumes of poetry have appeared from Chaucer even to Tennyson; but it seems to me that the essence of poetry lies hid in a marvelously condensed form within these few words. It will take you many an hour to suck out all their sweetness. There is an almost inconceivable depth of meaning in them; and of richness of assured experience and of sweet conclusions of a hallowed faith they are full to the brim.

"My God will hear me." It is prophetic; but the prophet has taken upon himself no unusual power, neither does he intend his prophecy to be true of himself alone. He puts this divine sentence into the mouth of every believer; every child of God may dare to say that his God will hear him.

"My God will hear me." It is a choice song for a lone harp, which is half afraid of the choir of musicians, and loves to have its strings touched in solitude. I feel as I repeat it that I want to sit down and quietly enjoy it. As I see the cows lie in the meadow quietly chewing the cud, so would I ruminate on these few but precious words. Let me hear the sounds again and again, till my tongue, learning their rhythmic melody, repeats as a matter of habitual delight the assurance, "My God will hear me."

The Lord is good, a stronghold in the day of trouble; and he knoweth them that trust in him.

Nahum 1: 7

10

This morning our desires go forth for growth in our acquaintance with the Lord Jesus. This was most blessedly perfect long before we had the slightest knowledge of Him. Before we had a being in the world we had a being in His heart. When we were enemies to Him, He knew us, our misery and our wickedness. When we wept bitterly in despairing repentance, and viewed Him only as a judge and a ruler, He viewed us as His brethren well beloved. He never mistook His chosen, but always beheld them as objects of His infinite affection. "The Lord knoweth them that are his."

Do not be afraid, Christ is your strength and righteousness. A wave comes against the side of the ship, but it does not hurt the ship, it only drives the wedges in tighter. The Master is at the helm—will that not assure your heart? It has floated over so many billows—will that not increase your confidence? It must, indeed, be a strong billow that will sink it now; there never shall be such a one.

Christ presents the perfect number of all His people to the Father

June

in the last day; not one shall perish. The ark of our salvation shall bring all its living freight into the haven of everlasting rest.

Although the fig tree shall not blossom . . . yet I will rejoice in the Lord, I will joy in the God of my salvation.

Habakkuk 3: 17, 18

It was a divine song which Habakkuk sang, when in the night he said, "Although the fig tree shall not blossom, neither shall fruit be in the vines; the labor of the olive shall fail, and the fields shall yield no meat; the flock shall be cut off from the fold, and there shall be no herd in the stalls: yet I will rejoice in the Lord, I will joy in the God of my salvation." No man can make a song in the night of himself; he may attempt it, but he will find that a song in the night must be divinely inspired. O Chief Musician, let us not remain songless because affliction is upon us, tune our lips to the melody of thanksgiving.

Should it happen that, in the providence of God, you are a loser, you shall find that if the Lord pays you not back in the silver of earthly prosperity, He will discharge His promise in the gold of spiritual joy. Remember that a man's life consists not in the abundance of that which he possesses. To wear a guileless spirit, to have a heart void of offense, to have the favor and smile of God, is greater riches than the mines of Ophir could yield, or the traffic of Tyre could win. "Better is a dinner of herbs where love is, than a stalled ox and hatred therewith" (Prov. 15: 17). An ounce of heart's ease is worth a ton of gold.

Not by might, nor by power, but by my Spirit, saith the Lord of hosts.

Zechariah 4: 6

Could faith believe in a Being more answerable to all our needs, more helpful to our noblest longings? Allied to Jesus, we confidently aspire to such likeness to our Creator as it is possible for a creature to bear. Nor is the advantage less in the other direction, for here is a Man, bound to us by relationship and affection the most intense, who is not only tender to the last degree of our suffering nature, but is also as wise as He is brotherly, and as mighty to subdue our faults as He is gentle to bear with our frailties. His manhood brings Jesus down to us, but united with the divine nature it lifts us up to God. The Lord Jesus thus not only ministers to our comfort, but to our betterment, the greater concern.

Without Him we can do nothing, but by His almighty energy the most extraordinary results can be produced: everything depends upon His manifesting or concealing His power. Do we always look up to Him both for our inner life and our outward service with the respectful dependence which is fitting? Do we not too often run before His call and act independently of His aid? Let us humble ourselves this day for past neglects, and now entreat the heavenly dew to rest upon us, the sacred oil to anoint us, the celestial flame to burn within us. The Holy Ghost is no temporary gift—He abides with the saints. We have but to seek Him aright, and He will be found of us.

But unto you that fear my name shall the Sun of righteousness arise with healing in his wings.

Malachi 4: 2

13

"Heal my soul, for I have sinned against thee" (Ps. 41: 4). For this also the godly praise the name of the Lord, saying, "He heals all our diseases" (see Ps. 103: 3). What a transcendent comfort it is that in the person of Jesus "dwelleth all the fullness of the Godhead bodily"! My soul, whatever your disease may be, the great Physician can heal you. If He be God, there can be no limit to His power. Come just as you are, for He who is God can certainly restore you. None shall restrain the healing virtue which proceeds from Jesus our Lord. All His patients have been cured in the past, and shall be in the future, and you shall be one among them, my friend, if you will but rest yourself in Him.

June

14

The book of the generation of Jesus Christ, the son of David, the son of Abraham.

Matthew 1: 1

The book of the New Covenant begins with Jesus. Now look at the last verse, see how the Testament ends: "The grace of our Lord Jesus Christ be with you all. Amen." Jesus Christ appears in the first verse, and He appears in the last verse. Did He not say, "I am Alpha and Omega, the beginning and the ending"? The first line of the covenant of grace is Jesus Christ; the last line of the covenant of grace is Jesus Christ; and all in between is the Lord Jesus Christ.

Oh what blessings have come to us through Jesus Christ! Through His name we have received remission of sins, in His name we are justified, in His name we are sanctified, in His name we shall be glorified, even as in Him we were chosen from before the foundation of the world. My tongue can never tell you even the commencement of His greatness. Who shall declare His generation? The fringe, the hem of His infinite glories, who can touch? He is unspeakable. As for His glory, I may say, "O Lord our Lord, how excellent is thy name in all the earth! who hast set thy glory above the heavens." All glory and honor be unto Him in whom are comprehended all the blessings whereby God has enriched His people in time and in eternity.

15

Blessed are they which do hunger and thirst after righteousness: for they shall be filled.

Matthew 5: 6

"On the last day, that great day of the feast, Jesus stood and cried, saying, If any man thirst, let him come unto me, and drink!" (John 7: 37). No other distinction is made but that of thirst. No waiting or preparation is so much as hinted at. Drinking represents a reception for which no fitness is required. Sinful lips may touch the stream of divine love, they cannot pollute it, but shall themselves be purified. Jesus is the fount of hope. Dear reader, hear the dear

Redeemer's loving voice as He cries to each of us, "If any man thirst, let him come unto me and drink."

If our Lord is so ready to heal the sick and bless the needy, then, my soul, don't be slow to put yourself in His way, that He may smile on you. Be not slack in asking, if He be so abundant in bestowing. Give earnest heed to His Word now, that Jesus may speak through it to your heart. Where He is to be found, there make your resort, that you may obtain His blessing. When He is present to heal, may He not heal you? But surely He is present even now, for He always comes to hearts which need Him. And do you not need Him? Ah, He knows how much! O Son of David, turn Your eye and look upon the distress which is now before You and make Your suppliant whole.

And lead us not into temptation, but deliver us from evil. . . .
Matthew 6: 13

16

What we are taught to seek or shun in prayer, we should equally pursue or avoid in action. Very earnestly, therefore, should we avoid temptation, seeking to walk guardedly in the path of obedience. We are not to enter the thicket in search of the lion. This lion may cross our path, or leap upon us from the thicket; but we have nothing to do with hunting him. He who meets with him, even though he wins the day, will find it a stern struggle. Let the Christian pray that he may be spared the encounter. Our Savior, who had experience of what temptation meant, thus earnestly admonished His disciples: "Pray that ye enter not into temptation."

And when Jesus was come into Peter's house, he saw his wife's mother laid, and sick of a fever.
Matthew 8: 14
Read Matthew 8: 14–17

17

Our Lord Jesus Christ had been having a heavy day: He had been to the synagogue, and He had preached and had wrought miracles;

June

He had moved in the midst of a great throng, and now that the Sabbath was drawing to a close He needed refreshment. It was most convenient that Peter had a house into which the Lord could go.

Though our Lord went to Peter's house to rest, He did not find it free from trouble. It was a hospital before He made it a palace. Peter's wife's mother was on her bed prostrate with "a great fever." Probably typhus of the worst kind was burning out her life.

Certain people attribute all sickness to the devil, and impute special sin to those who are grievously afflicted. This teaching is as false as it is cruel. "Whom the Lord loveth he chasteneth." Our sicknesses are of the Lord's appointing, however painful they may be, and we may without doubt say, as David did, "The Lord hath chastened me sore." "Lord, he whom thou lovest is sick" is still a truth. Even Peter's house, though it be the abode of a chosen saint, and leading apostle, whose very shadow would one day heal the sick, had a terrible fever in it which threatened death. Yet Jesus came where the fever polluted the air. If the disease had come, the great Physician had come also. We are not alarmed at the cross if Christ comes with it.

| **18** | *And he touched her hand, and the fever left her: and she arose, and ministered unto them.* |

Matthew 8: 15

When healed of her fever Peter's wife's mother had strength to perform a suitable ministry, such as the peculiar occasion required. She did for Jesus and the three companions that which was needful there and then. Jesus had had a hard day's preaching, and that is hungry work: He had spent a heavy day in healing, and that is exhausting work; and now He wanted somewhat to eat, and therefore He came into Peter's house. The principal worker there was laid aside, and so our Lord did not ask for refreshment. He always thought of others before Himself; and when He was faint and hungry He put back His own needs till He restored health to the fevered woman. This being done, the next necessary thing was that the wearied Preacher and Physician should be refreshed, and this the grateful woman attended to.

Now, dear friends, you who are converted may minister to Christ in a way which is as necessary as the service of His ablest preachers and pastors. There is something for you to do which will be a refreshment to Him and to His servants. He condescendingly permits it and will graciously accept it. You can personally minister to a personal Christ. You cannot do everything, but you can do something that will be acceptable to Him. You may; you can; and you ought. You owe your very life to Him. Come, spend that life in His service.

And Jesus saith unto him, The foxes have holes, and the birds of the air have nests; but the Son of man hath not where to lay his head.

Matthew 8: 20

19

How constantly our Master used the title, the "Son of man"! If He had chosen, He might always have spoken of Himself as the Son of God, the Everlasting Father, the Wonderful, the Counselor, the Prince of Peace; but behold the lowliness of Jesus! He prefers to call Himself the Son of man. Let us learn a lesson of humility from our Savior. Jesus loved manhood so much, that He delighted to honor it; and since it is a high honor, and, indeed, the greatest dignity of manhood, that Jesus is the Son of man, He is wont to display this name, that He may, as it were, hang royal stars upon the breast of manhood, and show forth the love of God to Abraham's seed.

Son of man—whenever He said that He shed a halo round the head of Adam's children. Jesus Christ called Himself the Son of man to express His oneness and sympathy with His people. He thus reminds us that He is one whom we may approach without fear. As a man, we may take to Him all our griefs and troubles, for He knows them by experience; in that He Himself has suffered as the "Son of man," He is able to aid and comfort us. All hail, blessed Jesus! inasmuch as You are evermore using the sweet name which acknowledges that You are a brother and a near kinsman, it is to us a dear token of Your grace, Your humility, Your love.

June

20

For whether is easier, to say, Thy sins be forgiven thee; or to say, Arise, and walk?

Matthew 9: 5

Behold one of the great Physician's mightiest arts; He has power to forgive sin! Before the ransom had been paid, before the blood had been literally sprinkled on the mercy seat, He had power to forgive sin. Does He not have power to do it now that He has died? He has boundless power now that He has finished transgression and made an end of sin. Hear Him pleading before the eternal Father, pointing to His wounds, urging the merit of His sacred passion! What power to forgive is here! "He is exalted on high to give repentance and remission of sins." The most crimson sins are removed by the crimson of His blood.

Poor souls! forget not the present Savior, who bids you look unto Him and be saved. *He* could heal you at once, but you prefer to wait for an angel and a wonder. To trust Him is a sure way to every blessing, and He is worthy of the most implicit confidence; but unbelief makes you prefer the cold porches of Bethesda (John 5: 2) to the warm bosom of His love. O that the Lord may turn His eye upon the multitudes who are in the situation today; may He forgive the slights which they have put upon His divine power, and call them by that sweet constraining voice, to rise from their beds of despair, and in the energy of faith take up their beds and walk.

21

But the very hairs of your head are all numbered.

Matthew 10: 30

There shall not a hair of your head perish, but yet that head may ache with weariness. It is for good, and only for good, that God thinks of us, and deals with us. Oh, that we could settle this in our hearts, and have done with dark forebodings! Though your way may now lie through dark ravines where the crags rise so steeply above you as to shut out the light of day, yet press onward, for the way is safe. Follow the Lord, for where the road is rough, you will be less likely to slip than in more smooth and slippery places. If the way be steep, you will the sooner ascend on high; or if your way inclines downward, you will the sooner feel the needful humiliation, and the more readily cease from yourself, and cast yourself upon your Lord. Though I may not yet be so old and gray-headed as many, yet one thing I know: that God has done unto me good, and not evil, all the days of my life; and I bear my public witness at this hour, that in very faithfulness He has afflicted me, and not one good thing has failed of all that He has promised me.

All things are delivered unto me of my Father: and no man knoweth the Son, but the Father; neither knoweth any man the Father, save the Son, and he to whomsoever the Son will reveal him. Come unto me, all ye that labor and are heavy laden, and I will give you rest.

Matthew 11: 27, 28

22

This kindly and gracious invitation needs only to be held up in different lights to give us different subjects of admiration. That it flowed like an anthem from our Savior's lips we perceive: in what connection it was spoken we may properly inquire. He had just made some important disclosures as to the covenant relations that existed between Himself and God the Father. This interesting revelation of heavenly truth becomes the basis upon which He offers an invitation to the toiling and oppressed children of men, and He assigns it as a reason why they should immediately avail themselves of His rest.

I must cease from creature helps and carnal rites, to rest myself upon Jesus. That is what my Savior means when He says, "Come unto me." The exhortation is very personal. "Come unto me," says He. He does not say come to My ministers to consult them, nor come to My sacraments to observe them, nor come to My Bible to study its teaching—interesting and advantageous as under some circumstances any or all of these counsels might be; but He invites us in the sweetest tone of friendship, saying, "Come unto me." For a poor sinner this is the truest means of succor. Let him resort to the blessed Lord Himself. To trust in a crucified

June

Savior is the way of salvation. Let him leave everything else and fly away to Christ, and look at His dear wounds.

23

Come unto me, all ye that labor and are heavy laden, and I will give you rest.

Matthew 11: 28

Those who have not worked hard think they will love heaven as a place of service. That is very true. But to the working man, to the man who toils with his brain or with his hands, it must ever be a sweet thought that there is a land where we shall rest. Oh! weary sons and daughters of Adam, you shall be still, you shall be quiet, you shall rest yourselves, for all are rich in heaven, all are happy there, all are peaceful. Toil, trouble, travail, and labor are words that cannot be spelled in heaven; they have no such things there, for they always rest.

24

Again, the kingdom of heaven is like unto a merchantman, seeking goodly pearls: who, when he had found one pearl of great price, went and sold all that he had, and bought it.

Matthew 13: 45, 46

Some ancient philosopher has said: "When the beams of the sun are contracted by a magnifying glass, upon one spot, then they cause fire, so when our thoughts are concentrated on one object they warm the heart and at last burn the truth into it."

There are many rays of light, but they are scattered. We get a little upon many things, while what is wanted is one great truth, and so much upon it as shall fix it on the heart, and set the soul blazing with it. This is the fault of many lives; they are squandered upon a dozen objects, whereas if they were economized for one, they would be mighty lives, known in the present and honored in the future.

June

*And they did all eat, and were filled: and they took up of
the fragments that remained twelve baskets full.*

Matthew 14: 20
Read Matthew 14: 13–21

Care is always taken by Christ to pick up all the broken pieces.
The Lord All-sufficient is yet the God of economy. Since Jesus
could create as much food as ever He pleased, you might have
thought that it was hardly worth His while to gather up the fragments; and yet He did so. Waste is of Satan, not of God. God is
not lavish of creation, nor prodigal of miracles.

Though the Lord can raise up in this place, if He pleases, fifty
ministers in an instant, He may not do so; but what He would
have us do is to make use of such powers as we have. If we are
only fragments our place is not the ground, but the basket. We
must not allow ourselves to be thrown away, or to be consumed
by an animal passion, or to be left to decay; but we must be in
the Lord's store, ready to be used when the time comes. We shall
be of some use one of these days, if we are willing to be used.

Beginning to sink, he cried, saying, Lord, save me.

Matthew 14: 30

Sinking times are praying times with the Lord's servants. At the
beginning of his watery adventure, Peter neglected prayer. But
when he began to sink, his danger made him a beggar, and his
cry though late was not too late. In our hours of bodily pain and
mental anguish, we find ourselves as naturally driven to prayer
as the wreck is driven upon the shore by the waves. The fox goes
to its hole for protection; the bird flies to the wood for shelter;
even so the tried believer runs to the mercy seat for safety. Heav-
en's great harbor of refuge is all-prayer; thousands of weather-
beaten vessels have found a haven there, and the moment a storm
comes on, it is wise for us to make for it under full sail.

June

Short prayers are long enough. There are but three words in Peter's petition, but they were sufficient for his purpose. Not length but strength is desirable. A sense of need is a mighty teacher of brevity. If our prayers had less of the tail feathers of pride and more wing, they would be all the better. Verbiage is to devotion as chaff is to the wheat. Precious things lie in small scope, and all that is real prayer in many a long address might have been uttered in a petition as short as Peter's.

Our extremities are the Lord's opportunity. The moment a keen sense of danger forces an anxious cry from us, the ear of Jesus hears, and with Him ear and heart go together, and the hand does not long linger. At the last moment we appeal to the Master, but His swift hand makes up for our delays by instant and effectual action. Are we nearly engulfed by the boisterous waters of affliction? Let us then lift up our souls unto our Savior, and we may rest assured that He will not suffer us to perish. When we can do nothing, Jesus can do all things; let us enlist His powerful aid upon our side, and all will be well.

And she said, Truth, Lord: yet the dogs eat of the crumbs which fall from their masters' table.

Matthew 15: 27

My sins are many, but oh! it is nothing to Jesus to take them all away. "It will be but a small thing for *Him* to give me full remission, although it will be an infinite blessing for *me* to receive it." The woman opens her soul wide, expecting great things of Jesus, and He fills it with His love. Dear reader, do the same. She laid fast hold upon Him, drew arguments even out of His words; she believed great things of Him, and she thus overcame Him. *She won the victory by believing in Him.* Her case is an instance of prevailing faith; and if we would conquer like her, we must imitate her.

"To whom do you belong?" Reader, let me assist you in your response. *Have you been "born again"?* If you have, you belong to Christ; but without the new birth you cannot be His. *In whom do you trust?* For those who believe in Jesus are the sons of God. *Whose work are you doing?* You are sure to serve your master, for he whom you serve is thereby owned to be your lord. *What is your conversation?* Is it heavenly, or is it earthly? *What have you learned of your master?* If you have served your time with Jesus, it will be said of you, as it was of Peter and John, "They took knowledge of them, that they had been with Jesus" (Acts 4: 13).

While he spake, behold, a bright cloud overshadowed them: and behold a voice out of the cloud, which said, This is my beloved son, in whom I am well pleased; hear ye him.
Matthew 17: 5
Read Acts 3: 22–26

28

Observe at the outset the words, *"Behold, a bright cloud overshadowed them."* When God draws near to man it is absolutely necessary that His glory should be veiled. No man can see His face and live. Hence the cloud, in this instance, and in other cases; hence that thick veil which hung over the entrance to the most holy place; hence the need of the incense to fill that place with smoke when the high priest once a year went within the veil; hence above all the need of the body and the manhood of Christ that the Godhead may be softened to our view. The God shines graciously through the Man, and we behold the brightness of the Father's glory without being blinded thereby.

There must be a cloud. Yet it was a *bright* cloud which in this case yielded the shadow, and not a thick darkness like that which became the canopy of Deity at the giving of the Law. Then Mount Sinai was altogether on a smoke, and the Lord sat enthroned amid thick darkness. On other occasions we read, "He made darkness his secret place; his pavilion round about him were dark waters and thick clouds of the skies"; but now on Tabor, where God bears peaceful witness to His well-beloved Son, He veils Himself in a brightness significant of His good pleasure toward the sons of men.

June

29

And Jesus came and touched them, and said, Arise, be not afraid.

Matthew 17: 7

When Jesus came to earth, one of the things He did was, *He touched them.* This is to me most precious: as they lie there all fainting He touches Peter, James, and John, just as in after days we read, "He laid his right hand upon me, saying unto me, Fear not." That was His way of healing those diseased with leprosy. The blind man He touched and gave him sight, and the dead maiden was thus revived. Oh, the power of His touch!

Our touch of Jesus saves us; what will not His touch of us do? We are so much made up of feeling, after all, that we want to know that the Lord really feels for us, and will enter so tenderly into our case as to touch us. That touch reassures our fainting hearts, and we know our Lord to be Emmanuel, God with us.

Sympathy! This is the meaning of that human touch of a hand which is nevertheless divine. Oh, how sweetly Christ has touched us by being a partaker in all that is human! He touched us everywhere: in poverty, for He had not where to lay His head; in thirst, for He sat by the well and said, "Give me to drink"; in anguish, for He was betrayed by His friend.

He has touched us in depression of spirit, for He cried, "My soul is exceeding sorrowful even unto death." He is touched with a feeling of our infirmities, "for he was tempted in all points like as we are." The hand of Jesus is laid upon us, and in the strength which it gives, a man might dash through hell and climb to heaven. Ezra said, "I was strengthened as the hand of the Lord my God was upon me." Touched with the almighty Sufferer's sacred sympathy, we glory in tribulation, and triumph in death. Is not this more effective evidence of the truth of the gospel and of the commission of Christ than if the Lord God should again speak out of a cloud? To feel the wondrous power of Christ strengthening our hearts, surely this is the most certain witness.

30

Even so it is not the will of your Father which is in heaven, that one of these little ones should perish.

Matthew 18: 14

It is this same Father God who tells his children, "Return unto the Lord thy God" (Hosea 14: 1). Where we first found salvation

June

we shall find it again: at the foot of Christ's cross, confessing sin. Moreover, the Lord will have us obey His voice according to all that He has commanded us, and we must do this with all our heart and all our soul, and then our captivity shall end.

Often depression of spirit and great misery of soul are removed as soon as we quit our idols and bow ourselves in obedience before the living God. We may return to Zion's citizenship, and that speedily. Lord, turn our captivity!

July

1

With God all things are possible.

Matthew 19: 26

There is no elevation of grace, no attainment of spirituality, no clearness of assurance, no post of duty, which is not open to you if you have but the power to believe. Lay aside your sackcloth and ashes, and rise to the dignity of your true position. The golden throne of assurance is waiting for you! The crown of communion with Jesus is ready to bedeck your brow. Wrap yourself in scarlet and fine linen and fare sumptuously every day; if you believe, your land shall flow with milk and honey, and your soul shall be satisfied as with marrow and fatness. Gather golden sheaves of grace, for they await you in the fields of faith. "All things are possible to him that believeth" (Mark 9: 23).

2

All things, whatsoever ye shall ask in prayer, believing, ye shall receive.

Matthew 21: 22

Without the heart prayer is a nullity, and *when there is but little heart, prayer is a failure.* He that prays with little desire asks God to refuse him. If you go through your prayer, and your mind is wandering up and down about a thousand vanities, your desires are feeble, and your supplication will effect little. Prayer must be fervent to be effectual; it must be ardent to be acceptable. If the utter failure of your prayer would not greatly grieve you, and if its success would not much gratify you, then depend upon it, you will have to wait long at mercy's gate before it will admit you. "The kingdom of heaven suffereth violence, and the violent take it by force." Importunity is indispensable: our Lord has given us many parables to that effect. To play at praying will never do: heart and soul must be fully awake; for no sleepy prayer can enter heaven. We must praise God with our whole heart, and we must pray in the same manner. If a double-minded man may not expect to receive anything of the Lord, neither may a half-hearted man. Above all things, keep your heart with all diligence if you would speed to the throne.

And sent forth his servants to call them that were bidden to the wedding: and they would not come. . . . Then saith he to his servants, The wedding is ready, but they which were bidden were not worthy. Go ye therefore into the highways, and as many as ye shall find, bid to the marriage.
Matthew 22: 3, 8, 9

3

If those who were first bidden had put in an appearance, they would have come arrayed in their own scarlet and fine linen. Some of the gentlemen would have bought a new suit on purpose. You may depend upon it, all the skilled women in the city would have been employed to get their ladyships ready for the banquet, that they might have honor in the court that day. Now these fine clothes would have been more for the glory of those who came in them, than for the honor of the king.

There was nothing of this among those who were gathered from the highways. They were in sorry gear. It was difficult, perhaps, in some cases, to tell which was the original stuff of their garments, so patched and mended were they. Anyhow, they were a ragged regiment; and what was the consequence? Why, then they must all be dressed in the prince's own livery, and all the glory of their apparel must be unto him.

He said to his servants, "Go to my wardrobe. Bring forth changes of raiment." Everyone that came in to the feast was invited to put on the king's wedding garments. When he came in to see the guests, it was a grand sight, for everyone was royally arrayed.

July

The king's wedding robes were much better than his subjects' best suits. It was a grand sight to see so many all in one royal livery; every guest wearing the uniform of mercy.

So is it with us poor sinners, saved by grace. If we had possessed any true righteousness of our own we should have worn it; but now we count our own righteousness but dross and dung that we may win Christ and be found in Him. His righteousness decorates all the saints: they could not be better arrayed. Thus is the feast made more glorious than it otherwise would have been, and the wedding is furnished with guests.

So those servants went out into the highways, and gathered together all as many as they found, both bad and good: and the wedding was furnished with guests.

Matthew 22: 10

"The wedding was furnished with guests." Guests are a part of the furniture of a wedding feast. You may pile on your gold and silver plate, hang up your banners, load your tables, and sound your music; but if you have no guests the feast is a failure. It is our solemn conviction that the Lord our God has never failed yet, and that He never will fail. We believe that the Lord's eternal purpose will stand, and that He will do all His pleasure. God's greatest work is redemption; will He fail in it? Salvation is the focus of His glory; shall this be frustrated? If God were to fail in connection with the cross, it would be a failure indeed; God would be dishonored, and His crown jewels cast into the mire. But it shall not be.

Turn to the parable, and we find *there were sufficient guests:* "the wedding was furnished with guests." There were as many guests as were necessary to the honor of the king, and his son, and his bride. Oh yes, in the gathering up and consummation of all things, the wedding of the Lord Jesus will be amply furnished with guests: "He shall see of the travail of his soul, and shall be satisfied." Satan may whisper disaster and disappointment to us at this hour, and for the moment it may seem as if the forces of darkness triumphed; but the end is not yet. The will of God, so full of grace and mercy, shall be accomplished, the preparations of grace shall be used, and the purpose of love fulfilled. As the wedding was furnished with guests so shall heaven be filled with "a number which no man can number."

Then shall the King say unto them on his right hand, Come, ye blessed of my Father, inherit the kingdom prepared for you from the foundation of the world. . . .

Matthew 25: 34

5

We have sat at the table of the Lord's love, and said, "Nothing but the infinite can satisfy me; I am such a great sinner that I must have infinite merit to wash my sin away"; but we have had our sin removed, and found that there was merit to spare; we have had our hunger relieved at the feast of sacred love, and found that there was an abundance of spiritual meat remaining. Yes, there are graces to which we have not attained; places of fellowship nearer to Christ which we have not reached; and heights of communion which our feet have not climbed. At every banquet of love there are many baskets of fragments left. Let us magnify the liberality of our glorious Redeemer.

He draws us to closer communion with Himself. We have been sitting on the doorstep of God's house, and He bids us advance into the banqueting hall and sup with Him, but we decline the honor. There are secret rooms not yet opened to us; Jesus invites us to enter them, but we hold back. Shame on our cold hearts! We are but poor lovers of our sweet Lord Jesus, not fit to be His servants, much less to be His brides, and yet He has exalted us to be bone of His bone, and flesh of His flesh, married to Him by a glorious marriage covenant. Herein is love!

For this is the blood of the new testament, which is shed for many for the remission of sins.

Matthew 26: 28

6

We know from Holy Scripture that this doctrine of the death of Christ is the very core of Christianity. Leave out the cross, and you have killed the religion of Jesus. Atonement by the blood of Jesus is not an *arm* of Christian truth; it is the *heart* of it. Even as the Lord said of the animal, "the blood is the life thereof," so is it true of the gospel; the sacrificial death of Jesus is the vital point of our profession. I know nothing of Christianity without the blood of Christ. No teaching is healthy which throws the cross into the background.

Let us endeavor to make amends for the dishonor done to our divine Master by those who deny or dishonor His vicarious sacrifice: let us abide steadfast in this faith while others waver, and preach Christ crucified if all else forbear. Grace, mercy, and peace be to all who exalt Christ crucified!

Thinkest thou that I cannot now pray to my Father, and he shall presently give me more than twelve legions of angels? But how then shall the Scriptures be fulfilled, that thus it must be?

Matthew 26: 53, 54

Our Lord speaks of angels that His Father would give Him, or send Him. We may interpret it that the Father would at once put at His disposal the glorious inhabitants of heaven. Think of seraphs at the disposal of the Man of Sorrows! He is despised and rejected of men, and yet angels that excel in strength are at His beck and call. Swift of wing, and quick of hand, and wise of thought, they are charmed to be the messengers of the Son of man, the servants of Jesus. Think of this, beloved, when you bow before the thorn-crowned head, and when you gaze upon the nailed hands and feet. Remember that angels and principalities and powers, and all the ranks of pure spirits, by whatever name they are named, were all at the beck of Jesus when He was newly past His agony, and was about to be led away bound, to the High Priest. He is our Lord and God, even at His lowest and weakest.

He trusted in God; let him deliver him now, if he will have him: for he said, I am the Son of God.

Matthew 27: 43

Well, what kind of a deliverance was that? Did the Father tear up the cross from the earth? Did He proceed to draw out the nails from the sacred hands and feet of His dear Son? Did He set Him down upon that "green hill far away, beyond the city wall," and place in His hand a sword of fire with which to smite His adversaries? Did He bid the earth open and swallow up all His foes? No; nothing of the kind. Jehovah did not interpose to spare His Son a single pang; but He let Him die. He let Him be taken as a dead man down from the cross and laid in a tomb. Jesus went through with His suffering to the bitter end. O, brothers and sisters, this may be God's way of delivering us. We have trusted in God that he would deliver us; and His rendering of His promise is that He will enable us to go through with it; we shall suffer to the last, and triumph in so doing.

Yet God's way of delivering those who trust in Him is *always the best way*. If the Father had taken His Son down from the cross, what would have been the result? Redemption unaccomplished, salvation work undone, and Jesus returning with His life-work unfinished. This would not have been deliverance, but defeat. It was much better for our Lord Jesus to die. Now He has paid the ransom for His elect, and having accomplished the great purpose of atonement, He has slept a while in the heart of the earth, and now has ascended to His throne in the endless glories of heaven. It was deliverance of the fullest kind; for from the pangs of His death has come the joy of life to His redeemed. It is not God's will that every mountain should be leveled, but that we should be the stronger for climbing the Hill Difficulty.

And there came a leper to him, beseeching him, and kneeling down to him, and saying unto him, If thou wilt, thou canst make me clean. And Jesus, moved with compassion, put forth his hand, and touched him, and saith unto him, I will; be thou clean.

Mark 1: 40, 41

9

It is well for us when prayers about our sorrows are linked with pleas concerning our sins—when being under God's hand, we are not wholly taken up with our pain, but remember our offenses against God. It is well, also to take both sorrow and sin to the same place. It was to God that David confessed his sin. Observe,

July

then, *we must take our sorrows to God.* Even your little sorrows you may roll upon God, for He counts the hairs of your head; and your great sorrows you may commit to Him, for He holds the ocean in the hollow of His hand.

It is easy work to pray when we are grounded, as to our desires, upon God's own promise. How can He that gave the Word refuse to keep it? Immutable veracity cannot demean itself by a lie, and eternal faithfulness cannot degrade itself by neglect. God must bless His Son, His covenant binds Him to it. That which the Spirit prompts us to ask for Jesus is that which God decrees to give Him. Whenever you are praying for the kingdom of Christ, let your eyes behold the dawning of the blessed day which draws near, when the Crucified shall receive His coronation in the place where men rejected Him.

And Jesus . . . saw much people, and was moved with compassion toward them, because they were as sheep not having a shepherd: and he began to teach them many things.

Mark 6: 34

Oh, how precious is Christ! How can it be that I have thought so little of Him? How is it I can go elsewhere for joy and comfort when He is so full, so rich, so satisfying? Fellow-believer, make a covenant in your heart, and ask the Lord to ratify it. Bid Him place you as a signet upon His finger, and as a bracelet upon His arm. "The sparrow has found a house, and the swallow a nest for herself where she may lay her young, even thine altars, O Lord of hosts, my King and my God" (Ps. 84: 3), and so too would I make my nest, my home, in You, and never from You may my soul go forth again, but may I nestle close to You, O Jesus, my true and only rest.

There are times when all the promises and doctrines of the Bible are of no avail, unless a precious hand shall apply them to us. To meet this need there is One, even the Spirit of truth, who takes the things of Jesus and applies them to us. Think not that Christ has placed His joys on heavenly shelves that we may climb up to them for ourselves, but He draws near, and sheds His peace abroad in our hearts. O Christian, if you are today laboring under deep distresses, your Father does not give you promises and then leave you to draw them from the Word, but the promises He has written in the Word He will write anew on your heart.

This is my beloved Son: hear him.

Mark 9: 7

If the Father says, "This is my Son," observe the graciousness of our adoption! With such a Son the Lord had no need of children. He did not make us His children because He needed sons, but because we needed a father. The infinite heart of the Father was well filled by the love of the Only-begotten. There was enough in Jesus to satisfy the love of the divine Father, and yet He would not rest till He had made Him "the firstborn among many brethren." Herein we ought to admire exceedingly the grace of God. "Behold what manner of love the Father hath bestowed upon us that we should be called the sons of God." When a man is childless, and desires an heir, it may be that he adopts a child to fill the vacancy which exists in his house; but the heavenly Father had no such want, for He says, "This is my beloved Son." Our adoption is, therefore, not for His gain, but for ours: it is a matter of divine charity, arising out of the spontaneous love of God. Thanks be unto the Father evermore!

He appeared first to Mary Magdalene.

Mark 16: 9

If we would see much of Christ, let us *serve* Him. Tell me who they are who sit most often under the banner of His love, and drink deepest draughts from the cup of communion, and I am sure they will be those who give most, who serve best, and who abide closest to the bleeding heart of their dear Lord. But notice

July

how Christ revealed Himself to this sorrowing one—by *a word,* "Mary." It needed but one word *in His voice,* and at once she knew him, and *her heart owned allegiance by another word,* her heart was too full to say more. That one word is most fitting. It implies obedience. She said, *"Master."*

He has been good to me in all my needs, trials, struggles, and sorrows. Never could there be a better Master, for His service is freedom, His rule is love. The ancient saints proved Him to be a good Master, and each of them rejoiced to sing, "I am thy servant, O Lord!" I will bear this witness before my friends and neighbors, for possibly they may be led by my testimony to seek my Lord Jesus as their Master. Oh that they would do so! They would never repent so wise a deed. If they would but take His easy yoke, they would find themselves in so royal a service that they would enlist in it forever.

| 13 | *And all they that heard it wondered at those things which were told them by the shepherds.* |

Luke 2: 18

"All they that heard it wondered at those things. . . ." We must not cease to wonder at the great marvels of our God. It would be very difficult to draw a line between holy wonder and *real worship;* for when the soul is overwhelmed with the majesty of God's glory, though it may not express itself in song, or even utter its voice with bowed head and humble prayer, yet it silently adores. Our incarnate God is to be worshiped as "the Wonderful." That God should consider His fallen creature, man, and should Himself undertake to be man's Redeemer, and to pay his ransom price, is, indeed, marvelous!

| 14 | *Simeon . . . was just and devout, waiting for the consolation of Israel: and the Holy Ghost was upon him.* |

Luke 2: 25

To Simeon Jesus was the consolation of Israel; and so He was. Before His actual appearance, His name was the day-star; cheering the darkness, and prophetic of the rising sun. To Him they looked with the same hope which cheers the nightly watcher, when from the lonely watch tower he sees the fairest of the stars, and hails her as the usher of the morning. When He was on earth, He must have been the consolation of all those who were privileged to be His companions. Like children they would tell Him of their griefs, and consider Him as their Father.

Oh! it must have been sweet to have lived with Christ. Surely, sorrows were then but joys in masks, because they gave an opportunity to go to Jesus to have them removed. Oh! would to God, some of us may say, that we could have lain our weary heads upon the bosom of Jesus, and that our birth had been in that happy era, when we might have heard His kind voice, when He said, "Let the weary ones come unto me." But hear how kindly Jesus speaks: "I will not leave you comfortless, for I will pray the Father, and He will send you another Comforter, that He may abide with you forever."

And Simon answering said unto him, Master, we have toiled all the night, and have taken nothing: nevertheless at thy word I will let down the net.

Luke 5: 5

A little stay on earth will make heaven more heavenly. Nothing makes rest so sweet as toil. Our battered armor and scarred countenances will render more illustrious our victory above, when we are welcomed to the seats of those who have overcome the world. We should not have full *fellowship with Christ* if we did not for a while sojourn below, for He was baptized with a baptism of suffering among men, and we must be baptized with the same if we would share His kingdom. Fellowship with Christ is so honorable that the sorest sorrow is a light price by which to procure it.

Prayer sometimes must pester like a petitioner at the gate, until the King comes forth to fill her bosom with the blessings which she seeks. The Lord, when He has given great faith, has been known to try it by long delayings. He has suffered His servants' voices to echo in their ears as from a brazen sky. Unanswered petitions are not unheard. By and by your suit shall prevail. Can

July

you not be content to wait a little? Will not your Lord's time be better than your time? By and by He will comfortably appear, to your soul's joy, and make you put away the sackcloth and ashes of long waiting, and put on the scarlet and fine linen of full fruition.

16

And why call ye me, Lord, Lord, and do not the things which I say? Whosoever cometh to me, and heareth my sayings, and doeth them, I will show you to whom he is like: He is like a man which built a house, and digged deep, and laid the foundation on a rock: and when the flood arose, the stream beat vehemently upon that house, and could not shake it; for it was founded upon a rock.

Luke 6: 46-48

It is a grand thing to have a faith which cannot be shaken. I saw one day a number of beech trees which had formed a wood: they had all fallen to the ground through a storm. The fact was they leaned upon one another to a great extent, and the thickness of the wood prevented each tree from getting a firm hold of the soil. They kept each other up and also constrained each other to grow up tall and thin, to the neglect of root growth. When the tempest forced down the first few trees the others readily followed one after the other. Close to that same spot I saw another tree in the open, bravely defying the blast, in solitary strength. The hurricane had beaten upon it but it had endured all its force unsheltered. That lone, brave tree seemed to be better rooted than before the storm.

I thought, "Is it not so with professors?" They often hold together, and help each other to grow up, but if they have not firm personal roothold, when a storm arises they fall in rows. A minister dies, or certain leaders are taken away, and over go the members by departure from the faith and from holiness. I would have you be self-contained, growing each man into Christ for himself, rooted and grounded in love and faith and every holy grace. Then when the worst storm that ever blew on mortal man shall come, it will be said of your faith, "It could not shake it."

*Return to thine own house, and show how great things God
hath done unto thee. And he went his way, and published
throughout the whole city how great things Jesus had done
unto him.*

Luke 8: 39
Read Luke 8: 26–39

17

This story illustrates beautifully that our Lord Jesus has not died
in vain. His death was sacrificial; He died as our substitute, because
death was the penalty of our sins, and because His substitution
was accepted of God. He has saved those for whom He made His
soul a sacrifice. By death He became like the kernel of wheat,
which brings forth much fruit. There must be a succession of children to Jesus; He is "the Father of the everlasting age." He shall
say, "Behold, I and the children whom thou hast given me."

First, then, here is what these children are to tell. It is to be a
story of *personal experience.* "Go home to thy friends and tell them
how great things the Lord has done for thee, and hath had compassion on thee." Not what you have believed, but what you have
felt; what you really know to be your own; not what great things
you have read, but what great things the Lord has *done for you;*
not alone what you have seen done in the great congregation,
and how great sinners have turned to God, but what the Lord
has done for *you.* And mark this: There is never a more interesting
story than that which a man tells about himself.

In that hour Jesus rejoiced in spirit.

Luke 10: 21

18

The Savior was "a man of sorrows," but every thoughtful mind
has discovered the fact that down deep in His innermost soul He
carried an inexhaustible treasury of refined and heavenly joy. Of
all the human race, there was never a man who had a deeper,
purer, or more abiding peace than our Lord Jesus Christ. "He
was anointed with the oil of gladness above His fellows." His vast
benevolence must, from the very nature of things, have afforded

July

Him the deepest possible delight, for benevolence is joy. There were a few remarkable seasons when this joy manifested itself. "At that hour Jesus rejoiced in spirit, and said, I thank thee, O Father, Lord of heaven and earth." Christ had His songs, though it was night with Him; though His face was marred, and His countenance had lost the luster of earthly happiness, yet sometimes it was lit up with a matchless splendor of unparalleled satisfaction, as He thought upon the recompense of the reward, and in the midst of the congregation sang His praise unto God.

In this, the Lord Jesus is a blessed picture of His church on earth. At this hour the church expects to walk in sympathy with her Lord along a thorny road; through much tribulation she is forcing her way to the crown. To bear the cross is her office, and to be scorned and counted an alien by her mother's children is her lot; and yet the church has a deep well of joy, of which none can drink but her own children. There are stores of wine, and oil, and corn, hidden in the midst of our Jerusalem, upon which the saints of God are evermore sustained and nurtured; and sometimes, as in our Savior's case, we have our seasons of intense delight, for "There is a river, the streams whereof shall make glad the city of our God." Exiles though we be, we rejoice in our King; yea, in Him we exceedingly rejoice, while in His name we set up our banners.

19	*The Holy Ghost shall teach you in the same hour what ye ought to say.* Luke 12: 12

The Holy Spirit who brooded over chaos, and brought order out of confusion, the mighty Spirit who came down at Pentecost in tongues of fire, with a sound like a mighty rushing wind—that same blessed Spirit will come to the hearts of the members of His church and comfort them. There are sorrows for which there is no solace within the reach of the creature; there is a ruin which it would baffle any mortal to retrieve. Happy for us that the Omnipotent comes to our aid. It is "he who telleth the number of the stars; calleth them by their names"; who also "healeth the broken in heart, and bindeth up their wounds" (Ps. 147: 3). There He is, rolling the stars along, filling heaven with wonder as He creates majestic orbs, and keeps them in their pathways, making the comet fling its gorgeous light across space and startle nations, holding the burning furnace of the sun in the hollow of His hand; yet He stoops down to minister to a desponding spirit, and to pour the oil and wine of heavenly comfort into a poor distracted heart! Yes, it is Zion that is to be comforted, but it is God himself who has promised to be her Comforter!

Come; for all things are now ready.

Luke 14: 17

| 20 |

The dispensation of the old covenant was that of distance. When God appeared even to His servant Moses, He said, "Draw not nigh hither: put off thy shoes from off thy feet"; and when He manifested Himself upon Mount Sinai to His own chosen and separated people, one of the first commands was, "Thou shalt set bounds about the mount." When the gospel came, we were placed on quite another footing. The word "Go" was exchanged for "Come"; distance was made to give place to nearness, and we who aforetime were afar off, were made nigh by the blood of Jesus Christ. "Come unto Me, all ye that labor and are heavy laden, and I will give you rest" (Matt. 11: 28).

Faith in Jesus is more than a match for worldly trials, temptations, and unbelief. It overcomes them all. The same absorbing principle shines in the faithful service of God; with an enthusiastic love for Jesus, difficulties are surmounted, sacrifices become pleasures, sufferings are honors. But if religion is thus a consuming passion in the heart, then it follows that there are many persons who profess religion, but have it not; for what they have will not bear this test. Examine yourself, my reader, on this point. Aaron's rod *proved* its heaven-given power. Is your religion doing so? If Christ be anything, He must be everything. Oh, rest not till love and faith in Jesus be the master passions of your soul!

July

21

Then drew near unto him all the publicans and sinners for to hear him. And the Pharisees and scribes murmured, saying, This man receiveth sinners. . . .

Luke 15: 1, 2

Does Christ receive us when we come to Him, notwithstanding all our past sinfulness? Does He never chide us for having tried all other refuges first? And is there none on earth like Him? Is He the best of all the good, the fairest of all the fair? Oh, then let us praise Him! Daughters of Jerusalem, extol Him with timbrel and harp! Now let the standards of pomp and pride be trampled under foot, but let the cross of Jesus, which the world frowns and scoffs at, be lifted on high. Oh for a throne of ivory for our King! Let Him be set on high forever, and let my soul sit at His footstool, and kiss His feet, and wash them with my tears.

How humbling it is to realize that "This man receiveth sinners"; not, however, that they may remain sinners, but He receives them that He may pardon their sins, justify their persons, cleanse their hearts by His purifying Word, preserve their souls by the indwelling of the Holy Spirit, and enable them to serve Him, to show forth His praise, and to have communion with Him. Into His heart's love He receives sinners, takes them from darkness, and wears them as jewels in His crown; plucks them as brands from the burning, and preserves them as costly monuments of His mercy. None are so precious in Jesus' sight as the sinners for whom He died.

22

I will arise and go to my father. . . .

Luke 15: 18
Read Luke 15: 11–32

Endeavor to know the Father, bury your head in His bosom in deep repentance, and confess that you are not worthy to be called His son; receive the kiss of His love; let the ring which is the token of His eternal faithfulness be on your finger; sit at His table and let your heart make merry in His grace. Then press forward and seek to know much of *the Son* of God; know Him as eternal God, and yet suffering, finite man; follow Him as He walks the waters with the tread of deity, and as He sits upon the well in the weariness of humanity. Be not satisfied unless you know much of Jesus Christ as your Friend, your Brother, your Husband, your all.

Come, O Lord my God; my soul invites You earnestly, and waits for You eagerly. Come to me, O Jesus, my well beloved, and plant fresh flowers in my garden, such as I see blooming in such perfection in Your matchless character! Come, O my Father, who are the Husbandman, and deal with me in Your tenderness and prudence! Come, O Holy Spirit, and bedew my whole nature, as the herbs are now moistened with the evening dews. Oh, that God would speak to me! Speak, Lord, for Your servant hears. Oh, that He would walk with me; I am ready to give up my whole heart and mind to Him. I am only asking what He delights to give.

Now that the dead are raised, even Moses showed at the bush, when he calleth the Lord the God of Abraham, and the God of Isaac, and the God of Jacob. For he is not the God of the dead, but of the living: for all live unto him.
Luke 20: 37, 38

23

This was the covenant, that they should have God to be their God, and that they should be God's people. O brothers, I do not know how to speak on such a blessing as this, though I live in the daily enjoyment of it. This God is our God. All that the Lord is, and all that He can do, He has given over to us, to be used on our behalf: the fullness of His grace and truth, the infinity of His love, the omnipotence of His power, the infallibility of His wisdom— all, all shall be used on our behalf.

The Lord has given Himself over to His people to be their inheritance; and on the other hand, we, poor weak feeble creatures as we are, are taken to be the peculiar treasure of the living God. "They shall be mine, saith the Lord of hosts, in that day when I make up my jewels."

"The Lord's portion is his people: Jacob is the lot of his inheritance." O what an honor it is that God should even say to you and to me—"I will be your God, and you shall be my people. Beyond the angels, beyond heaven, beyond all my other creatures,

July

I reserve you unto myself. I have loved you with an everlasting love. I will rest in my love to you. I will rejoice over you with singing."

24

Watch ye therefore, and pray always, that ye may be accounted worthy to escape all these things that shall come to pass, and to stand before the Son of man.

Luke 21: 36

Prayer is the lisping of the believing infant, the shout of the fighting believer, the requiem of the dying saint falling asleep in Jesus. It is the breath, the watchword, the comfort, the strength and honor of a Christian.

Spiritual mercies are good things, and not only good things, but the best things, so that you may well ask for them; for if no good things will be withholden, much more will none of the best things.

If you want power in prayer you must have purity in life.

If our faith is to grow exceedingly we must maintain constant communion with God.

Prayer must not be our chance work but our daily business, our habit and vocation. As artists give themselves to their models, and poets to their classical pursuits, so must we addict ourselves to prayer. We must be immersed in prayer as in our element, and so pray without ceasing. Lord, teach us to pray that we may be more prevalent in supplication.

The common fault with the most of us is our readiness to yield to distractions. Our thoughts go roving hither and thither, and we make little progress toward our desired end. Like quicksilver, our mind will not hold together, but rolls off this way and that. How great an evil this is! It injures us, and, what is worse, it insults our God.

25

But their eyes were holden that they should not know him.

Luke 24: 16

The disciples had heard His voice so often, and gazed upon that marred face so recently, that it is strange they did not recognize

Him. Yet is it not so with us also? We have not seen Jesus lately. We have been to His table, and we have not met Him there. We are in a dark trouble this day, and though He plainly says, "It is I, be not afraid," yet we cannot discern Him. Dear child of God, are you in this state? Faith alone can bring us to see Jesus. Let us make it our prayer, "Lord, open my eyes, that I may see my Savior present with me."

Be courageous concerning this, O Christian! Be not dispirited, as though your spiritual enemies could never be destroyed; you are Christ's, and sin has no right to you.

You are able to overcome them—not in your own strength—the weakest of them would be too much for you in that; but you can and will overcome them through the blood of the Lamb. Do not ask, "How shall I dispossess them, for they are greater and mightier than I?" But go to the strong for strength, wait humbly upon God, and the mighty God of Jacob will surely come to the rescue, and you will sing of victory through His grace.

Then he said unto them, O fools, and slow of heart to believe all that the prophets have spoken.

Luke 24: 25

26

The two disciples who walked to Emmaus and conversed together, and were sad, were true believers. The Lord Jesus Christ came to these two disciples, and took a walk of some seven miles with them to remove their sadness; for it is not the will of our Lord that His people should be cast down. The Savior does Himself that which He commanded the ancient prophet to do: "Comfort ye, comfort ye my people, saith your God. Speak ye comfortably to Jerusalem." Thus He spoke and thus He acts. He was pleased when He went away to send us another Comforter, because He wishes us to abound in comfort; but that promise proves that He was, and is, Himself a Comforter.

Do not dream, when you are sad, that your Lord has deserted you; rather reckon that for this very reason He will come to you. As her baby's cry quickens the mother's footsteps to come to him more speedily, so shall your griefs hasten the visits of your Lord.

July

He hears your groanings; He sees your tears. He will come to you as the God of all consolation.

27

But they constrained him, saying, Abide with us; for it is toward evening, and the day is far spent.

Luke 24: 29

"Abide with us, for . . . the day is far spent." Beloved, remember what you have heard of your Lord Jesus, and what He has done for you; make your heart the golden pot of manna to preserve the memorial of the heavenly bread whereon you have fed in days gone by. Let your memory treasure up everything about Christ which you have either felt, or known, or believed, and then let your fond affections hold *Him* fast forevermore. Love the person of your Lord! Bring forth the alabaster box of your heart, even though it be broken, and let all the precious ointment of your affection come streaming on His pierced feet.

28

And their eyes were opened, and they knew him; and he vanished [from] their sight.

Luke 24: 31

When the two disciples had reached Emmaus, and were refreshing themselves at the evening meal, the mysterious stranger who had so enchanted them upon the road, took bread and broke it, made Himself known to them, and then vanished out of their sight. They had constrained Him to abide with them, because the day was far spent; but now, although it was much later, their love was a lamp to their feet, yea, wings also; they forgot the darkness, their weariness was all gone, and forthwith they journeyed back the threescore furlongs to tell the glad news of a risen Lord, who had appeared to them by the way.

He sups with you because you find the house of the heart, and *you with Him* because He brings the provision. He could not sup with you if it were not in your heart; nor could you sup with Him if He did not bring the provision with Him. Fling wide, then, the portals of your soul. He will come with that love which you long to feel; He will come with that joy into which you cannot work your poor depressed spirit; He will bring the peace which now you have not. Only open the door to Him, and He will dwell there forever. Oh, wondrous love, that brings such a guest to dwell in such a heart!

And as they thus spake, Jesus himself stood in the midst of them, and saith unto them, Peace be unto you.

Luke 24: 36

29

In the resurrection our nature will be full of peace. Jesus Christ would not have said, "Peace be unto you" if there had not been a deep peace within Himself. He was calm and undisturbed. There was much peace about His whole life; but after the resurrection His peace becomes very conspicuous. There is no striving with scribes and Pharisees, there is no battling with anyone after our Lord is risen.

A French author has written of our Lord's forty days on earth after the resurrection under the title of *The Life of Jesus Christ in Glory.* Though rather misleading at first, the title is not so inaccurate as it appears; for His work was done, and His warfare was accomplished, and our Lord's life here was the beginning of His glory. Such shall be our life; we shall be flooded with eternal peace, and shall never again be tossed about with trouble, and sorrow, and distress, and persecution. An infinite serenity shall keep our body, soul, and spirit throughout eternity.

Behold my hands and my feet, that it is I myself: handle me, and see; for a spirit hath not flesh and bones, as ye see me have.

Luke 24: 39

30

Find if you can, beloved, one occasion in which Jesus inculcated doubt, or bade men dwell in uncertainty. The apostles of unbelief

July

are everywhere today, and they imagine that they are doing God service by spreading what they call "honest doubt." This is death to all joy! Poison to all peace! The Savior did not so. He would have them take extraordinary measures to get rid of their doubt.

"Handle me," He says. It was going a long way to say that, but He would sooner be handled than His people should doubt! Ordinarily it might not be meet for them to touch Him. Had He not said to the women, "Touch me not"? But what may not be allowable ordinarily becomes proper when necessity demands it. The removal of their doubt as to our Lord's resurrection needed that they should handle Him, and therefore He bids them do so.

O beloved, you who are troubled and vexed with thoughts, and therefore get no comfort out of your religion because of your mistrust, your Lord would have you come very near to Him, and put His gospel to any test which will satisfy you. He cannot bear you to doubt. He appeals tenderly, saying, "O thou of little faith, wherefore didst thou doubt?" He would at this moment still encourage you to taste and see that the Lord is good. He would have you believe in the substantial reality of His religion, and handle Him and see: trust Him largely and simply, as a child trusts his mother and knows no fear.

31	*And the Word was made flesh, and dwelt among us, (and we beheld his glory, the glory as of the only begotten of the Father,) full of grace and truth.* John 1: 14

Our God is full of truth. True have His promises been; not one has failed. I want none beside Him. In life He is my life, and in death He shall be the death of death; in poverty Christ is my riches; in sickness He makes my bed; in darkness He is my star, and in brightness He is my sun; He is the manna of the camp in the wilderness, and He shall be the new corn of the host when they come to Canaan. Jesus is to me all grace and no wrath, all truth and no falsehood: and of truth and grace He is full, infinitely full. My soul, this day, bless with all your might "the only Begotten."

August

The next day John seeth Jesus coming unto him, and saith, Behold the Lamb of God, which taketh away the sin of the world!

John 1: 29

1

Behold Him whom you cannot behold! Lift up your eyes to heaven and see Him, who stretched the heavens like a tent to dwell in, and then did weave into their tapestry, with golden needle, stars that glitter in the darkness. Mark Him who spread the earth, and created man upon it. He is all-sufficient, eternal, self-existent, unchangeable! Will you not reverence Him? He is good, He is loving, He is kind, He is gracious! See the bounties of His providence; behold the plentitude of His grace! Will you not love Jehovah, because He is Jehovah?

O my heart, put your treasure where you can never lose it. Put it in Christ; put all your affections in His person, all your hope in His glory, all your trust in His efficacious blood, all your joy in His presence, and then you will have put yourself and your all where you can never lose anything, because it is secure. Go, tell your secrets to that Friend that sticks closer than a brother. My heart, trust all your concerns with Him who never can be taken from you, who will never let you leave Him, even "Jesus Christ the same yesterday, and today, and forever."

He first findeth his own brother Simon.

John 1: 41

2

This case is an excellent pattern of all cases where spiritual life is vigorous. As soon as a man finds Christ, *he begins to find others.*

D.B.D.—8

August

I will not believe that you have tasted of the honey of the gospel if you keep it all to yourself. True grace puts an end to all spiritual monopoly. Andrew first found his own brother Simon, and then others.

Relationship has a very strong demand upon our first individual efforts. Andrew did well to begin with Simon. I doubt whether there are not some Christians giving away tracts at other people's houses who would do well to give away a tract (or genuine love) at their own; whether there are not some engaged in works of usefulness abroad who are neglecting their special sphere of usefulness at home. You may or may not be called to evangelize the people in any particular locality, but certainly you are called to minister to your own household, your own kinfolk and acquaintances.

Let your religion begin at home. Many merchants export their best commodities; the Christian should not. He should have a good witness wherever he goes, but let him be careful to put forth the sweetest fruit of spiritual life and testimony in his own family.

When Andrew went to find his brother, he little imagined how eminent Simon would become. Simon Peter was worth ten Andrews so far as we can gather from what is recorded of their exploits in sacred history; yet Andrew was the instrument God used to bring Simon to Himself. You may not have much talent yourself, and yet you may be the means God uses to draw one to Himself who will become eminent in grace and service.

3	*So Jesus came again into Cana of Galilee, where he made the water wine. And there was a certain nobleman, whose son was sick at Capernaum. When he heard that Jesus was come out of Judea into Galilee, he went unto him, and besought him that he would come down, and heal his son: for he was at the point of death.*

John 4: 46, 47

Observe that trouble led this courtly personage to Jesus. Had he been without trial, he might have lived forgetful of his God and Savior; but sorrow came to his house, and it was God's angel in disguise. It may be, dear friend, that you are in trouble right now;

and, if so, I pray that affliction may be the black horse upon which mercy shall ride to your door. It is a sad, sad thing with some men that the better the Lord deals with them in providence the worse return they make. On the other hand, there are hearts that turn to the Lord when He smites them. When they drift into deep waters, when they can scarcely find bread to eat, when sickness attacks their bodies, and especially when their children are smitten, then they begin to think of God, and better things. Blessed is the discipline of the great Father in such a case. It is well for the troubled if their tribulation bruises their hearts to repentance, and repentance leads them to seek and find pardon.

Search the Scriptures; for in them ye think ye have eternal life: and they are they which testify of me.

John 5: 39

4

"Search the Scriptures." The Greek word here rendered *search* signifies a strict, close, diligent search, such as men make when they are seeking gold, or hunters when they are in earnest after game. We must not be content with having given a superficial reading to a chapter or two, but with the candle of the Spirit we must deliberately seek out the hidden meaning of the word. Holy Scripture *requires searching*—much of it can only be learned by careful study. No man who merely skims the Book of God can profit thereby; we must dig and mine until we obtain the hid treasure. The Scriptures *claim searching*.

At this hour we rest in the promises of our faithful God, knowing that His words are full of truth and power; we rest in the doctrines of His Word, which are consolation itself; we rest in the covenant of His grace, which is a haven of delight. The person of Jesus is the quiet resting place of His people; and when we draw near to Him in the breaking of bread, in the hearing of the Word, the searching of the Scriptures, prayer, or praise, we find any form of approach to Him to be the return of peace to our spirits. The God of Peace gives perfect peace to those whose hearts are stayed upon Him.

August

*Our fathers did eat manna in the desert; as it is written,
He gave them bread from heaven to eat. . . . Your fathers
did eat manna in the wilderness, and are dead.*

John 6: 31, 49

Manna had a sweetness all its own. I cannot tell you exactly how
it tasted. Some said that it tasted like wafers made with honey.
The Jewish notion is that it tasted according to every man's own
taste; so that if he preferred this flavor or that, the manna had
that flavor to him, and thus it was to each one a personal and
peculiar delicacy. This I know—that there is a sweetness about
my Lord which is precisely that which delights *me*. I cannot communicate it to you, for you must each one taste for himself. I believe
that our Lord has a flavor to me different from that which He
could have to you, because our circumstances and desires somewhat
differ. Though there is in the great church of God, a sweet community of delight in the Lord, yet each believer has his own special
delight. All Israel could claim all Canaan, and yet every Israelite
had a little plot of land that was his own; and so all believers can
claim all Christ, and yet each believer has a special portion which
is altogether his own.

Oh, the sweetness that there is in the bread that came down
from heaven!

I am that bread of life.

John 6: 48

You will observe that our Lord here speaks concerning Himself.
He speaks not of His words merely, nor of His offices, nor of His
work, but of Himself. "I am that bread of life." And herein He
teaches us all to fix our eye mainly upon His blessed person, and
to think of Himself first and foremost. He is the center and soul
of all. There is a tendency about us all to get away from Jesus,
and to look rather to the streams than to the Fountain-head. Why
are we more taken up with bits of glass that sparkle in the light
than with the sun himself?

That tree of life, in the midst of the Paradise of God—we forget to eat of that; and we wander to the borders of the garden, to pluck the fruit of the forbidden tree of the knowledge of good and evil. He is wisest who does not wander, but keeps to Calvary, and is content to speak only of Jesus crucified.

"God forbid," said one who was a great and a wise man— "God forbid that I should glory, save in the cross of our Lord Jesus Christ." Paul would have considered it a terrible calamity if he had become fascinated, or even influenced, by the speculations of the cultured men of his period: he felt that the atoning sacrifice deserved all his admiration, and he had none to spare for anything else.

This is the bread which cometh down from heaven, that a man may eat thereof, and not die.

John 6: 50

7

Feeding upon Jesus assures us an immortal blessedness; we shall never die. If we have fed on Christ, we shall fall asleep, but it will be in Jesus. Some whom we love have lately fallen asleep: they will awake with Him in the morning. But we shall never die. We shall only pass into a higher stage of life: for that food on which we feed shall be in us the pledge of an immortality equal to the immortality of the Christ who has become our bread.

I am the living bread which came down from heaven: if any man eat this bread, he shall live for ever: and the bread that I will give is my flesh, which I will give for the life of the world.

John 6: 51

8

The Lord Jesus Christ is living bread. Bread such as we get from the baker is in itself dead; and if you put it to dead lips, there are two dead things together, and nothing can come of the contact. But our Lord Jesus Christ is living bread; and when He touches

August

the dead lips of an unregenerate sinner, life comes into him. He brings life even to those who are dead in sin. He says, "Young man, arise," and he sits up upon the bier. He takes a little girl by her hand, and says, *"Talitha cumi*—Maid, arise," and she sits up in her bed. He calls to Lazarus, who by this time stinks, and He says, "Lazarus, come forth," and he comes forth, wearing his grave-clothes. Lazarus has shuffled down from the niche in the cave, and he has made his way out of the damps of the cold sepulcher. Oh, what a wonderful Christ this is, who is not only bread for the living, but life for the dead!

9

He that eateth my flesh, and drinketh my blood, dwelleth in me, and I in him.

John 6: 56

To feed upon Christ means to meditate much upon Him—to think much of Him. Brothers, there are many sweet doctrines in the Bible which I delight to make my own by reading, marking, learning, and inwardly digesting them; for they are parts of the great circle of truth which is revealed of God. But I find that I am never so comforted, strengthened, and sustained, as by deliberately considering Jesus Christ's precious death and atoning sacrifice. His sacrifice is the center of the circle, the focus of the light. There is a charm, a divine fascination, about His wounds.

O sacred head, once wounded! I could forever gaze, admire, and adore! There is no beauty in all the world like that which is seen in the countenance "more marred than that of any man." This one vision is enough for all eyes for all time. There is no sustenance to the heart like the sustenance that comes of His flesh and His blood, given up in anguish and in death to work out our redemption. Beloved, this is the bread of heaven. "Take, eat," says He, "this is my body, which is broken for you." What food is this! What life ought that to be which is nourished by such bread!

As the living Father hath sent me, and I live by the Father; so he that eateth me, even he shall live by me.

John 6: 57

10

Jesus has said, "him that cometh to me I will in no wise cast out." You may summon a poor man before the magistrate, and say, "He is a thief, for he stole bread from my counter." You may put him in prison for the theft, though I hope you would not if hunger drove him to the act; but you cannot get your bread away from him if he has eaten it. So, if you come to Christ, and take him into yourself, He is yours, and you shall live by Him. Jesus says, "He that eateth me, even he shall live by me." Not death, nor hell, nor time, nor eternity, can take Jesus away when once you have Him within you. "Who shall separate us from the love of Christ?" Swallow, then, the divine truth. Let it go down quickly, for fear anybody should come before it has fully entered into your soul. Once there, it is yours! They say that possession is nine points of the law; and I should think in the case of eating that it is the whole ten points, or any other number of points, for there is no getting repossession of that which a man has actually eaten. Get Christ, and Christ is yours—yours by a kind of possession which will never be disputed before the courts of heaven.

This, then, is to feed upon Christ—to believe that which is revealed about Him, and then to appropriate Him to yourself by personal faith.

Many of the people therefore, when they heard this saying, said, Of a truth this is the Prophet. Others said, This is the Christ.

John 7: 40, 41

11

My brethren, every one of our Lord's offices is a wellspring of comfort. Is He prophet, priest, and king? Is He friend? Is He brother? Is He husband? Is He head? Every way and everywhere we lean the weight of our soul's great business upon Him, and He is our all in all.

Besides, there is this sweet thought, that He is *our representative.*

August

Do you not know that of old He was our covenant head, and stood for us in the great transactions of eternity? Like as the first Adam headed up the race, and stood for us—alas, I must correct myself—*fell* for us, and we fell in Him; so now has the second Adam taken up within Himself all His people and stood for them, and kept for them the covenant, so that now it is ordered in all things and sure, and every blessing of it is infallibly secured to all the seed. Believers must and shall possess the covenanted inheritance because Jesus represents them, and on their behalf has taken possession of the estate of God.

Whatever Christ is His people are in Him. They were crucified in Him, they were dead in Him, they were buried in Him, they are risen in Him; in Him they live eternally, in Him they sit gloriously at the right hand of God, "who has raised us up together, and made us sit together in the heavenly places in Christ Jesus."

In Him we are "accepted in the Beloved," both now and forever; and this, I say, is the essence of the whole gospel. He who preaches Christ preaches the gospel; He who does not preach Christ, preaches no gospel.

12	*Now we know that God heareth not sinners: but if any man be a worshipper of God, and doeth his will, him he heareth.* John 9: 31

This new believer, the lame man healed by Jesus, believed in the power of the prayers of simple people so to move the mind of God that He would exert His hand in providence and His influence over the hearts of men. Never let us imagine that the doctrine of the fixity of events, or the supremacy of law, as the philosophers call it, is at all contrary to the truth that prayer is effectual for its own ends and purposes.

In olden times a warrior was going forth to battle for his country, and a certain preacher of the Word said to him, "My prayer is made continually for you that you may be victorious." The warrior, in his philosophic doubt, replied that he saw no use in the promised prayers; for if God had determined to give him victory, he would have it without prayer; and if fate had decreed that he should be defeated, prayers could not prevent it. To which the godly man very properly replied, "Then take off you helmet and your coat of mail, and hang up your sword and buckler. Go not forth to battle at all with your men-at-arms; for, indeed, if the Lord is to conquer your enemies He can do it without your weapons, and if He will not prosper you, it is in vain for you to mount your war-horse." The argument of the warrior, when carried out, answers itself: there is, in truth, no force in it. The net result of such doubt would be absolute inaction. We know and are persuaded that our prayers will avail much. By our power in prayer God's power will be set in motion, and by that force all will be accomplished which shall be for His glory and for our good.

And when he putteth forth his own sheep, he goeth before them, and the sheep follow him: for they know his voice.
John 10: 4

| 13 |

Christ appears as a Shepherd to His own sheep, not to others, As soon as He appears, His own sheep perceive Him—they trust Him, they are prepared to follow Him; He knows them, and they know Him—there is a mutual knowledge—there is a constant connection between them. Thus the one mark, the sure mark, the infallible mark of regeneration and adoption is a hearty faith in the appointed Redeemer. Reader, are you in doubt, are you uncertain whether you bear the secret mark of God's children? Then let not an hour pass over your head till you have said, "Search me, O God, and know my heart."

Our good Shepherd has in His flock sheep with a variety of experiences; some are strong in the Lord, and others are weak in faith; but He is impartial in His care for all His sheep, and the weakest lamb is as dear to Him as the most advanced in the flock. Lambs are wont to lag behind, prone to wander, and apt to grow weary; but from all the danger of these infirmities the Shepherd protects them with His arm of power. He finds newborn souls, like your lambs, ready to perish—He nourishes them till life becomes vigorous; He finds weak minds ready to faint and die—He consoles them and renews their strength.

August

My sheep hear my voice, and I know tnem, and they follow me: and I give unto them eternal life; and they shall never perish, neither shall any man pluck them out of my hand. My Father, which gave them me, is greater than all; and no man is able to pluck them out of my Father's hand.

John 10: 27–29

"I give unto my sheep," says He, "eternal life; and they shall never perish, neither shall any man pluck them out of my hand." What do you say to this, O trembling, feeble mind? Is this not a precious mercy, that coming to Christ, you do not come to one who will treat you well for a little while, and then send you away, but He will receive you and make you His bride, and you will be His forever. Receive no longer the spirit of bondage again to fear, but the spirit of adoption whereby you can cry, "Abba, Father!" Oh, the grace of these words, "I will in no wise cast out!"

Believer, do you remember that rapturous day when you first realized pardon through Jesus the sin-bearer? Can you not make glad confession, and say, "My soul recalls her day of deliverance with delight. Laden with guilt and full of fears, I saw my Savior as my Substitute, and I laid my hand upon Him; oh! how timidly at first, but courage grew, and confidence was confirmed, until I leaned my soul entirely upon Him; and now it is my unceasing joy to know that my sins are no longer imputed to me, but laid upon Him, as were the debts of the wounded traveler. Jesus, like the good Samaritan, has said of all my future sinfulness, 'Set that to my account.'"

And not that nation only, but that also he should gather together in one the children of God that were scattered abroad.

John 11: 52

Oh, that the Lord would see in these days fully and evidently the fulfillment of this prophecy in the happy unity of His visible church! Sinners hate each other while they wander in their different ways; but when the Lord brings them together by His grace, then love is born in their hearts. What enmities are cast out by the power of divine grace! When lusts are conquered, wars and fightings cease. God is not the author of confusion, but of peace.

In that visible community which stands for the Church of God—I mean the combined external organization of Christendom—there are many divisions and fierce heart-burnings; but in the real Church of God, that spiritual body which the Holy Spirit inhabits, these evils are buried. The truly spiritual are really one in heart. You may meet with a man from whom you differ in many respects, but if the life of God is in him and in yourself also, you will feel a kinship with him of the nearest kind. Often have I read books which have awakened in my soul a sense of true brotherhood with their authors, although I have known them to be of a church opposed to many of my own views. If they praise my divine Lord, if they speak of the inner life, and touch upon communion with God, and if they do this with that unction and living power which are the tokens of the Holy Spirit, then my heart cleaves to them, be they who they may.

We would see Jesus.

John 12: 21

16

Is this your condition, my reader, at this moment? Have you but one desire, and is that after Christ? Then you are not far from the kingdom of heaven. Have you but one wish in your heart, and that one wish that you may be washed from all your sins in Jesus' blood? Can you really say, "I would give all I have to be a Christian; I would give up everything I have and hope for, if I might but feel that I have an interest in Christ?" Then, despite all your fears, be of good cheer, the Lord loves you, and you shall come out into daylight soon, and rejoice in the liberty wherewith Christ makes men free.

Are you willing, dear reader, to receive Christ? Then there is no difficulty in the way; Christ will be your guest; His own power is working with you, making you willing. What an honor to entertain the Son of God! The heaven of heavens cannot contain Him, and yet He condescends to find a house within our hearts! We are not worthy that He should come under our roof, but what an unutterable privilege when He condescends to enter! For

August

then He makes a feast, and causes us to feast with Him upon royal dainties; we sit at a banquet where He gives immortality to those who feed thereon. Blessed among the sons of Adam is he who entertains the Lord.

17

If any man serve me, let him follow me; and where I am, there shall also my servant be. . . .

John 12: 26

Christians are not to be praised for neglected duties under the pretense of having secret fellowship with Jesus: it is not sitting, but *sitting at Jesus' feet,* which is commendable. Do not think that activity is in itself an evil: it is a great blessing and a means of grace to us. Those who have most fellowship with Christ are not recluses or hermits, but indefatigable laborers who are toiling for Jesus, and who, in their toil, have Him side by side with them, so that they are workers together with God. Let us remember, then, in anything we have to do for Jesus, that we can do it, and should do it, in close communion with Him.

Whole-heartedness shows itself in *perseverance;* there may be failure at first, but the earnest worker will say, "It is the Lord's work, and it must be done; my Lord has bidden me do it, and in His strength I will accomplish it." Christian, are you thus "with all your heart" serving your Master? Remember the earnestness of Jesus! Think what heart-work was His! He could say, "The zeal of thine house hath eaten me up" (Ps. 69: 9; John 2: 7). When He sweat great drops of blood, it was no light burden He had to carry upon those blessed shoulders; and when He poured out His heart, it was no weak effort He was making for the salvation of His people.

18

If ye had known me, ye should have known my Father also: and from henceforth ye know him, and have seen him.

John 14: 7

The more you know about Christ, the less will you be satisfied with superficial views of Him; and the more deeply you study

August

His life and the fullness of His Grace which shines in all His offices, the more truly will you see the King in His beauty. Long more and more to see Jesus. *Meditation and contemplation* are often like windows of agate, and gates of carbuncle, through which we behold the Redeemer. Meditation puts the telescope to the eye, and enables us to see Jesus better than we could have seen Him if we had lived in the days of His flesh. Would that we were more taken up with the person, the work, the beauty of our incarnate Lord.

I will not leave you comfortless: I will come to you.
John 14: 18

19

You will notice that the margin reads, "I will not leave you orphans: I will come to you." In the absence of our Lord Jesus Christ, the disciples were like children deprived of their parents. During the three years in which He had been with them, He had solved all their difficulties, borne all their burdens, and supplied all their needs. Whenever a case was too hard or too heavy for them, they took it to Him. When their enemies well nigh overcame them, Jesus came to the rescue, and turned the tide of battle. They were all happy and safe enough while the Master was with them; He walked in their midst like a father amid a large family of children, making all the household glad. But now He was about to be taken from them by an ignominious death, and they might well feel that they would be like little children deprived of their natural and beloved protector.

Our Savior knew the fear that was in their hearts, and before they could express it, He removed it by saying, in effect, "You shall not be left alone in this wild and desert world; though I must be absent from you in the flesh, yet I will be present with you in a more efficacious manner; I will come to you spiritually, and you shall derive from My spiritual presence even more good than you could have had from My bodily presence, had I still continued in your midst."

August

20

But the Comforter, which is the Holy Ghost, whom the Father will send in my name, he shall teach you all things, and bring all things to your remembrance, whatsoever I have said unto you.

John 14: 26

The Savior when He departed from this world, provided for all the wants of His people, not so much by giving them divers benefits, as by promising them the presence of a gracious Person who should supply to them all that their spiritual needs might demand. I trust there are many of us who know in some degree the value of the promise, "I will send the Comforter unto you;" and that we know that when that Comforter comes, He brings us all good things. We have not to look in one place for quickening, and in another place for comfort, in another for instruction, and in a fourth for illumination; but when we receive the Spirit, we have all things in one. I may say of Him, as of Jesus Christ, "In him dwelleth all the fulness of the Godhead bodily" (Col. 2: 9). In Jesus it dwelt in a real human nature, physical as well as spiritual, but in the Holy Spirit we have the same fullness of deity, but He comes in and dwells, resides in His people.

21

Now ye are clean through the word which I have spoken unto you.

John 15: 3

Many can bring the Scriptures to the mind, but the Lord alone can prepare the mind to receive the Scriptures. Our Lord Jesus differs from all other teachers; they reach the ear, but He instructs the heart; they deal with the outward letter, but He imparts an inward taste for the truth, by which we perceive its savor and spirit. The most unlearned men become ripe scholars in the school of grace when the Lord Jesus by His Holy Spirit unfolds the mysteries of the kingdom to them, and grants the divine anointing by which they are enabled to behold the invisible. Happy are we if we have had our understandings cleared and strengthened by the Master!

A clear proof of the divine origin of Scripture is afforded by its portrait of the Perfect Man. Jesus is sinless in thought, and word, and deed; His enemies are unable to find a fault in Him either of excess or defect. Nowhere else in the world have we such another portrait of man; it would be superfluous to say that nowhere have we such another man. Jesus is unique; He is original, with peculiarities all His own, but without any divergence from the straight line of rectitude. He is not a recluse, whose character would have few relationships, and therefore few tests, but one living in the fierce light of a King among Men, coming into relation with the world in a thousand ways.

I am the vine, ye are the branches. He that abideth in me, and I in him, the same bringeth forth much fruit; for without me ye can do nothing. . . . Every branch in me that beareth not fruit he taketh away: and every branch that beareth fruit, he purgeth it, that it may bring forth more fruit.

John 15: 5, 1

22

"He purgeth it, that it may bring forth more fruit." If you bring forth fruit, you will have to endure affliction. But this affliction works out such precious results, that the Christian who is the subject of it must learn to rejoice in tribulations, because as his tribulations abound, so his consolations abound by Christ Jesus. Rest assured, if you are a child of God, you will be no stranger to the rod. Sooner or later every bar of gold must pass through the fire. You will be delivered from clinging to the present, and made to long for those eternal things which are so soon to be revealed to you.

If ye abide in me, and my words abide in you, ye shall ask what ye will, and it shall be done unto you.

John 15: 7

23

What is your desire this day? Is it set upon heavenly things? Do you desire liberty in close communication with God? Do you aspire to know the heights, and depths, and lengths, and breadths? Then you must draw near to Jesus; you must get a clear sight of Him in His preciousness and completeness. He who understands Christ, receives an anointing from the Holy One, by which he knows all things. Are you saying, "O that He would dwell in my bosom"? "Would that he would make my heart His dwelling-place forever"? Open the door, beloved, and He will come into your souls. He has long been knocking, and He will sup with you, and you with Him.

Success is certain when the Lord has promised it. Although you may have pleaded month after month without evidence of answer, it is not possible that the Lord should be deaf when His people are earnest in a matter which concerns His glory. Delayed answers often set the heart searching itself, and so lead to contrition and spiritual reformation.

Reader, do not fall into the sin of unbelief, but continue in prayer and watching. Plead the precious blood with unceasing importunity, and it shall be with you according to your desire.

As the Father hath loved me, so have I loved you: continue ye in my love.

John 15: 9

The Father loves the Son *without any end,* and thus does the Son love His people. Rest confident that even down to the grave Christ will go with you, and that up again from it He will be your Guide to the celestial hills. Moreover, the Father loves the Son *without any measure,* and the same immeasurable love the Son bestows upon His chosen ones. The whole heart of Christ is dedicated to His people. He "loved us and gave himself for us." His is a love which passes knowledge. Ah! we have indeed a precious Savior, one who loves without measure, without change, without beginning, without end, even as the Father loves Him!

Then Simon Peter having a sword drew it, and smote the high priest's servant, and cut off his right ear.

John 18: 10

Would you like to be throughout life screened from all affliction? I think I hear a great many say, "I should." Would you? Would you be always free from sickness, poverty, care, bereavement, slander, persecution? How, then, could that word be true, "I have chosen thee in the furnace of affliction"? What would that text mean, "What son is he whom the Father chasteneth not?"

Jesus said, "Except a man take up his cross and follow me, he cannot be my disciple." Are you to be an exception to the rule? Oh, do not kick against suffering, for in so doing you may be fighting against God. When Peter drew his sword he was unconsciously fighting to prevent our redemption. When we struggle against tribulation or persecution we may be warring against untold benefit. Do you desire to ride through the world like princes? Do not desire such a dangerous fate; for how then could the Scriptures be fulfilled, that the disciple is not above his Lord? Bow your spirit before the majesty of Scripture, and patiently endure all things for the elect's sake.

Then came the soldiers, and brake the legs of the first, and of the other which was crucified with him.

John 19: 32
Read John 19: 32-37

| 26 |

Soldiers go at once to perform the hideous operation, and they commence with the two malefactors. It is a striking fact that the penitent thief, although he was to be in Paradise with his Lord that day, was not, therefore, delivered from the excruciating agony occasioned by the breaking of his legs. We are saved from eternal misery, not from temporary pain. Our Savior, by our salvation, gives no pledge to us that we shall be screened from suffering in this life.

It is true, as the proverb has it, "All things come alike to all: there is one even to the righteous, and to the wicked; to the clean, and to the unclean." Accidents and diseases afflict the godly as well as the ungodly. Penitent or impenitent, we share the common lot of men, and are born to troubles as the sparks fly upward. You must not expect because you are pardoned, even if you have the assurance of it from Christ's own lips, that, therefore, you will escape tribulation; nay but from His gracious mouth you have the forewarning assurance that trial shall befall you; for Jesus said,

August

"These things I have spoken unto you, that in me ye might have peace. In the world ye shall have tribulation."

Suffering is not averted, but it is turned into a blessing. The penitent thief entered into Paradise that very day, but it was not without suffering; say, rather, that the terrible stroke was the actual means of the prompt fulfillment of his Lord's promise to him. By that blow he died that day; else might he have lingered long. How much we may any of us receive by the way of suffering it were hard to guess: perhaps, the promise that we shall be with our Lord in Paradise will be fulfilled in that way.

But when they came to Jesus, and saw that he was dead already, they brake not his legs.

John 19: 33

I can see in this passage also *the safety of the saints.* It is marvelous how full of eyes the things of Jesus are; for His unbroken bones look backward to the Paschal lamb, but they also look forward throughout all the history of the church to that day when He shall gather all His saints in one body, and none shall be missing. Not a bone of His mystical body shall be broken. There is a text in the Psalms which says of the righteous man—and all righteous men are conformed unto the image of Christ—"He keepeth all his bones: not one of them is broken." I do rejoice in the safety of Christ's elect; He shall not permit a bone of His redeemed body to be broken.

> For all the chosen seed
>   Shall meet around the throne,
> Shall bless the conduct of his grace,
>   And make his glories known.

A perfect Christ there shall be in the day of His appearing, when all the members of His body shall be joined to their glorious Head, who shall be crowned forever. Not one living member of Christ shall be absent: "Not a bone of him shall be broken." There shall be no lame, maimed Christ, no half-wrought redemption; but the purpose that He came to accomplish shall be perfectly achieved to the glory of His name.

But one of the soldiers with a spear pierced his side, and forthwith came there out blood and water.

John 19: 34

28

We see here the salvation of sinners. Jesus Christ's side is pierced to give to sinners the double cure of sin, the taking away of its guilt and power; but, better than this, sinners are to have their hearts broken by a sight of the Crucified. By this means also they are to obtain faith. "They shall look upon me whom they have pierced, and they shall mourn for him."

Beloved, our Lord Jesus came not only to save sinners, but to seek them: His death not only saves those who have faith, but it creates faith in those who have it not. The cross produces the faith and repentance which it demands. If you cannot come to Christ *with* faith and repentance, come to Christ *for* faith and repentance, for He can give them to you. He is pierced on purpose that you may be pricked to the heart. His blood, which freely flows, is shed for many for the remission of sins. What you have to do is just to look, and, as you look, those blessed feelings which are the marks of conversion and regeneration shall be wrought in you by a sight of Him.

Oh, blessed lesson! There is life in a look at the Crucified One. There is life at this moment for every one who will look to Him.

He, seeing this before, spake of the resurrection of Christ, that his soul was not left in hell, neither his flesh did see corruption.

Acts 2: 31

29

What is He now that He has left death, and all that belongs to it? What is He now that He shall hunger no more, neither thirst any more? He is much the same as He used to be; indeed He is altogether what He was, for He is "the same yesterday, today and forever."

In His appearance after death we are taught that *He is still anxious to create peace in the hearts of His people.* No sooner did He make Himself visible than He said, "Peace be unto you."

August

Beloved, your risen Lord wants you to be happy. When He was here on earth He said, "let not your hearts be troubled"; He says just the same to you today. He takes no delight in the distresses of His people. He would have His joy to be in them, that their joy may be full. He bids you rejoice in Him evermore.

30

Now when they saw the boldness of Peter and John, and perceived that they were unlearned and ignorant men, they marveled; and they took knowledge of them, that they had been with Jesus.

Acts 4: 13

What would that little company of disciples have been as they went through the streets of Jerusalem without their Lord? Conceive Him absent and no other Paraclete to fill his place, and you see no longer a powerful band of teachers equipped to revolutionize the world, but a company of fishermen, without intelligence and without influence, a band which in short time will melt under the influence of unbelief and cowardice. Christ was all in all to His people while He was here.

All that Jesus was, the Spirit of God is now to the church. He is "another Paraclete to abide with us for ever." If there be this day any power in the church of God, it is because the Holy Spirit is in the midst of her. If she be able to work any spiritual miracles, it is through the might of His indwelling. If there be any light in her instruction, if there be any life in her ministry, if there be any glory to God, if there be any good wrought among the sons of men, it is entirely because the Holy Spirit is still with her.

31

But Peter said, Ananias, why hath Satan filled thine heart to lie to the Holy Ghost, and to keep back part of the price of the land?

Acts 5: 3

Don't keep back part of the price! Make a full surrender of every motion of your heart; labor to have but one object and one aim, and for this purpose give God the keeping of your heart. Cry out for more of the divine influences of the Holy Spirit, so that when your soul is preserved and protected by Him it may be directed into one channel, and one only, that your life may run deep and pure, and clear and peaceful; its only banks being God's will, its only channel the love of Christ and a desire to please Him.

The hour is coming, and it may be even now is, when the Holy Ghost shall be poured out again in such a wonderful manner, that many shall run to and fro, and knowledge shall be increased— the knowledge of the Lord shall cover the earth as the waters cover the surface of the great deep; when His kingdom shall come, and His will shall be done on earth even as it is in heaven; when every one will see that verily the Spirit is poured out like water, and the rains are descending from above. For that let us pray; let us continually labor for it, and seek it of God.

September

Then Peter and the other apostles answered and said, We ought to obey God rather than men. . . . Watch ye, stand fast in the faith, quit you like men, be strong.

Acts 5: 29; 1 Corinthians 16: 13

Sometimes King Saul was among the prophets, easily turned into a prophet, and then afterwards among the witches; sometimes in one place and then another, and insincere in everything. How many such we have in every Christian assembly; men who are very easily molded. They have affectionate dispositions, very likely a tender conscience; but then the conscience is so remarkably tender, that when touched it seems to give, and you are afraid to probe deeper; it heals as soon as it is wounded. You may press them whichever way you wish, they are so elastic you can always win your purpose, but then they are not fixed in character and soon return to be what they were before.

Pray God to send a few men with "grit" in them; men, who when they know a thing to be right, will not turn away, or turn aside, or stop; men who will persevere all the more because there are difficulties to meet or foes to encounter; who stand all the more true to their Master because they are opposed; who, the more they are thrust into the fire, the hotter they become; who, just like the bow, the further the string is drawn the more powerfully it sends forth its arrows, and so the more they are trodden upon, the more mighty will they become in the cause of truth against error.

September

But he, being full of the Holy Ghost, looked up steadfastly into heaven, and saw the glory of God, and Jesus standing on the right hand of God.

Acts 7: 55
Read Esther 6: 1–11

2

The glory of God! How shall I describe it! I must set before you a strange scriptural picture. Mordecai must be made glorious for his fidelity to his king, and singular is the honor which his monarch ordains for him. This was the royal order: "Let the royal apparel be brought which the king useth to wear, and the horse that the king rideth upon, and the crown royal which is set upon his head: and let this apparel and horse be delivered to the hand of one of the king's most noble princes, that they may array the man withal whom the king delighteth to honor, and bring him on horseback through the street of the city, and proclaim before him, Thus shall it be done to the man whom the king delighteth to honor."

Can you not imagine the surprise of the Jew when robe and ring were put upon him, and when he found himself placed upon the king's horse? This may serve as a figure of that which will happen to us: we shall be glorified with the glory of God. The best robe, the best of heaven's array, shall be appointed unto us, and we shall dwell in the house of the Lord forever.

Highest of all our glory will be *the enjoyment of God Himself.* He will be our exceeding joy: this bliss will swallow up every other, the blessedness of God. "The Lord is my portion," says my soul. "Whom have I in heaven but thee? and there is none upon earth that I desire beside thee." Our God shall be our glory.

God anointed Jesus of Nazareth with the Holy Ghost and with power: who went about doing good, and healing all that were oppressed of the devil; for God was with him.

Acts 10: 38

3

Of the Savior, and only of the Savior, is it true in the fullest, broadest, and most unqualified sense: "He went about doing good." From this description it is evident that He did good *personally.* The

September

gospel writers constantly tell us that He touched the leper with His own finger, that He anointed the eyes of the blind, and that in cases where He was asked to speak the word only at a distance, He did not usually comply, but went Himself to the sick bed, and there personally brought about the cure. A lesson to us, if we would do good, to do it ourselves. "He hath left us an example that we should follow in His steps."

Since the first hour in which goodness came into conflict with evil, it has never ceased to be true in spiritual experience, that Satan hinders us. If we toil in the field, he seeks to break the plow; if we build the wall, he labors to cast down the stones; if we would serve God in suffering or in conflict, everywhere Satan hinders us. He hinders us when we are first coming to Jesus Christ. We had fierce conflicts with Satan when we first looked to the cross and lived. Now that we are saved, he endeavors to hinder the completeness of our personal character. "Let him that thinketh he standeth, take heed lest he fall."

Though he be not far from every one of us.

Acts 17: 27

When man disobeyed his God he died spiritually, and that death consisted in the separation of his soul from God. From that moment man began to think that God was faraway, and this has since been his religion in all ages. Either he has said, "There is no God"; or he has believed the visible creation to be God, which is much the same as having no God; or else he has thought God to be some faraway, mysterious Being who takes no note of man. Even after obtaining a better conception of God, he has thought Him hard to find and hard to be entreated of. Because his own heart is far from God, he imagines that God's heart is far from him. But it is not so. The living God is not far from any one of us; for "In him we live, and move, and have our being."

September

The nearness of God to man is a teaching of revelation. Look back to the record of the garden of Eden, and see an early evidence there of God's nearness to man. Adam, having transgressed, hid himself among the trees of the garden; but in his hiding place God sought him, and the voice of the Lord God was heard, walking among the trees of the garden, and saying, "Adam, where art thou?" Man will not seek God, but God seeks man. Though man's voice is not, "Where is my God?" yet God's voice is, "Adam, where art thou?"

And declared to be the Son of God with power, according to the Spirit of holiness, by the resurrection from the dead.
Romans 1: 4
Read Luke 24: 36–44

If He is not risen from the dead, then is our preaching vain, and your faith is also vain; you are yet in your sins. Justification receives its seal in the resurrection of Jesus Christ from the dead; not in His appearing as a phantom, but in His very self being loosed from death, and raised to a glorious life. This is God's mark of the acceptance of the word of the great Substitute, and of the justification of all for whom His atoning work was performed.

Note well that this is also our grand hope concerning those who are asleep. You have buried them forever if Christ was not raised from the dead. They have passed out of your sight, and they shall never again have fellowship with you, unless Jesus rose again from the dead; for the apostle makes the resurrection of all who are in Christ to hinge upon the resurrection of Christ. I do not feel it necessary, when I talk with the bereaved, to comfort them at all concerning those that are asleep in Christ, as to their souls: we know that they are forever with the Lord, and are supremely blessed, and, therefore, we need no further comfort. The only matter upon which we need consolation is that poor body, which once we loved so well, but which now we must leave in the cold clay. Yet the resurrection comes in as a final undoing of all that death has done.

September

For the invisible things of him from the creation of the world are clearly seen, being understood by the things that are made, even his eternal power and Godhead; so that they are without excuse.

Romans 1: 20

Beloved, God is everywhere. He is so present in all places that He is specially near to each person. His circumference is nowhere, but His center is everywhere. God is as much with you as if there were no other person in the world. His being near to you does not make Him far off from another. This truth is high, and we cannot attain to it, but it is none the less sure. God is near each one of us, observing us with exactness, perceiving the secret intents of our hearts. He is near us, feeling for us, and thinking of us. He is near us in active energy, ready to interpose and help us. He is near us in all places, and at all times. By night and by day He surrounds us. At this moment, "surely God is in this place."

7

Who was delivered for our offenses, and was raised again for our justification.

Romans 4: 25

Christ longed for the cross, because He looked upon it as the goal of all His exertions. He could never say "It is finished" on His throne: but on His cross He did cry it. He preferred the sufferings of Calvary to the honors of the multitude who crowded round about Him; for bless and heal them as He might, still was His work undone. In a sense He was saying: "I long for my sufferings, because they shall be the completion of my great work of grace." It is the end that brings the honor; it is the victory that crowns the warrior rather than the battle. And so Christ longed for this, His death, that He might see the completion of His labor.

Can you think what must have been the greatness of the atonement which was the substitution for all this agony which God would have cast upon us, if He had not poured it upon Christ?

And can you grasp the thought of the greatness of your Savior's mediation when He paid your debt, and paid it all at once; so

September

that there now remains not one cent of debt owing from Christ's people to their God, except a debt of love? Christ did pay it all, so that man is set free from all punishment, through what Jesus has done. Think you, then, how great His atonement since He has done all this.

By whom also we have access by faith into this grace wherein we stand, and rejoice in hope of the glory of God.

Romans 5: 2

8

Confident hope breeds inward joy. The man who knows that his hope of glory will never fail him because of the great love of God, of which he has tasted, that man will hear music at midnight; the mountains and the hills will break forth before him into singing wherever he goes. Especially in times of tribulation he will be found "rejoicing in hope of the glory of God." His profoundest comfort will often be enjoyed in his deepest affliction, because then the love of God will specially be revealed in his heart by the Holy Ghost, whose name is "the Comforter." Then he will perceive that the rod is dipped in mercy, that his losses are sent in fatherly love, and that his aches and pains are all measured out with gracious design. In our affliction God is doing nothing to us which we should not wish for ourselves if we were as wise and loving as God is. O friends! you do not want gold to make you glad, you do not even need health to make you glad; only get to know and feel divine love, and the fountains of delight are unsealed to you—you are introduced to the highest joy!

And not only so, but we glory in tribulations also; knowing that tribulation worketh patience.

Romans 5: 3

9

We glory in tribulations also, believing that we shall glorify God in them. We look forward to the time of old age, believing that

183

September

even then He is the same, and that in our days of decline He will carry us. We look forward to the advent of our Lord with delight; or, if that may not be in our day, we look to falling asleep upon the bosom of our Savior. Before us we see the resurrection morning and all its splendor: we anticipate the risen body, that glorified fabric in which our pure and perfect spirits shall dwell forever: we hear the voice of harpists harping with their harps, saluting the reign of Christ and the glorification of His people with Him. Below there is nothing before us now but that which is inexpressibly delightful; the day has long dawned with us, whose morning clouds have passed away; a day which grows warmer and brighter, and is nearing to the perfect day. A few more months, a few more years, and we shall be in the land of the unclouded sky. What will it be to be there! What will it be to be there for ever!

And hope maketh not ashamed; because the love of God is shed abroad in our hearts by the Holy Ghost which is given unto us.

Romans 5: 5

Pentecost is repeated in the heart of every believer. Let me give you a little bit of historical analogy to illustrate the text. The Lord's disciples were made to sorrow at His cross. Sore was the tribulation which came upon them as they thought upon His death, and His burial in Joseph's sepulcher. But after a little patience and experience, their hope revived; for their Lord rose from the dead, and they beheld Him ascending into heaven. Their hopes were bright concerning their Lord, who had gone into glory, and had left them a promise to come again, and to make them partakers of His victory. After that hope had been begotten in them, they were in due time made partakers of the Holy Spirit, whose divine influence was shed abroad upon them, so that they were filled with His power. Then were they made bold. They were not ashamed of their hope, but proclaimed it by the preaching of Peter and the rest of them. The Holy Spirit had visited them, and therefore they fearlessly proclaimed to the world the Lord Jesus, their hope of glory.

September

Truly, history repeats itself. The history of our Lord is the foreshadowing of the experience of all His people; that which happened to the Firstborn befell in measure all the brethren.

But God commended his love toward us, in that while we were yet sinners, Christ died for us. . . . For if, when we were enemies, we were reconciled to God by the death of his Son; much more, being reconciled, we shall be saved by his life.

Romans 5: 8, 10

11

This is just what the great Father did for us; and yet we were His enemies, living in alienation and in open rebellion against Him. Hear, O heavens, and wonder, O earth! He spared not His own Son, but freely delivered Him up for us all! "Herein is love, not that we loved God, but that God loved us, and sent his Son to be the propitiation for our sins" (1 John 4: 10). What gratitude this should create! What devotion it should bring! "This is *my* Son" (Matt. 17: 5). When you see Jesus on Tabor or on Calvary, you see God giving Himself to us, that we might not perish, but have everlasting life.

Does the Father say, "This is my Son"? What a Savior this must be! How confidently may you and I trust Him! If the Lord Jesus Christ be no common person, but nothing less than God Himself, who shall doubt His power to save? If He be God's only begotten Son, how safely we may trust our souls' affairs in His almighty hands!

Much more then, being now justified by his blood, we shall be saved from wrath through him.

Romans 5: 9

12

When Jesus died, an atonement was offered by Him and accepted by the Lord God, so that before the high court of heaven there

185

September

was a distinct removal of sin from the whole body of which Christ is the head. In the fullness of time each redeemed one individually accepts for himself the great atonement by an act of personal faith, but the atonement itself was made long before. I believe this to be one of the edges of the conquering weapon. We are to preach that the Son of God has come in the flesh and died for human sin, and that in dying He did not just make it possible for God to forgive, but He secured forgiveness for all who are in Him. He did not die to make men savable, but to save them. He came not that sin might be put aside at some future time, but to put it away there and then by the sacrifice of Himself; for by His death He "finished transgressions, made an end of sin, and brought in everlasting righteousness."

Believers may know that when Jesus died they were delivered from the claims of law, and when He rose again their justification was secured. The blood of the Lamb is a real price, which did effectually ransom. The blood of the Lamb is a real cleansing, which did really purge away sin. This we believe and declare; and by this sign we conquer. Christ crucified, Christ the sacrifice for sin, Christ the effectual redeemer of men, we will proclaim everywhere, and thus put to rout the powers of darkness.

13

There is therefore now no condemnation.

Romans 8: 1

Come, my soul, think of this. Believing in Jesus, you are actually and effectually cleared from guilt; you are led out of your prison. You are no more bound as a bondslave; you are delivered now from the bondage of the law; you are free from sin, and can walk about as a freeman; your Savior's blood has purchased your full pardon.

You have a right now to approach your Father's throne. No flames of vengeance are there to harm you now; no fiery sword; justice cannot touch the innocent. Your disabilities are taken away; once you were unable to see your Father's face: you can see it now. Once you could not speak with Him, but now you have access with boldness. Once there was the fear of hell in you, but now your fear is gone, for how can the guiltless be punished? He who believed is not condemned and cannot be punished. And more than all, the privileges you might have enjoyed if you had never sinned are yours now as if you had never sinned!

And if children, then heirs; heirs of God, and joint-heirs with Christ; if so be that we suffer with him, that we may also be glorified together.

Romans 8: 17

14

We must not imagine that we are suffering for Christ, and with Christ, if we are not in Christ. Beloved friend, are you trusting to Jesus only? If not, whatever you may have to mourn over on earth, you are not "suffering with Christ," and have no hope of reigning with Him in heaven. Neither are we to conclude that all a Christian's sufferings are sufferings with Christ, for *it is essential that we be called by God to suffer.* If we are rash and imprudent, and run into positions for which neither providence nor grace has fitted us, we ought to question whether we are not rather sinning than communing with Jesus.

We must manifest the spirit of Christ in meekness, gentleness, and forgiveness. Let us search and see if we truly *suffer with Jesus.* And if we do thus suffer, what is our "light affliction" compared with *reigning with Him?* Oh, it is so blessed to be in the furnace with Christ, and such an honor to stand in the pillory with Him, that if there were no future reward, we might count ourselves happy in present honor; but when the recompense is so eternal, so infinitely more than we had any right to expect, shall we not take up the cross with alacrity, and go on our way rejoicing?

Ourselves also, which have the firstfruits of the Spirit.

Romans 8: 23

15

But the first fruits were not the harvest, and the works of the Spirit in us at this moment, are not the consummation— the perfec-

September

tion is yet to come. We must not boast that we have attained, and so reckon the wave-sheaf to be all the produce of the year: we must hunger and thirst after righteousness, and pant for the day of full redemption. Dear reader, this day open your heart wide, and God will fill it. Groan within yourself for higher degrees of consecration, and your Lord will grant them to you, for He is able to do exceeding abundantly above what we ask, or even think.

Though we have brought forth some fruit unto Christ, and have a joyful hope that we are "plants of his own right hand planting," yet there are times when we feel very barren. Prayer is lifeless, love is cold, faith is weak, each grace in the garden of our heart languishes and droops. We are like flowers in the hot sun, requiring the refreshing shower. In such a condition what are we to do? "Sing, O barren . . . break forth into singing" (Isa. 54: 1). Sing, believer, for it will cheer your heart, and the hearts of other desolate ones. Sing on, for now that God makes you unsatisfied to be without fruit He will soon cover you with clusters.

Likewise the Spirit also helpeth our infirmities: for we know not what we should pray for as we ought: but the Spirit itself maketh intercession for us with groanings which cannot be uttered. And he that searcheth the hearts knoweth what is the mind of the Spirit, because he maketh intercession for the saints according to the will of God.

Romans 8: 26, 27

The Apostle Paul was writing to a tried and afflicted people, and one of his objects was to remind them of the rivers of comfort which were flowing near at hand. He first of all stirred up their pure minds by way of remembrance as to their sonship—for, said he, "as many as are led by the Spirit of God, they are the sons of God." They were, therefore, encouraged to take part and lot with Christ, the elder brother, with whom they had become joint heirs; and they were exhorted to suffer with Him, that they might afterward be glorified with him. All that they endured came from a Father's hand, and this should comfort them. A thousand sources of joy are opened in that one blessing of adoption. Blessed be the God and Father of our Lord Jesus Christ, by whom we have been begotten into the family of grace.

Who shall lay any thing to the charge of God's elect? It is God that justifieth.

Romans 8: 33

17

"*Who can* lay anything to the charge of God's elect?" Most blessed challenge! How unanswerable it is! Every sin of the elect was laid upon the great Champion of our salvation, and by the atonement carried away. There is no sin in God's book against His people. When the guilt of sin was taken away, the punishment of sin was removed. For the Christian there is no stroke from God's angry hand—no, not so much as a single frown of justice. The believer may be chastised by his Father, but God the Judge has nothing to say to the Christian, except "I have absolved thee: thou art acquitted."

Who is he that condemneth? Is it Christ that died; yea rather, that is risen again, who is even at the right hand of God, who also maketh intercession for us.

Romans 8: 34

18

Christ's cause is safe. Let not His church tremble, let her not think of putting out the hand of unbelief to steady the ark of the Lord. The history of the church is to be the history of Christ repeated: she is to be betrayed, she is to be scourged, she is to be falsely accused and spitted on; she may have her crucifixion and her death; but she will rise again. Her Master rose, and like Him she shall rise and receive glory. You can never kill the church till you can kill Christ; and you can never defeat her till you defeat the Lord Jesus, who already wears the crown of triumph. The grand old cause is safe. The outlook may be dark just now, and it may be unpopular to follow the Lamb wherever He goes; but the day

September

will come when they who do so shall walk in white, for they are worthy. The wheel will turn, and they who are lowest now shall soon be highest; they who have been with Him in the dust shall be with Him in His glory.

19

Even so then at this present time also there is a remnant according to the election of grace.

Romans 11: 5

The Lord has a people, "a remnant according to the election of grace," and for their sakes the earth remains yet a little while; but its end draws nearer every hour. "God hath appointed a day in the which he will judge the world in righteousness by the man Christ Jesus." An hour is set when mercy shall no longer hold back the axe from the barren tree, and forbearance shall no more restrain the angel with the sharp sickle from reaping the vintage of the earth.

Love now journeys to and fro among the sons of men, with the voice of trembling pathos, pleading with them to be reconciled to God; but her mission will come to an end, the day of grace will be over, and the reign of judgment will come.

Let us not reckon too much upon this world's enduring even for a little while; let us not set our love upon anything that is upon it; for here we have no continuing city. "The things which are seen are temporal"; the world therefore shall pass away, and all the works that are therein shall be burned up: even "the elements shall melt with fervent heat." There is a day coming when floods of fire shall be let loose: they shall fall from above, and burst upward from below, and all material things shall be melted in one common conflagration. The world is surely doomed! God has been gracious to it, but it is as a wreck drifting upon the rocks, or as a tree waiting for the axe. Believers in the testimony of God can joyfully say, "We, according to His promise, look for new heavens and a new earth, wherein dwells righteousness." Therefore we are not dismayed.

September

For of him, and through him, and to him, are all things: to whom be glory for ever.

Romans 11: 36

| 20 |

Beloved reader, what is your desperate case? What heavy matter confronts you right now? Bring it to your Father. The God of the prophets lives, and lives to help His saints. He will not suffer you to lack any good thing. Believe in the Lord of Hosts! Approach Him pleading the name of Jesus; you too shall see the finger of God working marvels for His people. According to your faith will it be unto you. In our hours of bodily pain and mental anguish, we find ourselves as naturally driven to prayer as the wreck is driven upon the shore by the waves.

Faith, then, we choose, rather than doubt, as the mainspring of our life.

Moreover, we may not refuse reliance upon God on the ground of our insignificance; for it is not conceivable that anything can be too little for God. The wonders of the microscope are quite as remarkable as those of the telescope; we may not set a bound to the Lord in one direction any more than in the other. He can and will show His divine skill in a man's life, as well as in a planet's orbit.

Witnesses are alive to testify to the Lord's making bare His arm on the behalf of those who trust Him. Any man may also put the principle to the test in his own instance; and it is memorable that none have done so in vain.

Let love be without dissimulation. . . . Be kindly affectioned one to another with brotherly love; in honor preferring one another.

Romans 12: 9, 10

| 21 |

A Christian ought to be a comforter, with kind words on his lips and sympathy in his heart; he should carry sunshine wherever he goes and diffuse happiness around him. If you see Jesus and abide in the light of His countenance habitually, your faces, your characters, your lives, will grow resplendent, even without your

September

knowing it. If the tender mercy of God has visited us, and done so much more for us than I can tell or than you can hear, let us ourselves exhibit tender mercy in our dealings with our fellow-men. He lives most and lives best who is the means of imparting spiritual life to others.

Consider the history of the Redeemer's love and a thousand enchanting acts of affection will suggest themselves, all of which have had for their design the weaving of the heart into Christ and the intertwisting of the thoughts and emotions of the renewed soul with the mind of Jesus. Nearness of life toward the Lamb will necessarily involve greatness of love to Him. As nearness to the sun increases the temperature of the various planets, so close communion with Jesus raises the heat of the affections toward Him. This alone is the true life of a Christian—its source, its sustenance, its fashion, its end, all gathered up in one name—Christ Jesus.

22	*But put ye on the Lord Jesus Christ, and make not provision for the flesh, to fulfil the lusts thereof.*

Romans 13: 14

There is no loss in being a Christian, and making God the first object; but make anything else your goal, and with all your running, should you run ever so well, you shall fall short of the mark; or if you gain it, you shall fall uncrowned, unhonored to the earth. "My soul, wait thou only upon God."

He that serves God in body, soul, and spirit, to the utmost of his power, finds new power given to him hour by hour, for God opens to him fresh springs.

The ideal Christian is one who has been made alive with a life which he lives for God.

23	*For the kingdom of God is not meat and drink; but righteous-ness, and peace, and joy in the Holy Ghost.*

Romans 14: 17

We shall never sing *Gloria in excelsis* except we pray to God *De profundis:* out of the depths must we cry, or we shall never behold glory in the highest. Prayer should be perfumed with love, saturated with love—love to our fellow saints, and love to Christ. One prevails in prayer only as he believes. The Holy Spirit is the Author of faith, and strengthens it so that we pray believing God's promise. Oh that this blessed combination of excellent graces, priceless and sweet as the spices of the merchant might be fragrant within us because the Holy Spirit is in our hearts! Most blessed Comforter, exert Your mighty power within us, helping our infirmities in prayer.

This age is peculiarly the dispensation of the Holy Spirit, in which Jesus cheers us not by His personal presence, as He shall do by and by, but by the indwelling and constant abiding of the Holy Spirit, who is evermore the Comforter of the church. It is His office to console the hearts of God's people. He convinces of sin; He illuminates and instructs; but still the main part of His work lies in making glad the hearts of the renewed, in confirming the weak, and lifting up all those who are bowed down. He does this by revealing Jesus to them. The Holy Spirit consoles, but Christ *is the consolation.*

Now I beseech you, brethren, for the Lord Jesus Christ's sake, and for the love of the Spirit, that ye strive together with me in your prayers to God for me.

Romans 15: 30

When we pray, we should make a point of praying for something distinctly. There is a general kind of praying, which fails from want of precision. It is as if a regiment of soldiers should all fire off their guns any way; possibly somebody would be killed, but the majority of the enemy would be missed. I believe that at the battle of Waterloo, there were no arms of precision; they had only the old Brown Bess, and though the battle was won, it has been said it took as much lead to kill a man as the weight of the man's body. This is a figure of the comparative failure of indistinct, generalizing prayer. If you pray any way, if it be with sincerity, a measure of blessing results from it; but it will take a great deal of such praying to accomplish much. But if you plead for certain mercies

September

definitely and distinctly, with firm unstaggering faith, you shall richly succeed.

25

Now the God of peace be with you all.

Romans 15: 33

"Now the God of peace." What a blessed name! In the Old Testament Scriptures He is the "Lord of Hosts"; but that is never the style in the New Testament. The "Lord of Hosts" is God as He was revealed under the old dispensation: in the majesty of His power, "the Lord is a man of war, the Lord is his name." But now that our Lord Jesus Christ has further unveiled the Father, we see Him as "the God of peace." Is not this a greater, sweeter, and more cheering title? O God of peace, we long for Your presence with us all!

When the God of peace makes peace with Himself, and so keeps our minds at peace within, He also creates peace with one another, so that we bear one another's burdens; and those who are strong are willing to bear the infirmities of the weak. "The God of peace be with you."

26

He that glorieth, let him glory in the Lord.

1 Corinthians 1: 31

Jesus wears all the glory which the pomp of heaven can bestow upon Him, which ten thousand times ten thousand angels can minister to Him. You cannot with your utmost stretch of imagination conceive His exceeding greatness: yet there will be a further revelation of it when He shall descend from heaven in great power, with all the holy angels—"Then shall he sit upon the throne of

September

his glory." Oh, the splendor of that glory! Nor is this the close, for eternity shall sound His praise. "Thy throne, O God, is forever and ever!" Reader, if you would joy in Christ's glory hereafter, He must be glorious in your sight now. Is He so?

But we speak the wisdom of God in a mystery, even the hidden wisdom, which God ordained before the world unto our glory.

1 Corinthians 2: 7
Read 1 Corinthians 2: 6–9

27

The essence of this mystery is *Christ Himself.* In these days certain would-be wise men are laboriously attempting to constitute a church without Christ, and to set forth a salvation without a Savior; but their Babel building is as a bowing wall and a tottering fence. The center of the blessed mystery of the gospel is *Christ Himself in His person.*

What a wonderful conception it was that ever the infinite God should take upon Himself the nature of man! It never would have occurred to men that such a condescension would be thought of. Even now that it has been done it is a great mystery of our faith. God and man in one person is the wonder of heaven, and earth, and hell. Well might David exclaim, "What is man, that thou art mindful of him? and the son of man, that thou visitest him?" The first thought of the incarnation was born in the unsearchably wise mind of God. It needed omnipotent omniscience to suggest the idea of "Immanuel, God with us." Think of it! The Infinite an infant, the Ancient of days a child, the Ever Blessed a man of sorrows and acquainted with grief! The idea is original, astounding, divine. Oh, that this blending of the two natures should ever have taken place!

Brethren, the heart of the gospel throbs in this truth. He who was made a little lower than the angels for the suffering of death is this day crowned with glory and honor, and made to have dominion over all the works of Jehovah's hands. This is the gospel indeed.

195

September

28

Eye hath not seen, nor ear heard, neither have entered into the heart of man, the things which God hath prepared for them that love him.

1 Corinthians 2: 9

Aged and mellow saints have so sweet a savor of Christ in them that their conversation is sweetly refreshing to him who delights to hear of the glories of redeeming love. They have tried the anchor in the hour of storm, they have tested the armor in the day of battle, they have proved the shadow of the great rock in the burning noontide in the weary land; therefore do they talk of those things, and of *Him* who is all these unto them. We must dive into the same waters if we would bring up the same pearls.

It is often remarked that after soul sorrow our pastors are more gifted with words in season, and their speech is more full of savor: this is to be accounted for by the sweet influence of grief when sanctified by the Holy Spirit. Blessed Redeemer, we delight in Your love, and Your presence is the light of our joys; but if Your brief withdrawals qualify us for glorifying You in cheering Your saints, we thank You for leaving us; as we seek You by night, it shall somewhat cheer us that You are blessing us even when You take away a blessing.

29

Know ye not that ye are the temple of God, and that the Spirit of God dwelleth in you?

1 Corinthians 3: 16

As the Spirit of God descended upon the Lord Jesus, the head, so He also, in measure, descends upon the members of the mystical body. His descent is to us after the same fashion as that in which it fell upon our Lord. There is often a singular *rapidity* about it; before we are aware, we are impelled onward and heavenward beyond all expectation. The brooding of the Spirit of God upon the face of the deep first produced *order and life,* and in our hearts He causes and fosters new life and light. Blessed Spirit, as You rested upon our dear Redeemer, even so rest upon us from this time forward and forever.

September

Words cannot set forth the preciousness of the Lord Jesus to His people as He indwells them through His Holy Spirit. Dear reader, what would you do in the world without Him, in the midst of its temptations and its cares? What would you do in the morning without Him, when you awake and look forward to the day's battle? What would you do at night, when you come home jaded and weary, if there were no door of fellowship between you and Christ? Blessed be His name, He will not suffer us to try our lot without Him, for Jesus never forsakes His own. Yet, let the thought of *what life would be without Him* enhance His preciousness.

Let a man so account of us, as of the ministers of Christ, and stewards of the mysteries of God.

1 Corinthians 4: 1
Read 1 Corinthians 4: 1–5

30

The gospel is the grand secret: the mystery of mysteries. It was hidden from ages and from generations, but is now made manifest to the saints. To the mass of mankind it was utterly unknown; and the chosen people, who saw something of it, only perceived it dimly through the smoke of sacrifices and the veil of types. It remained a mystery which wit could not guess nor invention unravel; and it must forever have continued a secret had not God in His infinite mercy been pleased to reveal it by the Holy Ghost.

In a still deeper sense it is even yet a hidden thing unless the Spirit of God has revealed it to us individually, for the revelation of the gospel in the Word of God does not of itself instruct men unto eternal life: the light is clear enough, but it shows nothing till the eyes are opened. Each separate individual must have Christ revealed to Him and in Him by the work of the Holy Ghost, or else he will remain in darkness even in the midst of gospel day. Blessed and happy are they to whom the Lord has laid open the divine secret which prophets and kings could not discover, which even angels desired to look into.

October

Doth God take care for oxen?

1 Corinthians 9: 9

The Lord cares for all things, and the meanest creatures share in His universal providence, but His particular providence is over His saints. "The angel of the Lord encampeth round about them that fear Him." "Precious shall their blood be in His sight." "Precious in the sight of the Lord is the death of His saints." "We know that all things work together for good to them that love God, to them that are the called according to His purpose." Let the fact that, while He is the Savior of all men, He is specially the Savior of them that believe, cheer and comfort you. You are His peculiar care; His regal treasure which He guards as the apple of His eye; His vineyard over which He watches day and night. "The very hairs of your head are all numbered."

Let the thought of His special love to you be a spiritual pain-killer, a dear quietus to your woe: "I will never leave thee, nor forsake thee." God says that as much to you as to any saint of old. Think that you see Him walking on the waters of your trouble, for He is there, and He is saying. "Fear not, it is I; be not afraid." Oh, those sweet words of Christ! May the Holy Ghost make you feel them as spoken to you; forget others for awhile—accept the voice of Jesus as addressed to you, and say, "Jesus whispers consolation; I cannot refuse it; I will sit under His shadow with great delight."

October

Wherefore let him that thinketh he standeth take heed lest he fall.

1 Corinthians 10: 12

2

An old adage has it: "Meadows may be occasionally flooded, but the marshes are drowned by the tide at every return thereof."

There is all this difference between the sins of the righteous and those of the ungodly. Surprised by temptation, true saints are flooded with a passing outburst of sin; but the wicked delight in transgression and live in it as in their element. The saint in his errors is a star under a cloud, but the sinner is darkness itself. The gracious may fall into iniquity, but the graceless run into it, wallow in it, and again and again return to it.

We are never out of the reach of temptation. Both at home and abroad, we are liable to meet with allurements to evil; the morning opens with peril, and the shades of evening find us still in jeopardy. They are well kept whom God keeps, but woe unto those who go forth into the world, or even dare to walk their own house unarmed. Those who think themselves secure are more exposed to danger than any others. The armor-bearer of sin is self-confidence. Be not secure. We need a watchman for the night, as well as a guardian for the day. Oh, for the constraining love of Jesus to keep us active and useful!

For I delivered into you first of all that which I also received, how that Christ died for our sins according to the Scriptures.

1 Corinthians 15: 3

3

The apostle would not have us forget that Christ died for us. That Christ should love us in heaven was a great thing; that He should then come down to earth and be born in Bethlehem was a greater thing. That He should live a life of obedience for our sakes was a wonderful thing; but that He should die, this is the climax of love's sacrifice: the summit of the Alp of love.

Some sights in the world astonish us once or twice, and then grow commonplace; but the cross of Christ grows upon us; the

October

more we know of it the more it surpasses knowledge. To a saint who has been saved two thousand years, the sacrifice of Calvary is even more a marvel than when first he saw it. That God Himself should take our nature, and that in that nature He should die a death like that of a felon upon a gibbet to save us who were His enemies, is a thing which could not be believed if it had been told us on less authority than the divine. It is altogether miraculous; and if you let it take possession of your soul, you will feel that there is nothing worth knowing, believing, or admiring when compared with this. Nothing can ever rival in interest the cross of Christ. Let us study what books we may, the knowledge of a crucified Savior will still remain the sublimest of all the sciences.

4

Who comforteth us in all our tribulation, that we may be able to comfort them which are in any trouble, by the comfort wherewith we ourselves are comforted of God.

2 Corinthians 1: 4

God employs His people to encourage one another. We should be glad that God usually works for man by man. It forms a bond of brotherhood, and being mutually dependent on one another, we are fused more completely into one family. Brethren, take Paul's words as God's message to you. Aim to comfort the sorrowful, and to cheer the desponding. Speak a word in season to him that is weary, and encourage those who are fearful to go on their way with gladness. God encourages *you* by His promises; Christ encourages *you* as He points to the heaven He has won for you, and the Spirit encourages *you* as He works in you to will and to do of His own will and pleasure.

Each of us has peculiar gifts and special manifestations; but the one object God has in view is the perfecting of the whole body of Christ. We must, therefore, bring our spiritual possessions and lay them at the apostles' feet, and make distribution unto all of what God has given to us. Keep back no part of the precious truth, but speak what you know, and testify what you have seen. Let not the toil, or darkness, or possible unbelief of your friends weigh one moment in the scale. Up, and be marching to the place of duty, and there tell what great things God has shown to your soul. We too must bear our witness concerning Jesus.

For we know that, if our earthly house of this tabernacle were dissolved, we have a building of God, a house not made with hands, eternal in the heavens.

2 Corinthians 5: 1
Read 2 Corinthians 5: 1–5

My text begins with the word, "For." Paul is always argumentative, the leaning of his mind is in that direction; hence, if he is cast down he has a reason for it, and if he is calm he can show just cause for his peace. Some religionists are deliriously happy, but they cannot tell you why. They see an enthusiastic crowd, and they catch the infection: their religion is purely emotional; I am not going to condemn it, yet show I unto you a more excellent way.

The joy which is not created by substantial causes is mere froth and foam, and soon vanishes away. If you have no principle at the back of your passion, your passion will burn down to a black ash, and you will look in vain for a living spark.

It was not so with Paul: he was a well-balanced man. If able to defy the present and rejoice in prospect of the future, he had a solid reason for so doing. Like Paul, let your heart be like a fiery, high-mettled steel, but take care that it is curbed and managed by discretion. An instructed Christian man is rational even in his ecstasies: ready to give a reason for the hope that is in him, when that hope seems to rise above all reason. He is glad, gladdest of the glad, but he knows the why and the wherefore of his gladness; and so he can bear the cruel test to which the world exposes spiritual joy. The true believer's peace . . . is a house built upon a foundation, a tree which has a firmly settled root, a star fixed in its sphere; and thus it is infinitely superior to the house upon the sand, the tree plucked up, the fleeting vapor of mere emotion. May God, the Holy Spirit, instruct us so that we may know the truth out of which solid happiness is sure to grow!

October

Now he that hath wrought us for the selfsame thing is God, who also hath given unto us the earnest of the Spirit.

2 Corinthians 5: 5

How very confidently Paul contemplates the prospect of death! He betrays no trembling apprehensions. With the calmness and serenity, not merely of resignation and submission, but of assurance and courage, he appears joyous and glad, and even charmed with the hope of having his body dissolved, and being clothed with the new body which God has prepared for His saints.

He who can talk of the grave and of the hereafter with such intelligence, thoughtfulness, faith, and strong desire as Paul did, is a man to be envied. Princes might well part with their crowns for such a sure and certain hope of immortality. Could emperors exchange their treasures, their honors, and their dominions, to stand side by side with the humble tentmaker in his poverty, they would be great gainers. Were they but able to say with him—"We are always confident, and willing rather to be absent from the body, and to be present with the Lord," they might well barter earthly rank for such a requital. This side of heaven what can be more heavenly than to be thoroughly prepared to pass through the river of death?

Therefore we are always confident, knowing that, whilst we are at home in the body, we are absent from the Lord: (For we walk by faith, not by sight:) We are confident, I say, and willing rather to be absent from the body, and to be present with the Lord. Wherefore we labor, that, whether present or absent, we may be accepted of him.

2 Corinthians 5: 6–9

Faith is always attended with a new nature. That is a point never to be forgotten. No man has faith in God, of a true kind, unless he has been born again. Faith in God is one of the first indications of regeneration. Now, if you have a new and holy nature, you are no longer moved towards sinful objects as you were before. The things that you once loved you now hate, and, therefore, you

October

will not run after them. You can hardly understand it, but so it is, that your thoughts and tastes are totally changed. You long for that very holiness which once it was irksome to hear of, and you loathe those very pursuits which were once your delight.

When the Lord renews us it is not half done; it is a total and radical change. If there were no work of the Holy Spirit connected with faith, and if faith were nothing more than human assent to truth, we might be blameworthy for preaching salvation through it; but since faith leads the van in the graces of the Spirit of God, and turns the rudder of the soul, we are more and more concerned to place faith where God places it, and we say without hesitation, "Believe on the Lord Jesus Christ, and thou shalt be saved." Remember you will thus be saved from the power of sin, and from the practice of sin, by being saved from the love of sin.

The love of Christ constraineth us. . . .
2 Corinthians 5: 14

8

Do you think, O Christian, that you can measure the love of Christ? Think of what His love has brought you—justification, adoption, sanctification, eternal life! The riches of His goodness are unsearchable! Oh, the breadth of the love of Christ! Shall such a love as this have half our hearts? Shall Jesus' marvelous loving-kindness and tender care meet with but faint response and tardy acknowledgment? O my soul, tune your heart to a glad song of thanksgiving! Go through the day rejoicing, for you are no desolate wanderer, but a beloved child, watched over, cared for, supplied, and defended by your Lord.

How comprehensive is the love of Jesus! There is no part of His people's interests which He does not consider, and there is nothing which concerns their welfare which is not important to Him. "The steps of a good man are ordered by the Lord: and he delighteth in his way" (Ps. 37: 23). Believer, rest assured that the heart of Jesus cares about your meaner affairs. The breadth of His tender love is such that you may resort to Him in all matters; for in all your afflictions He is afflicted, and like as a father pitieth

203

October

his children, so does He pity you. The meanest interest of all His saints are all borne upon the broad bosom of the Son of God.

And all things are of God, who hath reconciled us to himself by Jesus Christ, and hath given to us the ministry of reconciliation.

2 Corinthians 5: 18

The Lord must ever love us now that we are reconciled. He puts it thus—if God loved us when we were enemies, He will surely continue to love us now that we are friends. If Jesus died for us when we were rebels, He will refuse us nothing now that He has reconciled us. If He reconciled us by His death, surely He can and will save us by His life. If He died to reconcile enemies, surely He will preserve the reconciled.

Our hope has for the keystone of its arch the unchanging love of Jesus Christ, the same yesterday, and today, and forever. The Holy Ghost has so shed abroad the love of God in Christ Jesus in our hearts that we feel quite sure that none can separate us from it, and so long as we are not divided from it our hope of glory is sure as the throne of the Eternal.

Wherefore come out from among them, and be ye separate, saith the Lord, and touch not the unclean thing; and I will receive you.

2 Corinthians 6: 17

By coming out from the world, and following the Lord closely, *we come under the divine care and protection.* How wonderfully Abram was screened from evil! Jehovah was his shield. He was a stranger in the midst of enemies, but they did not molest him: an awe was upon them for Jehovah had said, "Touch not mine anointed, and do my prophets no harm." Wherever a true saint

October

goes, the Lord lays His commands on all the powers of nature and all the angels of heaven to take care of him.

When Abram was at peace God blessed him in all things; and if he went to war, God gave his enemies as driven stubble to his bow. If we are with God, God is with us. When God's will is our delight, God's providence is our inheritance. It is not so with you all: no, not even with all of you who profess to be Christians; but it is so with those of you who keep close to God's Word, and follow in will, in spirit, in belief, and in act, the example of His dear Son. O beloved, let us strive after this! Let us aim at perfect conformity to the will of God, for this will place us in quiet nearness to God.

Therefore, as ye abound in every thing, in faith, and utterance, and knowledge, and in all diligence, and in your love to us, see that ye abound in this grace also.

2 Corinthians 8: 7

Faith is not the mere belief that there is a God, though that we must have, for we cannot come to God except we "believe that he is, and that he is a rewarder of them that diligently seek him." We are to believe *in* God—that He is good, blessed, true, right, and therefore to be trusted, confided in, and praised. Whatever He may do, whatever He may say, God is not to be suspected, but believed in. You know what it is to believe in a man, do you not? To believe in a man, so that you follow him, and confide in him, and accept his advice? In that same way faith believes in God—not only believes that He is, but finds rest in His character, His Son, His promise, His covenant, His Word, and everything about Him.

Faith livingly and lovingly trusts in her God about everything. Especially must we believe in what God has revealed in Scripture—that it is verily and indeed a sure and infallible testimony to be received without question. We accept the Father's witness concerning Jesus, and take heed to it "as unto a light that shineth in a dark place."

October

Faith has specially to believe in Him who is the sum and substance of all this revelation, even Jesus Christ, who became God in human flesh that He might redeem our fallen nature from all the evils of sin, and raise it to eternal felicity. We believe *in* Christ, *on* Christ, and *upon* Christ; accepting Him because of the record which God has given to us concerning His Son, that He is the propitiation for our sins. We accept God's unspeakable gift, and receive Jesus as our all in all.

Therefore I take pleasure in infirmities, in reproaches, in necessities, in persecutions, in distresses for Christ's sake: for when I am weak, then am I strong.

2 Corinthians 12: 10

When we are weak we are strong, because then *we are driven away from self to God*. All strength is in God, and it is well to come to the one solitary storehouse and source of might. There is no power apart from God. As long as you and I look to the creature, we are looking to a cracked, broken cistern, that holds no water; but when we know that it is broken, and that there is not a drop of water in it, then we hasten to the great fountain and wellhead. While we rest in any measure upon self, or the creature, we are standing with one foot on the sand; but when we get right away from human nature because we are too weak to have the least reliance upon self whatever, then we have both feet on the rock, and this is safe standing.

If you believe in the living God, and if all your existence is by believing, you live at a mighty rate. But if you believe in God in a measure, and if, at the same time, you trust yourself in a measure, you are living at a dying rate, and half the joy which is possible to you is lost. You are taking in bread with one hand, and poison with the other: you are feeding your soul with substance and with shadow, and that makes a sorry mixture. When the shadow is clean taken away, and you have nothing but the substance, then you are a strong man, fed upon substantial meat.

October

Grace be to you, and peace, from God the Father, and from our Lord Jesus Christ, who gave himself for our sins, that he might deliver us from this present evil world, according to the will of God and our Father.

Galatians 1: 3, 4

13

Do not dissociate Jesus from our common manhood. It is a dark room which you are going through, but Jesus went through it before. It is a sharp fight which you are waging, but Jesus has stood foot to foot with the same enemy. Let us be of good cheer—Christ has borne the load before us, and the blood-stained footsteps of the King of glory may be seen along the road which we traverse at this hour. There is something sweeter yet—Jesus was tempted, but Jesus never sinned. Then, my soul, it is not needful for you to sin, for Jesus was a man, and if one man endured these temptations and sinned not, then in His power His members may also cease from sin.

Who gave himself for our sins, that he might deliver us from this present evil world, according to the will of God and our Father.

Galatians 1: 4

14

There is one great event, which every day attracts more admiration than do the sun, and moon, and stars. That event is the death of our Lord Jesus Christ. To it the eyes of all the saints who lived before the Christian era were always directed; and backwards, through the thousand years of history, the eyes of all modern saints are looking. Upon Christ, the angels in heaven perpetually gaze. "Which things the angels desire to look into," said the apostle. Upon Christ, the eyes of the redeemed are perpetually fixed; and thousands of pilgrims, through this world of tears, have no higher object for their faith.

O Children of God! death has lost its sting. It is sweet to die; to lie upon the breast of this Christ, and have one's soul kissed out of one's body by the lips of divine affection. And you who have lost friends, or who may be bereaved, sorrow not as those who are without hope. What a sweet thought the death of Christ

October

brings us concerning those who are departed! They are gone, my brethren; but do you know how far they have gone? The distance between the glorified spirits in heaven and the militant saints on earth seems great; but it is not so. We are not far from home.

But when the fulness of the time was come, God sent forth his Son, made of a woman, made under the law, to redeem them that were under the law, that we might receive the adoption of sons.

Galatians 4: 4, 5

Oh! how did heaven wonder! how did the stars stand still with astonishment! and how did the angels stay their songs a moment, when for the first time, God showed how He might be just and yet be gracious! "Oh, sinner," He said, "My heart has devised it; my Son, the pure and perfect, shall stand in your stead, and be accounted guilty, and you, the guilty, will stand in my Son's stead and be accounted righteous!" It would make us leap upon our feet in astonishment if we did but understand this thoroughly— the wonderful mystery of the transposition of Christ and the sinner. He came into the world to live as a man—and to die as God!

Because ye are sons, God hath sent forth the Spirit of his Son into your hearts, crying, Abba, Father.

Galatians 4: 6

The great King, immortal, invisible, the Divine person, called the Holy Ghost, the Holy Spirit: it is He who quickens the soul, or else it would lie dead forever; it is He who makes it tender, or else it would never feel; it is He who imparts efficacy to the Word preached, or else it could never reach further than the ear; it is He who breaks the heart, it is He who makes it whole.

There dwells upon this earth a mysterious Being, whose office is to renew the fallen and restore the wandering. We cannot see

October

Him, or hear Him, yet He dwells in some of us as Lord of our nature. His chosen residence is a broken heart and a contrite spirit.

God's Holy Spirit and man's sin cannot live together peaceably; they may both be in the same heart, but they cannot both reign there, nor can they both be quiet there; for "the Spirit lusteth against the flesh, and the flesh lusteth against the Spirit"; they cannot rest, but there will be a perpetual warring in the soul, so that the Christian will have to cry, "O wretched man that I am! who shall deliver me from the body of this death?" But in due time, the Spirit will drive out all sin, and will present us blameless before the throne of His Majesty with exceeding great joy.

But God forbid that I should glory, save in the cross of our Lord Jesus Christ, by whom the world is crucified unto me, and I unto the world.

Galatians 6: 14

17

In these words from Paul we see the cross in its proper perspective: *the cross of Christ's glory.* Man seeks to win his glory by the sacrifice of others—Christ by the sacrifice of Himself; men seek to get crowns of gold—He sought a crown of thorns; men think that glory lies in being exalted over others—Christ thought that His glory did lie in becoming "a worm and no man," a scoff and reproach among all who beheld Him. He stooped when He conquered; and He counted that the glory lay as much in the stooping as in the conquest.

Our God has made the day-spring from on high to visit us. Our life is bright with these visits as the sky with stars. Love is the vehicle of God's glory in us.

Who hath blessed us with all spiritual blessings.

Ephesians 1: 3

18

All the goodness of the past, the present, and the future, Christ bestows upon His people. In the mysterious ages of the past the Lord Jesus was His Father's first elect, and in His election He gave us an interest, for we were chosen in Him from before the

October

foundation of the world. He had from all eternity the prerogatives of Sonship, as His Father's only-begotten and well-beloved Son, and He has, in the riches of His grace, by adoption and regeneration, elevated us to sonship also, so that to us He has given "power to become the sons of God." The eternal covenant, based upon suretiship and confirmed by oath, is ours, for our strong consolation and security. In the everlasting settlements of predestinating wisdom and omnipotent decree, the eye of the Lord Jesus was ever fixed on us; and we may rest assured that in the whole roll of destiny there is not a line which militates against the interests of His redeemed.

The great betrothal of the Prince of Glory is ours, for it is to us that He is engaged, as the sacred nuptials shall before long declare to an assembled universe. The marvelous incarnation of the God of heaven, with all the amazing condescension and humiliation which attended it, is ours. The bloody sweat, the scourge, the cross, are ours forever. Whatever blissful consequences flow from perfect obedience, finished atonement, resurrection, ascension, or intercession, all are ours by His own gift. Upon His breastplate He is now bearing our names; and in His authoritative pleadings at the throne He remembers our persons and pleads our cause. His dominion over principalities and powers, and His absolute majesty in heaven, He employs for the benefit of them who trust in Him. His high estate is as much at our service as was His condition of abasement. He, who gave Himself for us in the depths of woe and death, does not withdraw the grant now that He is enthroned in the highest heavens.

According as he hath chosen us in him before the foundation of the world, that we should be holy and without blame before him in love.

Ephesians 1: 4

The sovereign choice of the Father, by which He elected us unto eternal life, before the earth was, is a matter of vast antiquity, since no date can be conceived for it by the mind of man. We were chosen from before the foundation of the world. *Everlasting love* went with the choice, for it was not a bare act of divine will

October

by which we were set apart, but the divine affections were concerned. The Father loved us in and from the beginning. Here is a theme for daily contemplation. *The eternal purpose* to redeem us from our foreseen ruin, to cleanse and sanctify us, and at last to glorify us, was of infinite antiquity, and runs side by side with immutable love and absolute sovereignty.

To the praise of the glory of his grace, wherein he hath made us accepted in the beloved.

Ephesians 1: 6
Read Ephesians 1: 3–10

20

That this was an act of pure grace there can be no doubt, for the verse runs, *"Wherein he hath made us accepted in the Beloved"*—that is, in His grace. There was no reason in ourselves why we should have been put into Christ, and so accepted; the reason lay in the heart of the Eternal Father Himself. He will have mercy on whom He will have mercy, and by this will we were saved. To the great First Cause we must ever trace the motive for our acceptance. Grace reigns supreme. It is a gracious acceptance of those who but for grace had been rejected. Do notice this, and dwell upon the truth, glorifying God.

"In the Beloved" is, as it were, within the gates of the city of refuge. You must abide within that wall of fire of which the cross is the center, or else you are not accepted. You must remain within the arms of the Well-beloved, living in the very heart of Christ, and then you shall know yourself to be "accepted in the Beloved." For Christ's sake, and because you are a part of Him, you shall be approved of the Father. He has taken you into covenant union, so that you can say with the favored apostle, "Truly our fellowship is with the Father and with his Son Jesus Christ."

That we should be to the praise of his glory, who first trusted in Christ. In whom ye also trusted, after that ye heard the word of truth, the gospel of your salvation.

Ephesians 1: 12, 13

21

Observe here the singular expression of the apostle—"That we should *be* to the praise of his glory." He does not say that we

211

October

should *sing* to the praise of our glorious God, though we will do that; nor that we should *suffer* to His praise, though we would not refuse to do that; nor that we should *work* to His praise, though by grace we will do that; but "that we should *be* to the praise of his glory." The very being of a believer is to the praise and glory of God. It is written, "Whether ye eat, or drink, or whatsoever ye do, do all to the glory of God"; but this is still more comprehensive, you are to *be* to His glory, your very existence is to *praise* Him. Your being, which is now turned into well-being, is to glorify the God of grace.

For by grace are ye saved through faith; and that not of yourselves: it is the gift of God. . . . he that cometh to God must believe that he is, and that he is a rewarder of them that diligently seek him.

Ephesians 2: 8; Hebrews 11: 6

If any of you desire to be saved by works, remember one sin will spoil your righteousness; one dust of this earth's dross will spoil the beauty of that perfect righteousness which God requires at your hands. If you would be saved by works, you must be as holy as the angels, you must be as pure and as immaculate as Jesus; for the Law requires perfection.

The power to receive is scarcely a power, and yet it is the only power needed for salvation. Come along and take what Christ freely gives you.

Believe in the Lord Jesus Christ, and believe intensely.

Coming to Christ is just the one essential thing for a sinner's salvation. He who comes not to Christ is yet in "the gall of bitterness and in the bonds of iniquity." Coming to Christ is the very first effect of regeneration. No sooner is the soul quickened than it at once discovers its lost estate, looks out for a refuge, and, believing Christ to be the only one, flies to Him and reposes in Him. Where there is not this coming to Christ, it is certain that there is as yet no quickening; where there is no quickening, the soul is dead in trespasses and sins, and being dead it cannot enter into the kingdom of heaven.

But now, in Christ Jesus, ye who sometimes were far off are made nigh by the blood of Christ.

Ephesians 2: 13

| 23 |

By what weapon can we drive away the adversary so as to come to God? Is it not written that we are made nigh by the blood? Is there not a new and living way consecrated for us? Have we not boldness to enter into the holiest by the blood of Jesus? We are sure of God's love when we see that Christ died for us; we are sure of God's favor when we see how that atonement has removed our transgressions far from us. We perceive our liberty to come to the Father, and therefore we each one say—

> I will approach thee—I will force
> My way through obstacles to thee;
> To thee for strength will have recourse,
> To thee for consolation flee!

Pleading the propitiation made by the blood of the Lamb, we dare draw nigh to God. Behold, the evil spirit makes way before us. The sacred name of Jesus is one before which he flees. This will drive away his blasphemous suggestions and foul insinuations better than anything that you can invent. The dog of hell knows the dread name which makes him lie down: we must confront him with the authority, and specially with the atonement of the Lamb of God. He will rage and rave all the more if we send Moses to him; for he derives his power from our breaches of the Law, and we cannot silence him unless we bring to him the great Lord who has kept the Law, and made it honorable.

I should preach among the Gentiles the unsearchable riches of Christ.

Ephesians 3: 8

| 24 |

To know Christ and be found in Him—oh, this is life, this is joy, this is marrow and fatness. *His unsearchable riches will be best known in eternity.* He will give you, on the way to heaven, all you need; your place of defense shall be the munitions of rocks, your bread shall be given you, and your waters shall be sure; but

October

it is there, *there,* where you shall hear the song of them that triumph, the shout of them that feast, and shall see the glorious and beloved One. The unsearchable riches of Christ! Lord, teach us more and more of Jesus, and we will tell out the good news to others.

To give to others is but sowing seed for ourselves. He who is so good a steward as to be willing to use his substance for his Lord, shall be entrusted with more. Friend of Jesus, are you rendering Him according to the benefit received? Much has been given you—what is your fruit? Have you done all? Can you not do more? To be selfish is to be wicked. God forbid that any of us should follow the ungenerous and destructive policy of living unto ourselves. Jesus pleased not Himself. All fullness dwells in Him, but of His fullness have we all received. O for Jesus' spirit, that from now on we may live not unto ourselves!

That Christ may dwell in your hearts by faith. . . . Let the word of Christ dwell in you richly in all wisdom. . . .

Ephesians 3: 17; Colossians 3: 16

Beyond measure it is desirable that we, as believers, should have the person of Jesus constantly before us, to inflame our love toward Him, and to increase our knowledge of Him. But to have Jesus ever near, the heart must be full of Him, welling up with His love, even to overrunning; hence the apostle prays "that Christ may *dwell in your hearts.*" See how near he would have Jesus to be! *"That he may dwell":* not that He may call upon you sometimes, as a casual visitor enters into a house and tarries for a night, but that He may *dwell,* that Jesus may become the Lord and Tenant of your heart.

That ye, being rooted and grounded in love, . . . know the love of Christ, which passeth knowledge, that ye might be filled with all the fulness of God.

Ephesians 3: 17–19

Oh! you kind and affectionate hearts, who are not rich in wealth, but who are rich in love—and that is the world's best wealth—

put this golden coin among your silver ones, and it will sanctify them.

The love of Christ casts not out the love of relatives, but it sanctifies our loves, and makes them sweeter far. Remember the love of men and women is very sweet. Oh! to have the love of Christ! for His love is "strong as death and mightier than the grave."

The most overpowering thought of all is that He loved us when there was nothing good in us whatever.

Do you know, O saint, how much the Lord loves you? Can you measure His love? Do you know how great is the affection of His soul toward you? Go measure heaven with a span; go weigh the mountains in the scales; go take the ocean's water, and tell each drop; go count the sand upon the sea's wide shore; and when you have accomplished this, you will be able to tell how much He loves you. He has loved you long, He has loved you well, He loved you ever, and He still shall love you; surely He is the One who can comfort you, because He loves.

Be ye therefore followers of God, as dear children. . . .
Ephesians 5: 1
Read Ephesians 5: 1, 2

27

"Be imitators of God, as beloved children" (RSV). I do not know of anything which would make us so useful to our fellow-men as this would do. What are we sent into the world for? Is it not that we may keep men in mind of God, whom they are most anxious to forget? If we are imitators of God, as dear children, they will be compelled to recollect that there is a God, for they will see His character reflected in ours. I have heard of an atheist who said he could get over every argument except the example of his godly mother: he could never answer that. A genuinely holy Christian is a beam of God's glory and a testimony to the being and the goodness of God. Men cannot forget that there is a God so long as they see His servants among them, dressed in the livery of holiness. We ought not only to be reminders of the careless, but teachers of the ignorant by our walk and conversation. When they look us up and down, and see how we live, they ought to

October

be learning somewhat of God. Holy men are the world's Bibles: those who read not the Testament, read our testimony.

28

Giving thanks always for all things unto God and the Father in the name of our Lord Jesus Christ.

Ephesians 5: 20

When we draw near to God, what is our strength with which to prevail in prayer? Is it not that we ask in the name of Jesus? If you leave out the name of Jesus, what are your prayers but a sounding brass and a tinkling cymbal? Prayer without the name of Jesus has no wings with which to fly up to God. This is that golden ladder whereby we climb up to the throne of God, and take unspeakable precious things out of the hand of the Eternal. That name prevails with God concerning everything, and so enables us to prevail with man; therefore, hold it fast, and deny not the faith; for what can you do if the truth and the name of Jesus be given up?

This name is our one *hope of victory.* As Constantine, in his dream, saw the cross, and took it for his emblem, with the motto, "By this sign I conquer," so today our only hope of victory for the gospel is that the cross of Christ displays it, and the name of Jesus is in it. His name is named on us, and in His name we will cast out devils, and do many mighty works, till His name shall be known and honored wherever the sun pursues his course, or the moon cheers the watches of the night.

29

That he might present it to himself a glorious church, not having spot, or wrinkle, or any such thing; but that it should be holy and without blemish.

Ephesians 5: 27

The holiest men, the most free from *impurity,* have always felt the effects of sin most. He whose garments are the whitest will best perceive the spots upon them. He whose crown shines the brightest, will know when he has lost a jewel. He who gives the most light to the world will always be able to discover his own darkness. The angels of heaven veil their faces; and the angels of God on earth, His chosen people, must always veil their faces with humility, when they think of what they were.

As you grow *downward* in humility seek also to grow *upward*, having nearer approaches to God in prayer and more intimate fellowship with Jesus.

Did you ever think of the love which Christ will manifest to you, when He shall present you without spot, or blemish, or any such thing, before His Father's throne? Well, pause and remember that He loves you at this hour as much as He will love you then; for He will be the same forever as He is today, and He is the same today as He will be forever. "As the Father hath loved me, even so have I loved you"; and a higher degree of love we cannot imagine. The Father loves His Son infinitely, and even so today, believer, does the Son of God love you!

Even as it is meet for me to think this of you all, because I have you in my heart. . . .

Philippians 1: 7

30

Paul wrote to the Philippians out of the fullness of his heart. Remember, that in proportion to the fullness of your heart will be the fullness of your life. Be empty-hearted and your life will be a meager, skeleton existence. Be full-hearted and your life will be full and strong, a thing that will tell upon the world. Keep, then, your peace with God firm within you. Keep close to this fact, that Jesus Christ has made peace between you and God. And keep your conscience still; then shall your heart be full and your soul strong to do your Master's work. Keep peace with God. This will keep your heart pure.

Is my conscience at peace? For, if my heart condemn me not, God is greater than my heart, and knows all things; if my conscience bear witness with me, that I am a partaker of the precious grace of salvation, then happy am I! I am one of those to whom God

October

has given the peace which passes all understanding. Now, why is this called "the peace of God"? Because it comes from God—because it was planned by God—because God gave His Son to make the peace—because God gives His Spirit to give the peace in the conscience—because, indeed, it is God Himself in the soul.

31

I pray that your love may abound yet more and more in knowledge and in all judgment.

Philippians 1: 9

"We love him because he first loved us." Here is the starting point of love's race. This is the rippling rill which afterwards swells into a river, the torch with which the pile of piety is kindled. The emancipated spirit loves the Savior for the freedom which He has conferred upon it; it beholds the agony with which the priceless gift was purchased, and it adores the bleeding Sufferer for the pains which He so generously endured.

On taking a survey of our whole life, we see that the kindness of God has run all through it like a silver thread.

There was never a soul yet that sincerely sought the Savior, who perished before he found Him. No; the gates of death shall never shut on you till the gates of grace have opened for you; till Christ has washed your sins away you shall never be baptized in Jordan's flood. Your life is secure, for this is God's constant plan— He keeps His own elect alive till the day of His grace, and then He takes them to Himself. And inasmuch as you know your need of a Savior, you are one of His, and you shall never die until you have found him. God sends the right messenger to the right man.

November

For to me to live is Christ, and to die is gain.
Philippians 1: 21
Read Philippians 1: 19–26

1

Certain Swiss peasants not very long ago were feeding their flocks on one of the lofty upland valleys. On one side of the pasture stood a number of *châlets,* or wooden huts, in which they were accustomed to live during the summer, poor shelters which were left as soon as the winter set in. One day they heard a strange rumbling up in the lofty Alps, and they understood what it meant; that a mass of rock or snow or ice had fallen, and would soon come crushing down in the form of an avalanche. In a brief space their fears were realized, for they saw a tremendous mass come rushing from above, bearing destruction in its course.

What did it destroy? Only the old, crazy *châlets;* that was all. Every man of the shepherds was safe, and untouched; the event was rather to them a matter which caused a Te Deum to be sung in the village church below than a subject for mourning and sorrow. They said, "The avalanche is terrible, but it has not slain the aged mother, nor crushed the babe in its cradle: it has injured none of us, but only buried a few hovels which we can soon rebuild."

Their case is a picture of ours. The avalanche of death will fall; but O saints, when it comes this is all it will do for you—your earthly house will be dissolved! Will you fret over so small a loss? No evil will come to you: the poor hut of the body will be buried beneath the earth, but as for yourself, what will you have to do but to sing an everlasting Te Deum unto Him who delivered you from death and danger, and raised you to His own right hand?

November

2

That I may know him, and the power of his resurrection, and the fellowship of his sufferings, being made conformable unto his death.

Philippians 3: 10

There is a time appointed for weakness and sickness, when we shall have to glorify God by suffering, and not by earnest activity. There is no single point in which we can hope to escape from the sharp arrows of affliction; out of our few days there is not one secure from sorrow. Beloved reader, set not your affections upon things of earth; but seek those things which are above, for *here* the moth devours, and the thief breaks through, but *there* all joys are perpetual and eternal. The path of trouble is the way home. Lord, make this thought a pillow for many a weary head!

3

Be careful for nothing; but in every thing by prayer and supplication with thanksgiving let your requests be made known unto God.

Philippians 4: 6

Doubtless the reader has been tried with the temptation to rely upon things which are seen, instead of resting alone upon the invisible God. Christians often look to man for help and counsel, and mar the noble simplicity of their reliance upon their God. Does this portion meet the eye of a child of God anxious about temporals, then would we reason with Him a while. You trust in Jesus, and only in Jesus, for your salvation; then why are you troubled? *"Because of my great care."* Is it not written, "Cast thy burden upon the Lord"?

4

Be careful for nothing; but in every thing by prayer and supplication with thanksgiving let your requests be made known unto God. And the peace of God, which passeth all understanding, shall keep your hearts and minds through Christ Jesus.

Philippians 4: 6, 7

No care but all prayer. No anxiety, but much joyful communion with God. Carry your desires to the Lord of your life, the guardian of your soul. Go to Him with two portions of prayer, and one of fragrant praise. Do not pray doubtfully, but thankfully. Consider that you have your petitions, and, therefore, thank God for His Grace.

Be not content with an interview now and then, but seek always to retain His company, for only in His presence do you have either comfort or safety. Jesus should not be to us a friend who calls upon us now and then, but one with whom we walk evermore. You have a difficult road before you; see, O traveler to heaven, that you go not without your Guide. You have to pass through the fiery furnace; enter it not, unless like Shadrach, Meshach, and Abednego, you have the Son of God to be your companion. In every condition you will need Jesus. Keep close to your Best Friend, and He will refresh and cheer you.

To whom God would make known what is the riches of the glory of this mystery among the Gentiles; which is Christ in you, the hope of glory.

Colossians 1: 27
Read Colossians 1: 24–29

5

Christ in you is Christ filling you. It is wonderful, when Christ once enters into a soul, how by degrees He occupies the whole of it.

Did you ever hear the legend of a man whose garden produced nothing else but weeds, till at last he met with a strange foreign flower of singular vitality? The story is that he sowed a handful of this seed in his overgrown garden, and left it to work its own sweet way. He slept and rose, and knew not how the seed was growing till on a day he opened the gate and saw a sight which much astounded him. He knew that the seed would produce a dainty flower and he looked for it; but he had little dreamed that the plant would cover the whole garden. So it was: the flower had exterminated every weed, till as he looked from one end to the other from wall to wall he could see nothing but the fair colors of that rare plant, and smell nothing but its delicious perfume.

Christ is that plant of renown. If He be sown in the soil of your soul, he will gradually eat out the roots of all ill weeds and poisonous plants, till over all your nature there shall be Christ in you. God

November

grant we may realize the picture in our own hearts, and then we shall be in Paradise.

6

As ye have therefore received Christ Jesus the Lord, so walk ye in him.

Colossians 2: 6

Oh! there is nothing that can so advantage you, nothing can so prosper you, so assist you, so make you walk toward heaven rapidly, so keep your head upward toward the sky, and your eyes radiant with glory, like the imitation of Jesus Christ. It is when by the power of the Holy Spirit, you are enabled to walk with Jesus in His very footsteps, and tread in His ways, you are most happy and you are most known to be the sons of God. For your sake, my brethren, I say, be like Christ.

To draw Him nearer to me, and myself nearer to Him, is the innermost longing of my soul.

Christ is the same; Christ's person never changes. Should He come on earth to visit us again, as certainly He will, we should find Him the same Jesus; as loving, as approachable, as generous, as kind, and though arrayed in nobler garments than He wore when first He visited earth, though no more the Man of Sorrows and grief's acquaintance, yet He would be the same person, unchanged by all His glories, His triumphs, and His joys. We bless Christ that amid His heavenly splendors His person is just the same, and His nature unaffected. "Jesus Christ the same yesterday, and today, and forever."

7

In him dwelleth all the fulness of the Godhead bodily. And ye are complete in him.

Colossians 2: 9, 10

All the attributes of Christ, as God and man, are at our disposal. All the fullness of the Godhead, whatever that marvelous term may comprehend, is ours to make us complete. He cannot endow us with the attributes of Deity; but He has done all that can be done, for He has made even His divine power and Godhead subservient to our salvation. How vast His grace, how firm His faithfulness, how unswerving His immutability, how infinite His power, how limitless His knowledge! All these are by the Lord Jesus made the pillars of the temple of salvation; and all, without diminution of their infinity, are covenanted to us as our perpetual inheritance.

And whatsoever ye do in word or deed, do all in the name of the Lord Jesus, giving thanks to God and the Father by him.

Colossians 3: 17

8

To learn how to discharge your duty as a witness for Christ, look at His example. He is always witnessing: by the well of Samaria, or in the Temple of Jerusalem, by the lake of Gennesaret, or on the mountain's brow. He witnesses so clearly and distinctly that there is no mistake in Him. Christian, make your life a clear testimony. Be as clear as the brook in which you may see every stone at the bottom. You need not *say*, "I am true," *be* true. Study your great Exemplar, and be filled with His Spirit. Remember that you need much teaching, much upholding, much grace, and much humility, if your witnessing is to be to your Master's glory.

No Christian is safe when his soul is lazy and self-satisfied, and his God is far from him. Every Christian is always safe as to the great matter of his standing in Christ, but he is not safe as regards his experience in holiness, and communion with Jesus in this life. Satan does not often attack a Christian who is living near God. It is when the Christian departs from his God, becomes spiritually starved, and endeavors to feed on vanities, that the devil discovers his vantage hour. He may sometimes stand foot to foot with the child of God who is active in his Master's service, but the battle is generally short. Oh for grace to walk humbly with our God!

As touching brotherly love ye need not that I write unto you: for ye yourselves are taught of God to love one another.
1 Thessalonians 4: 9

9

"*Whereby they have* made thee glad." And who are thus privileged to make the Savior glad? His church—His people. But is it possible?

November

He makes *us* glad, but how can *we make Him glad?* By *our love.*
See, loving heart, how He delights in you. When you lean your
head on His bosom, you not only receive, but you give Him joy;
when you gaze with love upon His all-glorious face, you not only
obtain comfort, but impart delight. Our *praise,* too, gives Him
joy—not the song of the lips alone, but the melody of the heart's
deep gratitude. He loves us, not for the value of what we give,
but for the motive from which the gift springs.

10

*Therefore let us not sleep, as do others; but let us watch and
be sober.*

1 Thessalonians 5: 6

When is the Christian most liable to sleep? Is it not *when his temporal circumstances are prosperous?* Have you not found it so? When
you had daily troubles to take to the throne of grace, were you
not more wakeful than you are now? Another dangerous time is
when all goes pleasantly in spiritual matters. There is no temptation half so dangerous as not being tempted. The distressed soul
does not sleep; it is after we enter into peaceful confidence and
full assurance that we are in danger of slumbering. The disciples
fell asleep after they had seen Jesus transfigured on the mountain
top. Take heed, joyous Christian; be as happy as you will, only
be watchful.

Many in waiting upon the Lord find immediate delight, but this
is not always the case. A deeper sense of sin may be given to
you instead of a sense of a pardon, and in such a case you will
have need of patience to bear the heavy blow. Ah! poor heart,
though Christ beat and bruise you, or even slay you, trust Him;
though He should seem to give you an angry word, believe in the
love of His heart. Do not, I beseech you, give up seeking or trusting
my Master because you have not yet obtained the conscious joy
which you long for. Cast yourself on Him, and perseveringly depend even where you cannot rejoicingly hope.

November

Rejoice evermore.

1 Thessalonians 5: 16

This is a sunny precept. When we read it we feel that the time of the singing of birds has come. Because Jesus has suffered, we are encouraged, commanded, and enabled to rejoice. Only the Man of Sorrows and His chosen apostle can teach for a precept such a word as this—"Rejoice evermore." Happy people who can be thus exhorted! We ought to rejoice that there is a command to rejoice. Glory be unto the God of happiness who bids His children be happy. Who can be sad, or silent, when the voice of the Beloved says, "Rejoice evermore"?

The Lord has not left it to our own option whether we will sorrow or rejoice; but He has pinned us down to it by positive injunction—"Rejoice evermore." Some things are to be done at one time, some at another; but rejoicing is for all times, forever, and forevermore, which I suppose, is more than ever, if more can be. Fill life's sea with joy up to the high-water mark. Spare not, stint not, when rejoicing is the order of the day. Run out to your full tether; sweep your largest circle when you use the golden compasses of joy.

Now our Lord Jesus Christ himself, and God, even our Father, which hath loved us, and hath given us everlasting consolation and good hope through grace, comfort your hearts, and stablish you in every good word and work.

2 Thessalonians 2: 16, 17

If it were not for the Father's love, there had never been a covenant of grace; if it were not for His infinite love, no atoning sacrifice had been provided; if it were not for His active love, no Holy Spirit would have quickened and renewed us; if it were not for His unchanging love, all that is good in us would soon pass away; if it were not for love almighty, love immutable, love unbounded, we should never hope to see the face of the King in His beauty in the land that is far off. He loves us, and therefore He leads us,

November

and feeds us, and keeps us evermore. Do not your hearts confess this? If that love could be suspended for a moment, if its outgoings were for an instant to cease, where would you be? We fall back upon the love of God as the final reason of our hope in Him.

And the grace of our Lord was exceeding abundant with faith and love which is in Christ Jesus.

1 Timothy 1: 14

Just so far as the Lord shall give us grace to suffer *for* Christ, to suffer *with* Christ, just so far does He honor us. Afflictions cannot sanctify us, except as they are used by Christ, as His mallet and His chisel. Our joys and our efforts cannot make us ready for heaven, apart from the hand of Jesus who fashioned our hearts aright, and prepared us to be partakers of the inheritance of the saints in light. Our griefs cannot mar the melody of our praise; we reckon them to be the bass part of our life's song. This vale of tears is but the pathway to the better country; this world of woe is but the stepping-stone to a world of bliss.

14

For there is one God, and one mediator between God and men, the man Christ Jesus.

1 Timothy 2: 5

Jesus is an indispensable Mediator. The only Mediator, so the text says. "Neither knoweth any man the Father, save the Son." There is none other that can approach unto God. It is Jesus Christ for your Savior, or else for you there is no Savior at all. Observe how that is. It is certain that no man knows God except Christ. It is equally certain that no man can come to God except by Christ. He says it peremptorily: "No man cometh to the Father but by me." Not less certain is it that no man can please the Father except through Christ, for "without faith it is impossible to please him."

November

No faith is worth having except the grace that is founded and based upon the Lord Jesus Christ, and Him only. Oh, then, souls, since you are shut up to it by a blessed necessity, say at once, "I will to the gracious Prince approach, and take Jesus to be my all in all."

I will therefore that men pray every where, lifting up holy hands, without wrath and doubting.
1 Timothy 2: 8

15

Paul was speaking here to all those who are part of the mystic body of Christ which is the church. Christian! learn to comfort yourself in God's gracious dealing toward the church. That which is so dear to your Master, should it not be dear above all else to you? What though your way be dark, can you not gladden your heart with the triumphs of His cross and the spread of His truth? Our own personal troubles are forgotten while we look, not only upon what God *has* done, and *is* doing for Zion, but on the glorious things He *will yet do* for His church. Try this recipe, O believer, whenever you are sad of heart and in heaviness of spirit: "Pray for the peace of Jerusalem," and your own soul shall be refreshed.

"Hallowed be thy name; thy kingdom come; thy will be done in earth as it is in heaven." Let not your prayers be all concerning your own sins, your own wants, your own imperfections, your own trials, but let them climb the starry ladder, and get up to Christ Himself, and then, as you draw nigh to the blood-sprinkled mercy-seat, offer this prayer continually, "Lord, extend the kingdom of thy dear Son." Such a petition, fervently presented, will elevate the spirit of all your devotions. Mind that you prove the sincerity of your prayer by laboring to promote the Lord's glory.

I will therefore that men pray every where, lifting up holy hands, without wrath and doubting.
1 Timothy 2: 8

16

Prayer is the certain forerunner of salvation. Sinner, you cannot pray and perish; prayer and perishing are two things that never

November

go together. I ask you not what your prayer is; it may be a groan, it may be a tear, but if it be a prayer from the inmost heart you will be saved; yet if from your heart you have learned to pray:

> Prayer is the breath of God in man,
> Returning whence it came.

And you cannot perish with God's breath in you. "Whosoever shall call upon the name of the Lord shall be saved!"

When no eye sees you except the eye of God, when darkness covers you, when you are shut up from the observation of mortals, even then be like Jesus Christ. Remember His ardent piety, His secret devotion—how, after laboriously preaching the whole day, He stole away at midnight to cry for help from His God. Recollect how His entire life was constantly sustained by fresh inspirations of the Holy Spirit, derived by prayer. Take care of your secret life: let it be such that you will not be ashamed to read at the last great day.

17

Who giveth us richly all things to enjoy.

1 Timothy 6: 17

Our Lord Jesus is ever giving and does not for a solitary instant withdraw His hand. As long as there is a vessel of grace not yet full to the brim, the oil shall not be stayed. He is a sun ever shining; He is manna always falling round the camp; He is a rock in the desert, ever sending out streams of life from His smitten side; the rain of His grace is always dropping; the river of His bounty is ever flowing, and the well-spring of His love is constantly overflowing. As the King can never die, so His grace can never fail. Daily we pluck His fruit, and daily His branches bend down to our hand with a fresh store of mercy. There are seven feast-days in His weeks, and as many as are the days, so many are the banquets in His years. Who has ever returned from His door unblessed? Who has ever risen from His table unsatisfied, or from His presence unblessed? His mercies are new every morning and fresh every evening. Who can know the number of His benefits, or recount the list of His bounties? Every grain of sand which drops from the glass of time is but the tardy follower of a myriad of mercies. The wings of our hours are covered with the silver of His kindness, and with the yellow gold of His affection. The river of time bears from the mountains of eternity the golden sands of His favor. The countless stars are but as the standard-bearers of a more innumerable host of blessings. Who can count the dust of the benefits which He bestows on Jacob, or tell the number of the fourth part of His mercies toward Israel? How shall my soul extol Him who daily loads me with benefits, and who crowns me with loving kindness? O that my praise could be as ceaseless as His bounty! O miserable tongue, how can you be silent? Wake up, I command you, lest I call you no more my glory, but my shame. "Awake, psaltery and harp: I myself will awake right early."

For God hath not given us the spirit of fear; but of power, and of love, and of a sound mind.

2 Timothy 1: 7

18

God plays no favorites in His love to His children. A child is a child to Him; He will not make him a hired servant; but he shall feast upon the fatted calf, and shall have the music and the dancing as much as if he had never gone astray. No chains are worn in the court of King Jesus. Our admission into full privileges may be gradual, but it is sure. Perhaps you are saying, "I wish I could enjoy the promises, and walk at liberty in my Lord's commands." "If thou believest with all thine heart, thou mayest." Loose the chains of your neck, O captive daughter, for Jesus makes you free.

Who hath saved us, . . . not according to our works, but according to his own purpose and grace, which was given us in Christ Jesus before the world began; but is now made manifest by the appearing of our Saviour Jesus Christ, who hath abolished death, and hath brought life and immortality to light through the gospel.

2 Timothy 1: 9, 10

19

Sinner, unconverted sinner, you have often tried to save yourself; but you have often failed. You have by your own power and might

November

sought to curb evil passions and sins; with you, I lament that all
your efforts have been unsuccessful. And I warn you, they will
be unsuccessful, for you never can save yourself by your own might;
with all the strength you have, you never can regenerate your
own soul; you never can cause yourself to be born again. And
though the new birth is absolutely necessary, it is absolutely impossible to you, unless God the Spirit shall do it.

By the sweet drawing of the Spirit, the sinner finds "a peace
with God which passeth all understanding, which keeps his heart
and mind through Jesus Christ our Lord." Now, you will plainly
perceive that all this may be done without any compulsion. Man
is as much drawn willingly, as if he were not drawn at all; and
he comes to Christ with full consent, with as full a consent as if
no secret influence had ever been exercised in his heart. But that
influence must be exercised, or else there never has been and
there never will be, any man who either can or will come to the
Lord Jesus Christ.

*For the which cause I also suffer these things: nevertheless
I am not ashamed; for I know whom I have believed, and
am persuaded that he is able to keep that I have committed
unto him against that day.*

2 Timothy 1: 12

We are not ashamed of the ground of our hope. Our hope rests
upon the solemn promises of God, which He made to us by His
prophets and apostles, and confirmed in the person and work of
His dear Son. Inasmuch as Jesus Christ died and rose from the
dead, we who are one with Him by faith are sure that we shall
rise again from the dead, and live with Him. The fact of Christ's
resurrection is the assurance of our resurrection, and His entrance
into glory is the pledge of our glorification, because we are made
one with Him by the purpose and grace of God. As we fell in
Adam by virtue of our being in him, so we rise and reign with
Jesus because we are in Him. God is not the God of the dead,
but of the living; yet is He the God of Abraham, of Isaac, and of
Jacob, and therefore these men are yet alive. Even thus do we

believe concerning all who die in the faith that they have not ceased to be, but they all live unto Him.

Therefore I endure all things for the elect's sake, that they may also obtain the salvation which is in Christ Jesus with eternal glory.

2 Timothy 2: 10

21

Our nature, our whole humanity, will be perfected at the day of the appearing of our Lord and Savior Jesus Christ, when the dead shall be raised incorruptible, and we that may then be alive shall be changed. Jesus has redeemed not only our souls, but our bodies. "Know ye not that your bodies are the temples of the Holy Ghost?" When the Lord shall deliver His captive people out of the land of the enemy, He will not leave a bone of one of them in the adversary's power. The dominion of death shall be utterly broken. Our entire nature shall be redeemed unto the living God in the day of the resurrection. After death, until that day, we shall be disembodied spirits; but in the adoption, to wit, the redemption of the body, we shall attain our full inheritance.

We are looking forward to a complete restoration. At this time the body is dead because of sin, and hence it suffers pain, and tends to decay; but the spirit is life because of righteousness: in the resurrection, however, the body shall be quickened also, and the resurrection shall be to the body what regeneration has been to the soul. Thus shall our humanity be completely delivered from the consequences of the fall. Perfect humanity is that which Jesus restores from sin and the grave; and this shall be ours in the day of His appearing.

Henceforth there is laid up for me a crown of righteousness, which the Lord, the righteous judge, shall give me at that day: and not to me only, but unto all them also that love his appearing.

2 Timothy 4: 8

22

It will always give a Christian the greatest calm, quiet, ease and peace, to think of the perfect righteousness of Christ. How often

November

are the saints of God downcast and sad! I do not think they ought to be. I do not think they would if they could always see their perfection in Christ.

When the believer says, "I live on Christ alone; I rest on Him solely for salvation; and I believe that, however unworthy, I am still saved in Jesus"; then there rises up as a motive of gratitude this thought—"Shall I not live to Christ? Shall I not love Him and serve Him, seeing that I am saved by His merits?" "The love of Christ constraineth us," "that they which live should not henceforth live unto themselves, but unto Him which died for them." If saved by imputed righteousness, we shall greatly value imparted righteousness.

| 23 | *For in that he himself hath suffered being tempted, he is able to succor them that are tempted.* |
| | Hebrews 2: 18 |

Though our Lord thus suffered being tempted, He suffered not in vain; for He was proved perfect through His sufferings, and fitted for His solemn office of High Priest to His people. From that fact I want you to gather fruit, because our heavenly Father means to bless you also. We cannot comfort others if we have never been comforted ourselves. I have heard—and I am sure that it is so—that there is no comforter for a widow like one who has lost her husband. Those who have had no children, and have never lost a child, may talk very kindly, but they cannot enter into a mother's broken heart as she bows over yonder little coffin. If you have never known what temptations mean, you make poor work when attempting to succor the tempted.

Our Lord obtained a blessing from suffering temptation; and you may do the same. Brother, the Lord means to make of you someone who shall be used like Barnabas to be a "son of consolation." He means to make a mother in Israel of you, my dear sister, that when you meet with others who are sorely cast down, you may know how to drop in a sweet word by which they shall be comforted. I think you will one day say, "It was worthwhile to go through that sorrow to be enabled to administer relief to that wounded heart." Will you not comfort others when you are delivered? I think you will. You will be ready and expert in the sacred surgery of consolation. Therefore be content to suffer being tempted, and look for the comforting fruit which all this shall produce in you.

Seeing therefore it remaineth that some must enter therein, and they to whom it was first preached entered not in because of unbelief.

Hebrews 4: 6

24

Instead of having wings as of an eagle to mount to heaven, a secret evil clips your wings, and you cannot rise. You say within yourself, "I have no faith, and I cannot expect to succeed with God without faith. I seem to have no love; or, if I have any, my heart lies asleep, and I cannot stir myself to plead with God. Oh, that I could come out of my prayer closet saying, *'Vici! Vici!'*—'I have overcome, I have overcome'; but alas! instead I groan in vain, and come away unsatisfied. I have been half dead, cold, and stolid, and I cannot hope that I have prevailed with God in prayer." Whenever you are in this condition, fly to the blood of the Lamb as your chief remedy. When you plead this master argument you will arouse yourself, and you will prevail with God. You will feel rest in pleading it, and a sweet assurance of success at the mercy-seat.

Seeing then that we have a great high priest, that is passed into the heavens, Jesus the Son of God, let us hold fast our profession.

Hebrews 4: 14

25

Ah! if we did but love Christ better, my brothers and sisters, if we lived nearer to the cross, if we knew more of the value of His blood, if we wept like Him over Jerusalem, if we felt more what it was for souls to perish, and what it was for men to be saved—if we did but rejoice with Christ in the prospect of His

November

seeing the travail of His soul, and being abundantly satisfied—if we did but delight more in the divine decree, that the kingdoms of this world *shall* be given to Christ, I am sure we should all of us find more ways and more means for the sending forth of the gospel of Christ.

Love to Christ smooths the path of duty, and wings the feet to travel it: it makes the life of sincere devotion.

Love has a clear eye; but it can see only one thing—it is blind to every interest but that of its Lord; it sees things in the light of His glory, and weighs actions in the scales of His honor; it counts royalty but drudgery if it cannot reign for Christ, but it delights in servitude as much as in honor, if it can thereby advance the Master's kingdom; its end sweetens all its means; its object lightens its toil, and removes its weariness.

Let us therefore come boldly unto the throne of grace, that we may obtain mercy, and find grace to help in time of need.

Hebrews 4: 16

Christ never lingers long with dumb souls; if there be no crying out to Him, He departs. What a marvelous influence prayer has upon our fellowship with Jesus! We may always measure one by the other. Those pray most fervently and frequently who have been constant attendants on the kind Intercessor; while, on the other hand, those who wrestle the hardest in supplication will hold the angel the longest. Joshua's voice stayed the sun in the heavens for a few hours; but the voice of prayer can detain the Sun of righteousness for months and even years.

Soldier of the cross! the hour is coming when the note of victory shall be proclaimed throughout the world. The battlements of the enemy must soon succumb; the swords of the mighty must soon be given up to the Lord of lords. What! soldier of the cross! in the day of victory would you have it said that you turned your back in the day of battle? Do you not wish to have a share in the conflict, that you may have a share in the victory? If you have even the hottest part of the battle, will you falter? You will have

November

the brightest part of the victory, if you are in the fiercest of the conflict.

Who in the days of his flesh, when he had offered up prayers and supplications with strong crying and tears unto him that was able to save him from death, and was heard in that he feared.

Hebrews 5: 7
Read Hebrews 5: 7–10

The Savior offered no petitions by way of mere form; His supplications arose out of an urgent sense of His need of heavenly aid. It is difficult to realize it, but so it is, that our divine and innocent Savior placed Himself in such a condition for our sakes that His needs were manifold. Of course, as God, He could come under no necessity; but being man, like ourselves, He did not permit the power of His Godhead to destroy the manlike weakness of the flesh. Hence He endured such necessities as we do, and resorted, as we must, to the one all-sufficient source of supply, approaching His Father by prayer.

He sought for blessings with prayers; He pleaded against evil with supplications. His approaches to God were many—both words are in the plural—"prayers and supplications"; and they were manifold in their character; for He presented prayers and supplications of all kinds. Specially in the garden He cried again and again, "If it be possible, let this cup pass from me." Now, trite as the observation may be, yet it is one that needs to be often repeated, that our Savior did really pray. When you, in your heaviness, shut the door of your chamber, and kneel down in prayer; when that prayer gathers strength, and you fall flat upon your face in agony; when you cry and weep before the Most High, under a sinking sense of need, it is hard for you to think that Jesus ever did the same. But He did so. He asked as really as you ask; He implored and besought, He entreated and wrestled, even as you must do. He knows the solitary place on Carmel, where Elias bowed his

235

November

head between his knees and cried seven times unto the Lord.
He knows the turning of the face to the wall and the weeping of
the sorrowful eyes, even as Hezekiah knew them. He can have
pity upon you in your loneliness, your distraction, your apparent
desertion, your sinking of heart, your sorrowfulness even unto
death. Look to Him then, in your night of weeping, and be of
good cheer.

28

Let us draw near with a true heart in full assurance of faith.
Hebrews 10: 22

It has been well said, "Nothing is easier than to doubt. A man of
moderate ability or learning can doubt more than the wisest men
believe." Faith demands knowledge, for it is an intelligent grace,
able and anxious to justify itself; but infidelity is not required to
give a reason for the doubt that is in it; a defiant mien and a
blustering tone answer its purpose. The acme of unbelief is to
know nothing. What is this but the apotheosis of ignorance?

A man may glide into agnosticism insensibly, and remain in it
languidly; but to believe is to be alive. Those who think faith to
be a childish business will have to make considerable advance toward manliness before they are able to test their own theory.

Faith must come out of active involvement in the Word of God.
We are not exacting when we demand that each candid man should
read the Bible for himself. In testing a book which professes to
be revelation of God's mind, we shall act unworthily if we trust
to others, be they who they may. Secondhand information lacks
assurance and vividness; a personal investigation is far more satisfactory and beneficial. Many other books have been warmly praised
by their readers; but we have never yet met with any other volume
which has commanded such frequent enthusiasm and such devoted
affection as the Bible; neither have we heard of one which answers
so many and such diverse purposes in connection with the lives
of men.

And let us consider one another to provoke unto love and to good works.

Hebrews 10: 24

29

We love Jesus when we are advanced in the divine life, from a participation with Him in the great work of His incarnation. We long to see our fellow-men turned from darkness to light, and we love Him as the sun of righteousness, who can alone illuminate them. We hate sin, and therefore we rejoice in Him as manifested to take away sin. We long for holier and happier times, and therefore we adore Him as the coming Ruler of all lands, who will bring a millennium with Him in the day of His appearing. Love the soul of every man with all the intensity of your being.

Only love seeks after love. If I desire the love of another it can surely only be because I myself have love toward him. We care not to be loved by those whom we do not love. It could be an embarrassment rather than an advantage to receive love from those to whom we would not return it. When God asks human love, it is because God is love. Whatever our frame or feeling, the heart of Jesus is full of love—love which was not caused by our good behavior, and is not diminished by our follies—love which is as sure in the night of darkness as in the brightness of the day of joy.

These all died in faith, not having received the promises, but having seen them afar off. . . .

Hebrews 11: 13

30

Behold the epitaph of all those blessed saints who fell asleep before the coming of our Lord! It matters nothing how else they died, this one point, in which they all agree, is the most worthy of record, "they all died in faith." In faith they lived—it was their comfort, their guide, their motive, and their support; and in the same spiritual grace they died, ending their life-song in the sweet strain in which they had so long continued. They did not die resting in the flesh or upon their own attainments; they made no advance

November

from their first way of acceptance with God, but held to the way of faith to the end.

Dying in faith has distinct reference to *the past*. They believed the promises which had gone before, and were assured that their sins were blotted out through the mercy of God. Dying in faith has to do with the present. These saints were confident of their acceptance with God, they enjoyed the beams of His love, and rested in His faithfulness. Dying in faith looks into *the future*. They fell asleep, affirming that the Messiah would surely come. Your course, through grace, is one of faith, and sight seldom cheers you: this has also been the pathway of the brightest and the best.

December

1

What a valiant leader is to an army, when his very presence inspires them with valor, when his wisdom and tact conduct them to certain victory, and when his influence over them nerves and strengthens them in the day of battle—all that, and more, is Jesus Christ to His disciples. What the shepherd is to the sheep, the sheep being foolish, and the shepherd alone wise; the sheep being defenseless, and the shepherd strong to protect them; the sheep being without power to provide for themselves in any degree, and the shepherd able to give them all they require—all that is Jesus Christ to His people.

He is not only the Founder but the Finisher of our system. Jesus is to us not only the doctor but the doctrine: "[He] is the way, and the truth, and the life" (John 14: 6). The disciple of Christ feels Jesus to be inexpressibly precious. He does not know how many uses Christ can be put to, but this he knows—Christ is all in all to him. As the Orientals say of the palm tree, that every fragment of it is of use, and there is scarcely any domestic arrangement into which the palm tree in some form or other does not enter, even so Jesus Christ is good for everything to His people, and there is nothing that they have to do or feel or know that is good or excellent, but Jesus Christ enters into it.

December

But ye are come unto mount Sion, and unto the City of the living God, the heavenly Jerusalem, and to an innumerable company of angels, to the general assembly and church of the firstborn, which are written in heaven, and to God the Judge of all, and to the spirits of just men made perfect.

Hebrews 12: 22, 23

When Jesus Christ came to build His temple, He found no mountain on which to build it; He had no mountain in our nature, He had to find a mountain in His own, and the mountain upon which He has built His church is the mountain of His own unchangeable affection, His own strong love, His own omnipotent grace and infallible truthfulness. It is this that constitutes the mountain upon which the church is built, and on this the foundation has been dug, and the great stones laid in the trenches with oaths and promises and blood to make them stand secure, even though earth should rock and all creation suffer decay.

If you would find God, He dwells on every hilltop and in every valley; God is everywhere in creation; but if you want a special display of Him, if you would know what is the secret place of the tabernacle of the Most High, the inner chamber of divinity, you must go where you find the church of true believers, for it is here He makes His continual residence known—in the hearts of the humble and contrite, who tremble at His word. Every church is to our Lord a more sublime thing than a constellation in the heavens; as He is precious to His saints, so are they precious to Him.

I will never leave thee.

Hebrews 13: 5

No promise is of private interpretation. Whatever God has said to any one saint, He has said to all. When He opens a well for one, it is that all may drink. When He opens a granary door to give out food, there may be some one starving man who is the occasion of its being opened, but all hungry saints may come and feed, too. Whether He gave the word to Abraham or to Moses matters not, O believer; He has given it to you as one of the covenanted seed. There is not a high blessing too lofty for you. Lift up now your eyes to the north and to the south, to the east and to the west, for all this is yours. Climb to Pisgah's top, and view the utmost limit of the divine promise, for the land is all your own. There is not a brook of living water of which you may not drink. If the land flows with milk and honey, eat the honey and drink the milk, for both are yours. Be bold to believe, for He has said, "I will never leave thee, nor forsake thee." In this promise, God gives to His people everything. "I will never leave thee."

Therefore, no attribute of God can cease to be engaged for us. Is He mighty? He will show Himself strong on the behalf of them that trust Him. Is He love? Then with loving-kindness will He have mercy upon us. Whatever attributes may compose the character of Deity, every one of them to its fullest extent shall be engaged on our side. To put everything in one, there is nothing you can want, there is nothing you can ask for, there is nothing you can need in time or in eternity, there is nothing living, nothing dying, there is nothing in this world, nothing in the next world, there is nothing now, nothing at the resurrection morning, nothing in heaven which is not contained in this text—"I will never leave thee, nor forsake thee."

Knowing this, that the trying of your faith worketh patience. But let patience have her perfect work, that ye may be perfect and entire, wanting nothing.

James 1: 3, 4

4

He who is never troubled cannot exercise patience. Angels cannot personally exhibit patience, since they are not capable of suffering. It is necessary to the possession and exercise of patience that we should be tried; and a great degree of patience can only come by a great degree of trial. You have heard of the patience of Job: did he learn it among his flocks, or with his camels, or with his children when they were feasting? Nay, he learned it when he sat among the ashes, and scraped himself with a potsherd, and

December

his heart was heavy because of the death of his children. Patience is a pearl which is only found in the deep seas of affliction; and only grace can find it there, bring it to the surface, and adorn the neck of faith therewith.

Blessed is the man that endureth temptation: for when he is tried, he shall receive the crown of life, which the Lord hath promised to them that love him.

James 1: 12

An old proverb has it, "The unsoundness of a vessel is not seen when it is empty; but when it is filled with water, then we shall see whether it will leak or no."

It is in our prosperity that we are tested. Men are not fully discovered to themselves till they are tried by fullness of success. Praise finds pride, wealth reveals selfishness, and learning discovers the leak of unbelief. Success is the crucible of character. Hence the prosperity which some welcome as an unmixed favor may far more rightly be regarded as an intense form of test. O Lord, preserve us when we are full as much as when we are empty.

"A garrison is not free from danger while it hath an enemy lodged within."

You may bolt all your doors, and fasten all your windows, but if the thieves have placed even a little child within doors who can draw the bolts for them, the house is still unprotected. All the sea outside a ship cannot do it damage till the water enters within and fills the hold. Hence, it is clear, our greatest danger is from within. All the devils in hell and tempters on earth could do us no injury if there were no corruption in our nature. Alas, our heart is our greatest enemy; this is the little home-born thief.

Confess your faults one to another, and pray one for another, that ye may be healed. The effectual fervent prayer of a righteous man availeth much.

James 5: 16

As an encouragement cheerfully to offer intercessory prayer, remember that *such prayer is the sweetest God ever hears,* for the prayer of Christ is of this character. His intercession must be the most acceptable of all supplications—and the more our prayer is like Christ's, the sweeter it will be; thus while petitions for ourselves will be accepted, our pleadings for others, having in them more of the fruits of the Spirit, more love, more faith, more brotherly kindness, will be, through the precious merits of Jesus, the sweetest oblation that we can offer to God, the very fat of our sacrifice. Remember, again, that *intercessory prayer is exceedingly prevalent.* What wonders it has worked.

That the trial of your faith, being much more precious than of gold that perisheth, though it be tried with fire, might be found into praise and honor and glory at the appearing of Jesus Christ.

1 Peter 1: 7

7

The Apostle declares that you must be tried even as gold must be put into the furnace: you have faith, and faith must be tested; it is according to its nature and divine purpose. The faith of Abraham was sharply tried, and so must the faith of all believers be (Heb. 11: 17). That your religion may be really solid metal, and not an imitation of it, or a mere gilded bauble, you must be tried. Your Master was tried: not without fighting did He win His crown; not without labor did He enter into His reward. There is a reason for our present affliction. God has a design in it—that He may have praise and glory and honor at the appearing of His dear Son; a praise, and glory, and honor in which we shall share. Come, then, brethren, if this fire is to be passed through, let us gird up our loins to dash through it. Let us not fear, for the Lord has said, "When thou passest through the fire I will be with thee, thou shalt not be burned; neither shall the flame kindle upon thee" (Isa. 43: 2). My brethren, if for a little time we must be tried, let us set our faces like flints to bear the trial. Let us not be intoxicated with sorrow or fear. Since God has a grand design in it, let us bow ourselves to His divine will, and only ask that His holy design may be fully answered. Let us hope to be sustained in the trial, and sanctified as the result of it, and let no unbelieving fear cast a cloud over our sky.

December

For even hereunto were ye called: because Christ also suffered for us, leaving us an example, that ye should follow his steps: who his own self bare our sins in his own body on the tree, that we, being dead to sins, should live unto righteousness: by whose stripes ye were healed.

1 Peter 2: 21, 24

Concerning the consciousness of evil in the past of our lives and the tendency to wrong-doing in our nature, the Bible is very clear, and it is most admirably explicit as to God's way of removing this barrier to our future progress. In Holy Scripture we see a most wise and gracious method for the putting away of guilt, without injury to the divine justice. The atonement offered by the Lord Jesus, who is the essence of the revelation of God, is an eminently satisfactory solution of the soul's sternest problem. Our feeling is that God, the universal Ruler, must do right, and must not, even for mercy's sake, relax the rule that evil done must bring evil as its consequence.

Christ had no transgressions of His own; He took ours upon His head; He never committed a wrong, but He took all my sin, and all yours, if you are a believer; concerning all His people, it is true, He bore their griefs and carried their sorrows in His own body on the tree. Sin may drag you ever so low, but Christ's great atonement is still under all. You may have descended into the deeps, but you cannot have fallen so low as "the uttermost"; and to the uttermost He saves.

Today *the world's one and only remedy* is the cross.

Who his own self bare our sins in his own body on the tree, that we, being dead to sins, should live unto righteousness: by whose stripes ye were healed.

1 Peter 2: 24

A prisoner was taken out to die, and as he rode along in the death cart his heart was heavy at the thought of death, and none could cheer him of all the throng. The gallows-tree was in sight, and this blotted out the sun for him. But lo, his prince came riding up in hot haste, bearing a free pardon. Then the man opened his eyes, and, as though he had risen from the dead, he returned to happy consciousness. The sight of his prince had chased all gloom away. He declared that he had never seen a fairer countenance in all his days: and when he read his pardon he vowed that no poetry should ever be dearer to his heart than those few lines of sovereign grace.

Friends, I remember well when I was in that death cart, and Jesus came to me with pardon. Death and hell were before me; but I rejoiced exceedingly when I saw the nailprints in His hands and feet, and the wound in His side. When He said, "Thy sins, which are many, are all forgiven thee," I thought I never saw such loveliness before, and never heard such music in all my days. Nay, it was not mere thought, I am sure my judgment was right. Eternity itself shall never disclose anything to me more sweet. My pardoning Lord has no peer nor rival. Oh, what a Christ is He who appeared to me, a guilty, condemned sinner, on the way to hell! Blessed be His name, He bore on the tree my curse, and shame, and death, and I am free.

Ye were as sheep going astray; but are now returned unto the Shepherd and Bishop of your souls.

1 Peter 2: 25

10

Friend, let this be your comfort, that God sees you when you begin to repent. He does not see you with His usual gaze, with which He looks on all men, but He sees you with an eye of intense interest. He has been looking on you in all your sin, and in all your sorrow, hoping that you would repent; and now He sees the first gleam of grace, and He beholds it with joy. No watcher on the lonely castle top ever saw the first gray light of morning with more joy than that with which God beholds the first desire in your heart.

As sure as God is God, if you this day are seeking Him aright, through Christ, the day will come when the kiss of full assurance shall be on you lip, when the arms of sovereign love shall embrace you, and you shall know it to be so. You may have despised Him, but you will know Him yet to be your Father and your Friend. You may have broken His Sabbaths and despised His Word; but

December

the day is coming when the Sabbath shall be your delight, and
His Word your treasure.

*Who is gone into heaven, and is on the right hand of God;
angels and authorities and powers being made subject unto
him.*

1 Peter 3: 22

Since Christ has gone into heaven and sits at the right hand of
God, *it shows which way we ought to go.* "I, if I be lifted up
from the earth, will draw all men unto me." He draws them to
the cross, and you may be sure He will draw them to the crown.
Do you think He has lost His attraction, now that He sits on the
throne? Not He. He is drawing us up right now. Let us send all
our thoughts upward; our desires, our rejoicings, our aspirations,
let them all climb Jacob's ladder up to the Lord. Oh that we could
at once rise to Him!

A pretty parable was given by one of our ministers, of a boy's
kite. He made it fly aloft: it rose up so high that he could no longer
see it. Still he said he had a kite, and he held fast by it. "Boy,
how do you know you have a kite?" "I can feel it pull," said he.
Today we feel our Jesus pull. He draws us with a far greater force
than a mere string. He is gone into heaven, and He draws us after
Him. Yield to His upward drawing!

*Humble yourselves therefore under the mighty hand of God,
that he may exalt you in due time.*

1 Peter 5: 6
Read 1 Peter 5: 1–5

Humble yourselves therefore under the hand of God as creatures
under the hand of the Creator. We are the clay, and You our
Potter, O Lord: it becomes us to be lowly. Humble yourselves
under the hand of God as criminals under the hand of their judge.
Cry, "Against thee, thee only, have I sinned, and done this evil

in thy sight: that thou mightest be justified when thou speakest, and be clear when thou judgest." Humble yourselves under the hand of God—as chastened children under a father's rod—for He chastens us for our profit, and right well do we deserve each smarting blow. Humble yourselves under the mighty hands of God, lastly, as servants under their Lord's word. Ask no questions about your Master's command, but go and do it; and when He rebukes you for shortcomings answer not again, but accept the reproof with bowed head and tearful eye, acknowledging that His rebuke is well deserved. Humble yourselves thus, dear brethren, in your daily lives, and God will exalt you in due time.

But the God of all grace, who hath called us unto his eternal glory by Christ Jesus, after that ye have suffered a while, make you perfect, stablish, strengthen, settle you.

1 Peter 5: 10
Read 1 Peter 5: 6–10

13

I reckon that glory to a saint means, first of all, *purified character*. The brightest glory that really can come to any one is the glory of character. Thus God's glory among men is His goodness, His mercy, His justice, His truth. But shall such poor creatures as we are ever to have perfect characters? Yes, we shall one day be perfectly holy. God's Holy Spirit, when He has finished His work, will leave in us no trace of sin: no temptation shall be able to touch us, there will be in us no relics of our past and fallen state. Oh, will that not be blessed?

For if God spared not the angels that sinned, but cast them down to hell, and delivered them into chains of darkness, to be reserved unto judgment.

2 Peter 2: 4
Read 2 Peter 2: 4–10

14

To think that men should stand where angels fall! We are by sovereign grace called to be as near to God as the angels ever were,

December

and in some respects we are nearer still. We are the bodyguard of Christ; His chosen ones with whom He communes. We are the table-companions of our Lord; we eat of His bread, and drink of His cup, and are made partakers with Him. We are lifted up to be one with Him, and are made to be "members of his body, of his flesh and of his bones"; yet God's eternal unbounded power keeps us in the day of temptation, and leads us so that if we go through the rivers we are not drowned, and when we pass through the fires we are not burned. Oh, the splendor of triumphant grace! Neither the glory of our calling, nor the unworthiness of our originals shall cause us to be traitors; we shall neither perish through pride nor lust; but the new nature within us shall overcome all sin, and abide faithful to the end.

15

If we walk in the light, as he is in the light. . . .

1 John 1: 7

As He is in the light! Can we ever attain to this? Shall we ever be able to walk as clearly in the light as He is whom we call "Our Father," of whom it is written, "God is light, and in him is no darkness at all"? Certainly, this is the model which is set before us, for the Savior Himself said, "Be ye perfect, even as your Father who is in heaven is perfect"; and although we may feel that we can never rival the perfection of God, yet we are to seek after it, and never be satisfied until we attain to it.

Be it ever in your remembrance, that to keep strictly in the path of your Savior's command is better than any outward form of religion; and to hearken to His precept with an attentive ear is better than to bring the fat of rams, or any other precious thing, to lay upon His altar. If you are failing to keep the least of Christ's commands to His disciples, I pray you be disobedient no longer. "To obey," even in the slightest and smallest thing, "is better than sacrifice." It is a blessed thing to be teachable as a little child, but it is a much more blessed thing, when one has been taught the lesson, to carry it out to the letter.

But if we walk in the light, as he is in the light, we have fellowship one with another, and the blood of Jesus Christ his Son cleanseth us from all sin.

1 John 1: 7

16

"The blood of Jesus Christ his Son cleanseth us from *all sin,"* not only from sin, but "from *all* sin." Reader, I cannot tell you the exceeding sweetness of this word, but I pray God the Holy Ghost to give you a taste of it. Manifold are our sins against God. Whether the bill be little or great, the same receipt can discharge one as the other. The blood of Jesus Christ is as blessed and divine a payment for the transgressions of blaspheming Peter as for the shortcomings of loving John; our iniquity is gone, all gone at once, and all gone forever. Blessed completeness! What a sweet theme to dwell upon as one begins another day.

If we confess our sins, he is faithful and just to forgive us our sins, and to cleanse us from all unrighteousness.

1 John 1: 9

17

It is quite certain that those whom Christ has washed in His precious blood need not make a confession of sin, as culprits or criminals, before God the Judge, for Christ has forever taken away all their sins, so that they no longer stand where they can be condemned; but having become children, and offending as children, ought they not every day to go before their heavenly Father and confess their sin, and acknowledge their iniquity? Nature teaches that it is the duty of erring children to make a confession to their earthly father, and the grace of God in the heart teaches us that we, as Christians, owe the same duty to our heavenly Father.

We have not so clear a view of Him as we could wish; we know not the heights and depths of His love; but we know of a surety that He is too good to withdraw from His trembling child the gift which he has been able to obtain. If we have faith as a grain of mustard seed, salvation is our present and eternal possession. If we cannot clasp the Lord in our hands with Simeon, if we dare not lean our heads upon His bosom with John, yet if we can venture

December

in the press behind Him, and touch the hem of His garment, we are made whole. Courage, timid one! your faith has saved you; go in peace. *"Being* justified by faith, *we have* peace with God."

18

If any man sin, we have an advocate with the Father, Jesus Christ the righteous.

1 John 2: 1

What words of tenderness, what sentences of persuasion, will the Anointed use when He stands up to plead for me! "Jesus Christ *the righteous."* This is not only His character, but also His plea. It is His character, and if the Righteous One be my Advocate, then my cause is good, or He would not have espoused it. It is His plea, for He meets the charge of unrighteousness against me by the plea that *He* is righteous. He declares Himself my substitute, and puts His obedience to my account. My soul, you have a friend well fitted to be your advocate; He cannot but succeed; leave yourself entirely in His hands.

It is our wisdom, as well as our necessity, to beseech God continually to strengthen that which He has wrought in us. We often forget that the Author of our faith must be the Preserver of it also. The lamp which was burning in the temple was never allowed to go out, but it had to be daily replenished with fresh oil; in like manner, our faith can only live by being sustained with the oil of grace, and we can only obtain this from God Himself.

Let us, then, day by day, go to our Lord for the grace and strength we need. We have a strong argument to plead, for it is *His own work of grace* which we ask Him to strengthen. Only let your faith take hold of His strength.

19

I write unto you, little children, because your sins are forgiven you for his name's sake.

1 John 2: 12

No human mind can adequately estimate the infinite value of the divine sacrifice, for as great as is the sin of God's people, the atone-

ment which takes it away is immeasurably greater. Therefore the
believer, even when sin rolls like a black flood, and the remembrance of the past is bitter, can yet stand before the blazing throne
of the great and holy God, and cry, "Who is he that condemneth?
It is Christ that died; yea, rather, that hath risen again." While
the recollection of his sin fills him with shame and sorrow, he at
the same time makes it a foil to show the brightness of mercy—
guilt is the dark night in which the fair star of divine love shines
with serene splendor.

*And this is the promise that he hath promised us, even eternal
life.*

> 1 John 2: 25

20

I wonder if John isn't here remembering the words he wrote down
in John 10: 28, "I give unto my sheep eternal life, and they shall
never perish, neither shall any pluck them out of my hand." You
have been taken into the family of God, and made His child; and
will your Father now disown you, or remove your name out of
the family register? You are also joined unto Christ in one spirit,
you are a "member of his body, of his flesh, and of his bones,"
and shall Christ be dismembered, and the Son of God divided?
Believing in my Lord I stand where the devils of hell cannot reach
me, and where the angels of God might envy me; for I can exclaim
in your name and in my own, "Who shall separate us from the
love of God, which is in Christ Jesus our Lord?" We challenge
earth and hell, time and eternity, to dissolve the blessed union
between Christ and His people. Who is he that can harm you if
you be followers of that which is good? If your confidence be in
the living God, who shall put you to shame?

*Hereby we know that he abideth in us, by the Spirit which
he hath given us.*

> 1 John 3: 24

21

Common, too common is the sin of forgetting the Holy Spirit. This
is folly and ingratitude. He deserves well at our hands, for He is

December

good, supremely good. As God, He is *good essentially*. He shares in the threefold ascription of holy, holy, holy, which ascends to the Triune Jehovah. Unmixed purity, and truth, and grace is He. He is *good benevolently*, tenderly bearing with our waywardness, striving with our rebellious wills; quickening us from our death in sin, and then training us for the skies as a loving nurse fosters her child. How generous, forgiving, and tender is this patient Spirit of God.

"Hold thou me up, and I shall be safe," we can pray to this Spirit with the Psalmist (119: 117). Having prayed, you must also watch; guarding every thought, word, and action with holy jealousy. Do not expose yourself unnecessarily; but if called to exposure, if you are bidden to go where the darts are flying, never venture forth without your shield; for the devil will rejoice that his hour of triumph is come, and will soon make you fall down wounded by his arrows. Though slain you cannot be, wounded you may be. "Be sober, be vigilant; danger may be in an hour when all seemeth securest to thee." Therefore take heed to your ways, and watch unto prayer. May the Holy Spirit guide us in all our ways.

22

Herein is love, not that we loved God, but that he loved us, and sent his Son to be the propitiation for our sins.

1 John 4: 10

We come nearer to John's meaning when we look at this negative as applying to those who do love God. "Not that we loved God"— that is, that our love to God, even when it does exist, and even when it influences our lives, is not worthy to be mentioned as a fountain of supply for love. The apostle points us away from it to something far more vast, and then he cries, "Herein is love!" I am looking for "the springs of the sea," and you point me to a little pool amid the rocks which has been filled by the flowing tide. I am glad to see that pool: how bright! how blue! how like the sea from whence it came! But do not point to this as the source of the great waterfloods; for if you do I shall smile at your childish ignorance, and point you to yon great rolling main which tosses its waves on high. What is your little pool to the vast Atlantic?

December

Do you point me to the love in the believer's heart, and say, "Herein is love"? You make me smile. I know that there is love in that true heart; but who can mention it in the presence of the great rolling ocean of the love of God, without bottom and without shore? The word *not* is not only upon my lip but in my heart as I think of the two things, *"Not* that we loved God, but that God loved us." What poor love ours is at its very best when compared with the love with which God loves us!

Beloved, if God so loved us, we ought also to love one another.
1 John 4: 11
Read 1 John 4: 7–12

23

They that are Christ's are filled with His love. "Every one that loveth is born of God, and knoweth God. He that loveth not knoweth not God; for God is love." God is the center of the believer's love; the saints are an inner circle specially beloved, and all mankind is embraced within the circumference of the ring of love.

The saints begin with love to God. That must ever hold the highest place; for God is the best and noblest being, and we owe Him all our hearts. Then comes, for Jesus' sake, love to all who are in Christ. There is a peculiarly near and dear relationship existing between one child of God and all the rest. Loving Him that begat, we love all them that are begotten of Him. Should not a child love his brothers with a tender, peculiar affection? This principle of love, once implanted, induces in the heart of the converted man a love towards all mankind. Not that he can take any complacency in the wicked; God Himself cannot do that; His holiness abhors all iniquity. The love desired is not the love of complacency, but the love of benevolence; so that we wish well, and to the utmost of our power would do well, unto all those that dwell upon the face of the earth. In this holy charity, this unselfish love, be imitators of God as dear children. Our heavenly Father is kind to the unthankful and to the evil, and so must we be; desiring that even the most abandoned may yet be rescued and made right and good. Love desires to create that which is lovable even in

December

the most unlovable of mankind, and God helping the effort, she succeeds.

24

Whosoever believeth that Jesus is the Christ is born of God: and every one that loveth him that begat loveth him also that is begotten of him. By this we know that we love the children of God, when we love God, and keep his commandments. For this is the love of God, that we keep his commandments.

1 John 5: 1–3

The love which the early Christians felt toward the Lord was not a quiet emotion which they hid within themselves in the secret chamber of their souls, and which they only spoke of when they met on the first day of the week and sang hymns in honor of Christ Jesus the crucified, but it was a passion with them of such a vehement and all-consuming energy, that it was visible in their actions, spoke in their common talk, and looked out of their eyes even in their commonest glances. Love to Jesus was a flame which fed upon the core and heart of their being; and, therefore, from its own force burned its way into the outer man, and shone there.

25

. . . Jesus Christ, who is the faithful witness, and the first-begotten of the dead, and the prince of the kings of the earth. Unto him that loved us, and washed us from our sins in his own blood. . . .

Revelation 1: 5

Dear friends, the last song in this world, the song of triumph, shall be full of God, and of no one else. Here you praise the instrument; today you look on this man and on that, and you say, "Thank God for this minister, and for this man!" But in that day, forgotten shall their names be for a season, even as the stars refuse to shine when the sun himself appears. The song shall be unto Jesus, and Jesus only; "Unto him that loved us, and hath washed us from our sins in his own blood, unto him be glory forever and ever. Amen."

No inferior hand has sketched even so much as the most minute parts of providence. It was all marked out, designed, and planned by the mind of the all-wise, all-knowing God. Hence, not even Christ's death was exempt from it. He that wings an angel and guides a sparrow, He that counts the hairs of our head, was not likely, when He took notice of such little things, to omit the greatest wonder of earth's miracles, the death of Christ. No; the blood-stained page of that book, the page which makes both past and future glorious with golden words—that blood-stained page, I say, was as much written of Jehovah as any other.

I know thy works, and where thou dwellest, even where Satan's seat is: and thou holdest fast my name, and hast not denied my faith.

Revelation 2: 13

26

The name of Christ is here made to be identical with the faith of Christ. "Thou holdest fast my name, and hast not denied my faith." The faith of Scripture has Christ for its center, Christ for its circumference, and Christ for its substance. To the Jews the Law was never in its proper place until it was laid in the ark, and covered with the mercy-seat; and I am sure believers never see the Law aright till they see it fulfilled in Christ Jesus. If it be so with the Law, how much more is it so with the gospel? The gospel is the gold ring, but Christ Jesus is the diamond which is set in it. When we hold fast the name of our Lord, then we have not denied the faith.

But how may the faith be denied? In several ways this may be done. Let me say it very tenderly, but very solemnly, some deny the faith, and let go the name of Jesus by *never confessing it.* Remember how the Lord puts this matter in the Gospels: "Whosoever shall confess me before men, him shall the Son of man also confess before the angels of God; but he that denieth me before men shall be denied before the angels of God." Here it is clear that to deny is the same thing as not confessing. I know people who almost boast of their neutrality. Permit me to remind you

December

of our Lord's own words: "He that is not with me is against me; and he that gathereth not with me scattereth abroad." Again He says, "Whosoever doth not bear his cross and come after me, cannot be my disciple." This text must bear hard upon those who have tried not exactly to hold with the hare nor yet to run with the hounds. These have hoped to find in their discretion the better part of valor; but, believe me, it is a valor which will be rewarded with everlasting contempt. This way you hope to lead an easy life. An easy life of such a kind will end in a very uneasy death. A life in which we have shunned the cross of Christ will lead to a state in which we shall miss the crown of glory. Oh, may we be like the church in Pergamos in holding to both the name and the faith!

And he said to me, These are they which came out of great tribulation, and have washed their robes, and made them white in the blood of the Lamb.

Revelation 7: 14

Oh! who shall measure the heights of the Savior's all-sufficiency? First, tell how high is sin, and, then, remember that as Noah's flood prevailed over the tops of earth's mountains, so the flood of Christ's redemption prevails over the tops of the mountains of our sins. In heaven's courts there are today men who once were sinners, but they have been washed—they have been sanctified. Ask them from where the brightness of their robes has come, and where their purity has been achieved, and they, with united breath, will tell you that they have washed their robes, and made them white in the blood of the Lamb.

They shall hunger no more, neither thirst any more; neither shall the sun light on them nor any heat.

Revelation 7: 16
Read Revelation 7: 13–17

We are assured that in heaven they have all their necessities prevented: "They shall hunger no more." To be supplied when we hunger is the mercy of earth; never to hunger at all is the plenitude of heaven. God will so fill the souls of His redeemed that they shall have no longings; their longings shall be prevented by their constant satisfaction. That which they enjoy will be more than they ever desired to enjoy, or ever imagined that they could be capable of enjoying. Imagination's utmost height never reached to the exceeding bliss and glory of the world to come. The saints confess in the glory that it never entered into their hearts to guess what God had prepared for them that love Him. Heaven shall exceed all the desires of God's people; they shall not, even with their enlarged capacities, be able to wish for anything which they do not already possess; so that they shall hunger no more, in the sense that they shall never long for more than they have.

They shall have done with the desires which it is right for them to have here—desires which intimate their present imperfection. Here it is their duty and their privilege to long after perfection, to be sighing and crying for a perfect deliverance from every shade of sin; but they shall not sigh and cry for this in glory, for they shall be without fault before the throne of God.

For the Lamb which is in the midst of the throne shall feed them, and shall lead them unto living fountains of waters.
Revelation 7: 17a

| 29 |

This is the reason for all the provision and enjoyment: the verse begins with the word *for*, signifying that this is the cause of all the felicity of the blessed, that the Lamb does feed and lead them.

Who is this that feeds them? It is *the Lamb.* I wish it were possible for me to communicate to you the enjoyment my own soul has had in meditating upon this blessed title "The Lamb," as it stands in this connection. Does it not teach us, first, that our comfort and life must come from our incarnate Savior—the Lamb? The expression is very peculiar: it is a figure, and no figure; a mixed metaphor, and yet most plain and clear! It is written, "The Lamb shall shepherd them." This is an accurate interpretation. How is that? A shepherd, and that shepherd a Lamb!

Here is the truth which the words contain—He that saves is a man like ourselves. He that provides for His people is Himself

December

one of them—"For which cause he is not ashamed to call them brethren." A lamb is a member of the flock; but in this case the Lamb is the shepherd of the flock: a shepherd who is also a lamb must be the most tender shepherd conceivable, the most sympathetic and brotherly guardian that can be. When a man is shepherd to sheep he should be compassionate, but he cannot be so tender as if he actually partook of their nature. In our case our Shepherd is to the full a partaker of our nature: we are men, and our Shepherd is a man. Thus to the saints, the Lamb is their hope, their comfort, their honor, their delight, their glory.

30 | *He shall lead them unto living fountains of waters: and God shall wipe away all tears from their eyes.*

Revelation 7: 17b

"He shall lead." That is another work of the Shepherd, to lead His flock—"He leads them to living fountains of waters." You may read it, "He shall guide them to fountains of waters of life"; it is but a variation of the same thought. Now, even in heaven the holy ones need guiding, and Jesus leads the way. While He is guiding, He points out to His people the secret founts and fresh springs which as yet they have not tasted. As eternity goes on, I have no doubt that the Savior will be indicating fresh delights to His redeemed. "Come hither," He says to His flock, "here are yet more flowing streams." He will lead them on and on, by the century, aye, by the millennium, from glory unto glory, onward and upward in growing knowledge and enjoyment. Continually will He conduct His flock to deeper mysteries and higher glories. Never will the inexhaustible God who has given Himself to be the portion of His people ever be fully known, so that there will eternally be sources of freshness and new delight, and the Shepherd will continue to lead His flock to these living fountains of water. He will guide them,

> "From glory unto glory" that ever lies before,
> Still widening, adoring, rejoicing more and more,
> Still following where he leadeth, from shining field to field,
> Himself our goal of glory, Revealer and Revealed!

December

He is Lord of lords, and King of kings: and they that are with him are called, and chosen, and faithful.
Revelation 17: 14

31

There is not a spider hanging on the king's wall but has its errand (Prov. 30: 28); there is not a nettle that grows in the corner of the churchyard but has its purpose; there is not a single insect fluttering in the breeze that does not accomplish some divine decree; and I will never have it that God created any man, especially any Christian man, to be a blank, and to be a nothing. He made you for an end. Find out what that end is; find out your niche, and fill it. If it be ever so little, if it is only to be a hewer of wood and a drawer of water, do something in this great battle for God and truth.

Our world has two forces; it has one tendency to run off at a tangent from its orbit; but the sun draws it by a centripetal power, and attracts it to itself. Oh! Christian, you will never walk aright, and keep in the orbit of truth, if it be not for the influence of Christ perpetually attracting you to the center. Christ is drawing you to Himself, to His likeness, to His character, to His love, to His bosom, and in that way you are kept from your natural tendency to fly off and to be lost in the wide fields of sin. Bless God, that Christ lifted up draws all His people unto Him.

Index

Index

Barnabas, 232
believing, 136, 163, 205–206, 212, 229, 236
Bethesda, 128
betrayal, 88
blessedness (*see* happiness)
blessings, 18, 19, 27, 32, 53, 55, 61, 66, 83, 124, 145–146, 151, 232, 241
Blood of Christ, 249, 255, 256
Bunyan, John, 105

calling, 107
Calvary (*see also* Cross), 73, 90, 139–140, 141, 161, 182, 199–200
Canaan (*see also* Promised Land), 156, 160
captivity, 134–135
character, 178, 242, 247
children of God, 143, 147, 169, 188, 203, 209–210, 215, 229, 247, 249, 251, 253
Christianity, 139–140
Church, 11, 12, 19, 27, 40–41, 76, 79–80, 116, 148, 166–167, 176, 189, 223–224, 227, 240
circumstances, 101, 160
City of Refuge, 42, 211
comfort, 22, 30, 36, 49, 63, 64, 80, 113, 144–145, 148–149, 153–154, 163, 181, 183, 188, 191–192, 220, 227, 232–233
concentration, 130
confession, 249
covenant, 10, 11, 12, 40, 56, 64, 79, 97, 102, 103, 115–116, 129, 139, 142, 149, 151, 164, 210, 223, 241
Cross (*see also* Calvary), 173, 182, 199–200, 207, 209, 216, 227, 244, 246

danger, 131–132
darkness, 7, 38–39, 133, 197, 217, 237
David, 23, 42–43, 52, 61, 63, 65, 81, 115–116, 141–142
death, 15, 27–28, 49, 77, 81, 87, 118, 161, 162, 180, 181, 202, 207, 218, 219, 231, 237–238
deliverance, 22, 26, 29, 37, 48, 62, 110, 140–141, 173, 231
disciples, 169, 176
Divine Providence, 9, 12–13, 16–17, 21, 22, 37–38, 40, 44, 67, 74, 99, 103–104, 105, 198, 241
doctrine, 59. 109, 110, 162

doubt, 31–32, 37, 40, 46–47, 58, 62, 63, 110, 155–156, 165, 236
dove, 8

Egyptians, 22–23, 24, 26, 90
Eleazar, 13
Elijah, 37, 104
Emmaus, 154
emotions, 201
encourage, 200–201
Ephraim, 19, 40
eternal life, 166, 171, 185, 202, 206, 210–211, 219, 258

faith, 15, 16, 20, 22, 29, 35, 39, 42, 44, 46, 50, 58, 61, 63, 82, 85, 112–113, 119, 132–133, 145–146, 149, 153, 165, 175, 191, 202–203, 205–206, 226–227, 236, 237–238, 255
family, 158
fate, 164–165
fellowship, 61, 139, 145–146, 154–155, 167–168, 234, 247–248
first fruits, 187–188
forgiveness of sin, 55, 92–93, 128, 150, 166, 186, 244–245, 249, 250–251
freedom, 95
friend(s), 88–89, 105, 129–130

Gethsemane, 73, 91, 98–99
glory, 43, 69, 110, 133, 137–138, 144, 155, 179, 184, 194–195, 209, 211–212, 247
gospel, 197, 255
grace, 11, 12, 14, 28, 36, 45, 69, 93, 105, 117, 124, 136, 138, 153, 158, 182, 211, 218, 247–248, 250
guidance, 15, 99, 102–103, 109, 252, 258

Hagar, 22
Haman, 50
happiness, 55, 62, 89, 93
harmony, 56, 57, 100
healing, 123, 125, 128, 134, 164, 179–180
heart(s), 136–137, 166–167, 170, 175, 180, 209, 217, 242
heaven, 28, 40, 48, 57, 67, 75, 87, 107, 108–109, 130, 139, 145, 184, 207–208, 213–214, 246, 256–257
hell, 54, 187
help, 102
holiness, 7, 29, 31, 117, 203
Holy Spirit, 8, 11, 14, 23, 27, 33, 39, 47, 48, 49, 62, 65, 66, 70, 76, 80, 85, 94,

Index

ONE IN A MILLION
Derek Williams

The story of Billy Graham with Mission England

'There is no doubt that the three months during which I shared in Mission England were one of the highlights of my entire Ministry'. Billy Graham

Outlining the six regional missions in England during 1984, Derek Williams carefully links personal encounters with an interesting insight into what went on behind the scenes.

192 pages (including 16 pages of colour photographs)

ISBN 0-85009-054-7

£1.95

HE BEGAN WITH EVE
Joyce Landorf

Best-selling author Joyce Landorf's warm insight and wit beckon the modern world to learn from women of the Bible in this collection of fast moving character sketches. Using 'sanctified imagination', she puts herself into the sandals of these women as they confront all the trauma, emotions and excitement of life today.

ISBN 0-85009-058-X

£1.95

PRAYER: KEY TO REVIVAL
Paul Y Cho with R. Whitney Manzano

The secret behind the growth of the largest church in the world!

'No man can schedule a revival', Dr Cho has said, 'for God alone is the giver of life. But . . . when 'the fullness of time' is come and prayer ascends from a few earnest hearts, then history teaches it is time for the tide of revival to sweep in once more.'

This perspective is born of Dr Cho's conviction that while revival is the sovereign work of the Holy Spirit, the earnest prayers of God's people must work with the Spirit. It is then that He moves anew in the hearts of unbelievers.

ISBN 0-85009-059-8

£1.95

YOU CAN MAKE A DIFFERENCE
Tony Campolo

This book challenges young people to make their lives count for Christ. Tony Campolo uniquely identifies with young people in their own situation, then shows how they can use the power of God to change their world. With his incomparable blend of humour and serious biblical insights, the author deals with commitment, vocation, dating and discipleship.

ISBN 0-85009-056-3

£1.95

IT'S FRIDAY BUT SUNDAY'S COMIN'
Tony Campolo

'This book is Campolo at his best . . . in a world of mealie-mouthed compromise, it is long overdue and very welcome.'
Peter Meadows

This book is sensitive to the needs of both youth and adults for agape love, deeper than the cultural myth of romanticism . . . for acceptance and wholeness . . . for knowledge of God. It's bold claim is that while the world metes out its 'Fridays' of doom and gloom, the resurrection is the last work – 'Sunday's comin'!'

ISBN 0-85009-057-1

£1.60

EVIDENCE FOR JOY
Josh McDowell and Dale Bellis

Unlocking the secrets to love, acceptance and security

Reasons for faith are never a mere academic exercise for the authors. In this book they first show how Christian faith rests in a person, not a system; that it is intelligent, not blind; and that it is objective, rather than subjective. They then devote most of their work to a challenging discussion of how this kind of faith relates to our felt needs – for love, for acceptance and for security.

ISBN 0-85009-055-5

£1.95

THE DREAM
Keith Miller

In the Dream, Keith Miller invites us to go on an imaginative journey with him to try to look at ourselves and the church the way God might look at us.

It is not always a happy journey. In many ways, the story shows, we in God's church have let Him down – failing to love and forgive one another, by failing to reach outside ourselves and help those who are in need.

The book is pervaded with a sense of the Lord's sadness and righteous anger over these sins. But it also shines with His overwhelming love, concern and forgiveness. It is fundamentally, a book of hope.

ISBN 0-85009-061-X

£1.40